SCIENCE EDUCATION FOR ELEMENTARY TEACHERS

An Investigation-Based Approach

Ann Benbow

Colin Mably

WADSWORTH

THOMSON LEARNING

Australia • Canada • Mexico • Singapore • Spain
United Kingdom • United States

We dedicate this book to our collective family,
who are legion in number and diverse in opinion.

We especially want to thank our parents, teachers all,
who didn't give up on us, despite everything.

Education Editor: Dan Alpert
Development Editor: Tangelique Williams
Editorial Assistant: Alex Orr
Marketing Manager: Becky Tollerson
Project Manager, Editorial Production: Trudy Brown
Print/Media Buyer: Tandra Jorgensen
Permissions Editor: Bob Kauser
Production Service: Johnstone Associates

Illustrator: Colin Mably
Text Designer: Kelly Shoemaker
Cover Designer: Bill Stanton
Cover Images: Top: Stone/David Young Wolff;
  Bottom: Stone/Daniel Bosler
Compositor: Thompson Type
Text and Cover Printer: Webcom Ltd.

Printed in Canada
1 2 3 4 5 6 7 05 04 03 02 01

For permission to use material from this text, contact us by
Web: http://www.thomsonrights.com
Fax: 1-800-730-2215
Phone: 1-800-730-2214

Library of Congress Cataloging-in-Publication Data
Benbow, Ann.
    Science education for elementary teachers : an investigation-
based approach / Ann Benbow and Colin Mably.
        p. cm.
    Includes bibliographical references and index.
    ISBN 0-7668-0090-3
    1. Science—Study and teaching (Elementary) 2. Science—
Methodology. 3. Concept learning. I. Mably, Colin. II. Title.

LB1585 .B33 2002
372.3'5044—dc21
                                    2001026566

Wadsworth/Thomson Learning
10 Davis Drive
Belmont, CA 94002-3098
USA

For more information about our products, contact us:
Thomson Learning Academic Resource Center
1-800-423-0563
http://www.wadsworth.com

International Headquarters
Thomson Learning
International Division
290 Harbor Drive, 2nd Floor
Stamford, CT 06902-7477
USA

UK/Europe/Middle East/South Africa
Thomson Learning
Berkshire House
168-173 High Holborn
London WC1V 7AA
United Kingdom

Asia
Thomson Learning
60 Albert Street, #15-01
Albert Complex
Singapore 189969

Canada
Nelson Thomson Learning
1120 Birchmount Road
Toronto, Ontario M1K 5G4
Canada

CONTENTS

2 **PARTS OF LIVING THINGS HAVE CERTAIN FUNCTIONS**
Investigating the Way Animals' Body Parts Work   **21**

3 **THE PROPERTIES OF MATERIALS**
Investigating Containers   **39**

4 **FORCES AND MOTION**
Investigating What Causes Things to Move   **59**

5   CHEMICAL REACTIONS FORM NEW SUBSTANCES
Investigating Chemical Reactions   75

8 ENERGY IS TRANSFORMED
Investigating Energy and Its Transformations   **125**

9 EARTH SYSTEMS CHANGE
Investigating Weather Patterns   **143**

PART II CONTENT AND PEDAGOGY   173

11 The Nuts and Bolts of Teaching Elementary Science   175

12 Planning a Science Investigation   189

13 How Children Learn   197

ABOUT THE AUTHORS

Ann Benbow and Colin Mably have been active in the field of science education for many years. First teachers, then teacher educators, Ann and Colin have been responsible for the development of several National Science Foundation curriculum projects, including *Foundations and Challenges to Encourage Technology-Based Science* (*FACETS*, American Chemical Society), *Investigating Earth Systems* (*IES*, American Geological Institute), and *Science in a Technical World* (*STW*, American Chemical Society). They are adjunct professors at the University of Maryland, College Park, and at Loyola College, Baltimore, where they teach elementary science methods and inservice science education programs.

Ann Benbow is a biologist with a Ph.D. in curriculum and instruction and a Master's degree in science education, both from the University of Maryland. During twelve years at the American Chemical Society, Ann was editor of *WonderScience*, a monthly magazine for elementary students, then principal investigator for two NSF-funded projects—*FACETS*, and *Operation Chemistry*, a nationwide teacher training program. Ann has been a consultant and advisor to numerous science education organizations, including the American Association for the Advancement of Science, the National Science Foundation, and the American Geological Institute.

Colin Mably was graduated from the University of Oxford Institute of Education, with postgraduate study at the Froebel Institute of the University of London. Colin taught for ten years in elementary schools. He then became a teacher educator, first at London University's Furzedown College, and later as principal lecturer at the University of East London. He co-developed *Modular Investigations into Science and Technology (MIST)*, an award-winning UK videodisc-based elementary science curriculum, a project to which Ann Benbow became a consultant. Working with Ann as a co-developer on *FACETS*, Colin was also an instructor for *Operation Chemistry* and video coordinator for *STW*. He continues to work on a variety of science education projects.

TO THE STUDENT

The audience for this book is the beginning elementary science teacher. We define a *beginning elementary science teacher* in two ways: (1) a student teacher, working on a preservice college program, and (2) a teacher in the first year of teaching. If you belong to the first category, your journey toward science teaching is likely to start with a preservice course in elementary science methods. It will continue through your student teaching experience, to the point where you are able to take on your first teaching job. In the past, the end of preservice might have been seen as the end of the journey, arriving as a qualified teacher who is employable by a school district. However, as any experienced teacher will tell you, the first year of teaching, more than any other, is a huge learning experience. While your preservice program can lay the groundwork for what you will encounter in schools, it is during that first year that you experience, and take responsibility for, the day-to-day reality of becoming a professional educator. This is why we include your preservice program and your first teaching year under the term *beginning teacher*. Beyond your first year of teaching, you will still need to engage in continuing professional development, just as physicians and lawyers do. However, the starting-out stage has its own special challenges and problems.

The Exciting Challenge of Science Teaching

First experiences with teaching are always challenging, whatever the subject. Teaching science for the first time can be even more challenging because of the nature of the subject and materials involved. This will be especially true if you feel that there are gaps in your own knowledge of science concepts and processes. In this you will not be alone. Many teachers of science, at all levels, have those same feelings. The introduction of national and local standards has placed science as an important subject in elementary schools. As a result, many experienced elementary teachers are taking on a broader range of science topics than they have in the past. If your own science knowledge about an area is just developing, you share a common situation with them and can count on some support.

Science education today is firmly oriented toward "learning through inquiry"—that is, investigating science questions rather than teaching science facts. This will allow you to experience science learning through children's eyes, giving you a valuable appreciation of the learning dimensions involved. Science teaching today is much more about working with your children in investigating scientific questions, and far less about being an expert scientist.

Scientific investigations are "naturals" for engaging your children's curiosity, both in and out of the classroom. They also are excellent instructional hooks, and entry points into other curricular areas such as mathematics, reading, social studies, language arts, music, physical education, and more. For example, your children can read science trade books for language arts and reading lessons; use the mathematical skills of measurement and graphing during a science experiment; learn about the social impact of a science discovery in social studies; investigate the science of sound in music; explore the physics and biology of exercise in physical education; and make many more cross-curricular connections. Science is involved, to some degree or another, with almost every other form of human understanding. In turn, science depends on other subject areas itself, especially mathematics and language arts.

You need to be aware that an understanding of science concepts and processes is essential for making intelligent decisions in life, as well as for approaching life's problems logically and systematically. As citizens, both you and the children you teach need to be scientifically literate to participate in society's decision-making processes in a useful and informed way.

Your Role as a Teacher of Science

Being a teacher of science involves being a guide and helper to your students as they investigate scientific ideas and questions. You do not need to have all the answers to the questions that will arise as your children explore, research, design, invent, and search for explanations. Science teaching is an unfolding process: it consists of posing questions, investigating those questions in a variety of ways, finding some answers, raising more questions, and continually moving forward in search of connections, solutions, themes, patterns, relationships, and, always, more questions. This is what scientists do. What you need to know is how to direct your children to resources that will help them find answers to their own questions. You also need to know a number of ways in which your children can explore their scientific questions and those posed by others.

This approach to science teaching and learning may differ significantly from your own experience as a student. Science teaching came under the microscope beginning in the late 1980s, and the result has been something of a revolution in terms of the traditional methods of instruction. In particular, the introduction of national, state, and local teaching standards now drives science education. (*Note:* See Chapter 18, "Using Curriculum Standards as a Teaching Resource" for specific details.)

How This Book Can Help

The core of this book consists of ten exemplary science investigations. They make up the first ten chapters because they illustrate a variety of ways in which your children can investigate many types of science questions. Each is based on a "science as inquiry" approach that is advocated by national standards. Some are more suitable for the early grades, while others are appropriate for children at upper elementary levels. (The grade level is indicated in each exemplar.) Together, they offer a range of types of investigations. For example, some are short-term, others long-term; some involve classroom experiments, others field study; some have children gathering data from direct observations, others have them gathering data from libraries, CD-ROMs, Web sites, parents, community members, or self-conducted surveys. From within these ten investigations you can gain experience of most forms of scientific inquiry, all of which can later be used for other investigations.

Each investigation focuses on a different area within the range of sciences or science content areas. Collectively, they cover the broad range of scientific concepts for which elementary children need to begin developing an understanding. Learning scientific ideas and processes takes time. The ten exemplars are only a small part of the story for your children as they progress through their elementary years. They will need to revisit each topic many times, delving more deeply into each area before moving on to middle school. But the essential range of areas is included, to allow you to get a sense of the big picture as a beginning teacher of science.

College and the School Classroom

These exemplars have been designed for two purposes:

1. *For use in a preservice college program: for your science methods course and in student teaching.* While in methods, you may first take on the role of an elementary student, although working at your own level, trying the investigations with your professor as "teacher." This will give you an experiential understanding of learning science in the way you will later be teaching. You will feel what it is like to engage in science understanding though an inquiry approach. You may also learn some new scientific concepts and processes. Doing this will prepare you for your student teaching in schools where you will be able to reinterpret your own experience for the children.

2. *For you to use, either in whole or in part, during your first year of teaching.* Even though the school in which you begin teaching may have a district-designed science curriculum, or might have adopted a particular basal curriculum, you will still find these investigations useful as alternatives or extensions. In the event that there is no basal curriculum, then these exemplars will provide you with a good starting point for that first year. You will be able to take the experiences you have had with these exemplary lessons and apply them to the science program your school is using.

Common Elements in the Exemplars

There are important common elements in the exemplars that reflect what is currently accepted as good science teaching practice. These elements are:

- Children are afforded the opportunity to express what they already know about a topic before they begin any investigations. This gives you, their teacher, the chance to assess their prior knowledge, including any informal ideas. (*Note:* Please see the later section headed "Children's Informal Ideas."

- As much as possible, children investigate questions about the world around them.

- Children start with everyday objects, events, living things, and phenomena in formulating questions to investigate.

- Children use their senses and, where appropriate, tools, to make, record, and analyze their observations.

- Children share their observations with each other and discuss what they might mean, in terms of the questions that can be investigated.

- Children consult with each other, and with their teacher, to decide on ways of investigating their questions.

- Children make predictions about possible outcomes for their investigations, based upon their prior knowledge, research, and reasoning.

- Children are asked to record their reasons for their predictions, when making predictions is appropriate to the investigation.

- Children explore their investigative questions by designing and running "fair tests" using any resources that are available to them (manipulatives, measuring devices, models, the outdoors, information resources, their teacher and other experts, as well as each other) and record the results.

- Children review their results and look for patterns and relationships that answer or explain their investigation questions.

- Children arrive at conclusions about the question they are investigating and attempt to tie them into a bigger, real-world picture.

- Children communicate the results of their investigations to others in a form that can be seen and understood.

- Children work with each other and their teacher to identify underlying science themes and big ideas that help to explain the results of their investigation.

- Children formulate new questions to explore, based upon the results of their original investigation.

- Children work independently, in pairs, or in small groups, based upon the nature of the investigation and the readiness of the children.

- Children revisit their original ideas about the topic they have investigated, to determine how their ideas have changed and expanded.

- Children reflect upon the processes they used to investigate, acknowledging what worked and didn't work for them.

The processes of scientific investigation are extremely important for your children to recognize, understand, and practice. This systematic way of exploring a question is a key part of "being scientific" and also a skill that they can use throughout their lives.

While it is important that your children understand science concepts and how they connect to one another, they should be learning these through their investigations and certainly not through a process of rote memorization. No one person could possibly know all of what is encompassed by "science," although it is important to comprehend the overarching themes and big ideas upon which the sciences are based. This is especially so since the body of knowledge called science is continually changing. As scientists make greater use of rapidly advancing technologies, "facts" that have been accepted for many years are being called into question. This is because scientists are now able to extend their senses through instrumentation to detect the formerly undetectable. We know more about space, the oceans, genetics, physics, subatomic particles, life through time, and many other topics than we have ever known before.

Children's Informal Ideas

A crucial element in the learning process lies with the learner, in terms of what the learner already knows or does not know. This is a key part of the approach to learning upon which all the exemplars are based. We all incorporate new ideas into what we already know or believe. In any learning moment, our minds are not simply empty spaces waiting to be filled. Instead, we bring to that moment any prior learning that seems relevant to help us interpret the new idea or ideas. As the term suggests, we *construct* meaning. This is a building process.

Even more important is the notion that the ideas we already have may be challenged by new ideas that somehow conflict with our current thinking. When we come across something we don't understand, or something with which we are unfamiliar, our minds try to make the best possible sense of it, using what we already know. Sometimes, when we do not have sufficient prior knowledge, or when the new idea is too complex to understand easily, this process can lead us to form an inaccurate understanding or explanation. This is sometimes referred to as a *misconception* and sometimes as a *naive idea,* though a better descriptor is probably an *informal idea.* That is, we have an understanding that does not conform to the commonly accepted explanation. (*Note:* See Chapter 13, "How Children Learn," for an explanation of the *constructivist* approach to learning.)

Science ideas and concepts, because of their complex nature, can easily prompt *informal ideas* or explanations, especially in young children whose intellectual development level is still immature. Many, perhaps most, will have some informal ideas about a scientific phenomenon or concept. So do most adults, especially if the idea they have was formed in childhood and has never been challenged enough for them to revise their understanding. Almost certainly, you yourself have some informal ideas with regard to science, some of which may be changed as you work through this book and begin teaching science.

It is crucial in science teaching and learning to give children the opportunity to share what they already think about a science idea. Obviously, it is common sense for you as a teacher discover this, so that you can provide the kind of science experiences that will help your children progress from their current understanding to new and more accurate ideas. It is also important for your children, because once they have articulated their current ideas they will be better able to compare these with new, more-accepted scientific ideas and explanations. To help you with this learning area, the following points are worth noting and remembering:

- Children have *informal ideas* about science based on the experiences that they have had with science phenomena.

- Children's *informal ideas* may be perfectly logical in their eyes given their experiences and intellectual development stages.

- Children's *informal ideas* should be respected. (They are not *wrong* so much as *different;* not a *misconception,* so much as a *preconception.*)

- Your job is to find out what children's *informal ideas* are and then help them toward a better understanding through hands-on activities, investigations, and interactions with both peers and adults.

- Children can only cope with ideas that come within the limits of their intellectual development. With young children, this means they can only form ideas through interaction with concrete things that they can observe and manipulate. They cannot think in abstract terms until a later developmental stage. Children at the elementary-school level may be between stages of intellectual development, sometimes thinking at a higher level, sometimes at a lower level, depending on the circumstances.

- An elementary class may be one grade level, but there will be great variety among children in terms of their development and level of science ideas. You need to take these individual differences into account when planning instruction.

Other Important Aspects of Elementary Science Education

While the ten exemplar investigations represent the core of this book, there are many other important aspects of science teaching with which you need to become familiar.

These components are covered in the remaining chapters of the book, and all of them will be important to you far beyond your first year of teaching. Some of these are very practical, such as Chapter 11, "The Nuts and Bolts of Teaching Elementary Science." This chapter describes how to set up your classroom for science, procure and manage materials, identify and use external resources, handle safety issues, manage your students during investigations, and more. Others chapters deal with current issues within science education that are likely have an impact on your professional responsibilities as a science teacher. (Again, see Chapter 18.) Still others provide insights into developing your own strategies for continuing professional development, (See Chapter 17, "Evaluating Your Own Science Teaching and Professional Growth.") There are also chapters on such topics as selecting appropriate science curricula, planning science lessons, assessing your children in science, teaching science in a cross-curricular fashion, dealing with diversity, and other useful areas.

The Research Base for This Book

It is worth remembering that science, like mathematics, is a universal discipline. While subjects like language arts, social science, and music may vary in content from country to country, or from culture to culture, the body of science knowledge is largely the same throughout the world. Different societies may place stronger emphasis on some particular parts of scientific knowledge, use different measures (English or metric units), or describe science in different languages, but the science itself remains reasonably constant. Similarly, the research base for science is international, both in terms of the actual research and the dissemination of research findings.

Science education research has an international perspective. However, cultural differences, the ways in which educational curricula and systems are managed, and differing teaching and learning styles from one country to another limit the universality of such research. While there is considerable sharing of science education research findings within English-speaking countries, even this can be constrained by variations in educational practice, favored theories about children's cognitive development, and traditional expectations of student learning.

In the United Sates, research into science education has received much attention in recent years. This has been greatly influenced by the move to develop science education standards. In research terms, the prime example of this is Project 2061 of the American Association for the Advancement of Science (AAAS), which made a wide-ranging analysis of existing science education research literature, both domestic and international. The project also created 25-person school-based research and development teams, at six sites around the country. These teams' task was, over one year, to develop models of science education for grades K–12 based on current research and their own knowledge of school practice. Consultation and technical assistance were provided by university faculty.

The results from both the literature analysis and the work of the teams were first extensively reviewed and then compiled into a research base for the Project 2061 publication *Benchmarks for Science Literacy.* Published in 1993, the book details precise statements (*benchmarks*) of what science education concepts, processes, attitudes and skills students should be expected to know at grade levels K–2, 3–5, 6–8, and 9–12. It is fair to say that the research base for *Benchmarks for Science Literacy* represents one of the most comprehensive studies ever made in science education.

Most science education research is conducted by relatively small specialist groups or individuals in universities or education research centers. While some of these findings are reported in professional journals and in other ways, they are usually published as an individual journal article, or at best as part of a collection of articles focusing upon a particular topic. Few researchers or research agencies have the human and financial resources needed to conduct a systematic review of science education research across the board. The resources invested in *the Benchmarks for Science Literacy* research base, coupled with the rigorous methodology of its compilation, make it by far the most comprehensive study completed to date. It is therefore the watershed research resource for current science education in general, and this book in particular.

The *Benchmarks for Science Literacy* research base was available as a resource for the developers of the *National Science Education Standards,* produced by the National Research Council, and published three years later in 1996. While this publication did not create a new science education research base, it did engage in very wide consultation with the science and educational community. As well as producing another set of statements, called *content standards,* about what students should be expected to know at different grade levels, it also focused upon the broader issues of science teaching, professional development for teachers of science, assessment in science education, science education programs standards, and science education system standards. These standards, and the rationales given for them, represent another powerful resource for anyone considering science teaching.

Though not strictly a research base, the *National Standards for Science Education* represents the collaborative thinking and views of the science education community at large. It influences new research, informs science curriculum developers, and provides the basis for state and school-district curricula nationally. In this sense, it provides another clear research resource base for this book.

While the research backgrounds of these two authoritative sources inform the basis of this book, many other research studies and findings are drawn upon to support its particular components. Thinking about science education is also a question of thinking about education. The study of teaching and learning, or *pedagogy,* is a well-established educational research field—derived in part from theories of child development, cognitive psychology, social psychology, sociology—and informed by practice. Serious consideration of these researched pedagogical elements is embedded within the design of the ten exemplar lessons (Chapters 1 to 10), the basis of which is described in Chapter 13, "How Children Learn."

Where appropriate, research citations are given at those points in the book to which they are most directly related. For example, relevant research items are shown for each of the exemplar lessons. All citations and references are listed in the bibliography at the end of the book. While we encourage readers to refer to the research base of this book wherever possible, we recognize that the pressing priorities of planning to teach children science may preclude the complete study of this important dimension. However, we feel it is crucial for all teachers of science to become familiar and make use of at least the *Benchmarks for Science Literacy* and the *National Science Education Standards*. Approaching the research base with the benefit of some firsthand classroom teaching experience is usually more interesting and motivating than reading it cold!

Lastly, this book draws heavily on the authors' own wide experience of elementary school teaching, preservice and inservice teacher education in science, and substantial work in science curriculum development and informal science education. This experience provides a practical body of understanding about the realities of teaching and learning science in elementary education, both in and out of the classroom.

Becoming and Being a Teacher of Science

We hope that *Science Education for Elementary Teachers: An Investigation-based Approach* will be useful to you, both in your preservice career and as a guide for your first year in the classroom. If you follow its message faithfully, you will realize that it is up to you as a teacher to take responsibility for your own professional development, both during and beyond these first steps. Teachers typically learn as much or more during teaching than do their students. With this in mind, look on your science teaching as an adventure for you and your students, and as an exciting chance to learn and explore science with them.

ACKNOWLEDGMENTS

We would first like to thank the many students and colleagues with whom it has been our privilege to work over the years, and from all of whom we learned more than we taught. Special thanks go to Jay Whitney, who initially persuaded us to work on this project; to Judy Johnstone, who kept our noses to the grindstone and has a wicked sense of humor; to Trudy Brown, who steered the production ship safely into harbor; and especially to Dan Alpert, whose faith in the concept and championship on our behalf made this book possible.

We are also deeply indebted to the following reviewers: Angela Battaglia, University of Utah; John R. Cannon, University of Nevada, Reno; Lynn S. Freeman, University of Houston; Gassia Gerges, University of Memphis; Ann S. Hernandez, University of Saint Francis; Linda Cronin Jones, University of Florida; Margaret King, Ohio University; Martha J. Kurtz, Central Washington University; Judith L. Lemons, Hannibal–LaGrange College; Judy Reinhartz, University of Texas–Arlington.

TO THE INSTRUCTOR

This book is for everyone who teaches elementary science methods. For some of you, the Instructor's Edition can be used as a guide to extend your existing programs. For others, it may provide an organizational framework for your methods course. Some of you may want to structure your own program closely around this material, while others can be counted upon to find alternative science methods that suit their particular teaching style or preference. Keeping this diversity in mind, we respectfully address all our colleagues who, like us, care passionately about giving prospective teachers the best opportunities to become thoroughly professional teachers of elementary science.

NSES and Benchmarks

An important feature of *Science Education for Elementary Teachers* is that is derived from, and informed by, both the *Benchmarks for Science Literacy* of the American Association for the Advancement of Science's Project 2061 (1993), and the National Research Council's *National Science Education Standards* (NSES), 1996. Within *NSES*, the *Standards for Professional Development for Teachers of Science*, (NSES, Chapter 4, pages 55–73) are particularly relevant for faculty. Here, many important elements that govern teacher education are identified, detailed, and debated. From this array, one standard may be most apposite, and it underpins the approach taken in this methods text:

> **Standard A:**
> *"Professional development for teachers of science requires learning essential science content through the perspectives and methods of inquiry. . . ."*
>
> (*NSES*, Ch. 4, p. 59)

Our driving concern is for the children with whom beginning teachers work in school classrooms. They, and their parents, have the right to expect quality science teaching that draws on the best knowledge available about science education. This places a heavy burden on a beginning teacher, who is asked to deliver high quality, yet has only limited experience upon which to draw—and at a stage in a teaching career that brings numerous other pressures and concerns. Our intention is to address and ease this problem for beginning teachers and the children they teach.

The Research Base

While the research base for this book is derived from many sources, including our own extensive experience in the field, we would argue that the central research is that which underlies the *Benchmarks* and *Standards*. The development of these two sources represents a depth of research scrutiny and consensus building unparalleled in the history of science education. Its results not only suggest what students should be expected to know and understand but also, in the case of the *Standards*, what *teachers* should know, understand, and be able to do professionally. In turning our attention to methods courses, we are attempting to shift the traditional balance between the practical vocational elements that students need—and schools expect them to have—and the more traditional approach that has often emphasized scholastic theory. Both are important of course, but the balance has often been skewed.

Bridging Preservice and Beginning Teaching

This book is designed as a survival guide to bridge the gap between a student's college-based methods course and that first year of teaching. The ten teaching exemplars of Part I form the basis of a methods course and undergird student teaching practice, while providing samples of specific investigations for students to use in the classroom during their first year of teaching.

These science investigations model good science teaching practice in the elementary classroom. They cover a variety of science concepts, instructional approaches, and topic areas that are suitable for various levels of elementary students. While the exemplars do not, by any interpretation, constitute an elementary science "curriculum," they can serve as starting points for further investigations when teachers are in their own classrooms.

The Exemplars

Part I of this book is comprised of the exemplar investigations, while Part II contains the more theoretical and generic material. While this order may seem unconventional, it mirrors common constructivist ideas about the relationship between theory and practice. Constructivist thinking holds that theory is best understood through reflection on firsthand experiences. By "doing" first, the learner has a vital tool with which to explore the whats and whys that arise. Certainly you can choose to use the book in reverse order if that is your preference.

The ten exemplars have been carefully selected to provide a cross section of science curriculum content. Recognizing that methods courses are relatively short, we have constructed the exemplars in a manner that integrates most aspects of elementary science education. Students working through these exemplars in methods class, and then adapting them for student teaching, will, at the very least, have covered many of the key issues raised by *Benchmarks* and *Standards* in a practical way. The exemplars also provide an experiential base from which to approach more theoretical science-education issues and considerations.

These exemplars are also designed to address some of the needs of pre-service elementary teachers who may not have had extensive science experiences in either their formal or informal education. Each exemplar includes a section on science background for the topic, as well as information on what children might already understand about that topic. There are also sample questions that your students might want to ask children during their practice teaching, to further explore how children think about science.

The exemplars also serve as illustrations of how science can be taught, using a modified learning cycle approach, through such practices as:

- Emphasizing hands-on activities
- Employing cooperative learning
- Emphasizing problem solving through science processes
- Assessing prior knowledge of concepts and skills
- Using everyday objects
- Accessing external resources
- Using the outdoors as a laboratory
- Incorporating community resources
- Taking a cross-curricular approach
- Beginning with national science education standards
- Doing performance assessment
- Eliciting student records of data
- Asking open-ended questions
- Offering opportunities for peer teaching and assessment
- Availing oneself of available technology

Pedagogy, Theory, and Practical Considerations

The supporting chapters of Part II cover the more theoretical and generic issues involved in teaching elementary science. They are intended to help students understand the context within which science teaching takes place. Experience suggests that beginning teachers are mainly focused upon the dynamics of the classroom—and particularly their performance within it. At this stage in their professional development, new teachers are less likely to be interested in, or easily assimilate, the vast range of complex philosophical, psychological, and sociological theories that underlie education practice. We have therefore been selective, including only those topics that seem to us to be paramount for a beginning teacher. They include:

- The nuts and bolts of teaching science (managing the logistics and materials of teaching elementary science)
- How children learn (learning theories supporting particular approaches to science teaching at the elementary level)
- Selecting an elementary science curriculum (what to look for when choosing an effective science program)
- Evaluating your own science teaching (how to assess one's own progress in teaching elementary science)

- Using curriculum standards as a teaching resource (how to use *the National Science Education Standards* and *Benchmarks for Science Literacy*)
- Planning a science investigation (how to decide exactly what to teach and how to teach it, so that children learn specific knowledge and skills)
- Cross-curricular teaching and learning (partnering with colleagues to teach science across the curriculum)
- Dealing with diversity (how to address the needs of all students in one's classroom)
- The role of assessment in elementary science teaching (how to determine what the children know and are able to do as a result of their science instruction)

The chapters of Part II were written to provide useful information and support for beginning elementary teachers as they plan, teach, and grow as science education professionals.

Many elementary science methods courses emphasize the application of science teaching research findings to classroom practice. For this to be effective, it requires that preservice teachers have numerous examples of good, research-based practice. The ten instructional exemplars in this book are designed to help beginning teachers cross the bridge from theory to practice. By using the lessons in methods class, in early field placements, and in the student teaching experience, teachers can discover what works for them and their students in the field.

Teaching Science Methods

One possible use of the exemplars is for practice teaching in science methods class. The methods class trial of the lessons can help the students to reflect on such important aspects of their teaching as:

- How to determine students' understanding of concepts
- How to organize materials
- How to gauge time for instruction
- How to group students to their best advantage
- How to manage a class during science
- How and when to ask questions that clarify students' ideas and provide feedback on their understanding
- How to work with colleagues in a cross-curricular fashion
- How to develop concepts through a number of examples and experiences
- How to assess student performance in a variety of ways
- How to recognize the components of a "good" science investigation
- How to reflect upon and improve one's own practice

As the methods students try out the exemplars with each other, they can adapt the lessons to use with elementary children in their field experiences. They can also adapt the lessons for children of different ages and abilities. After determining how well the lessons work with children, the students can discuss in methods class (or in the student teaching seminar) what was successful, what was not, and why. This entire process will help students become aware of their own teaching styles and how well those styles fit with effective science teaching practice.

As science methods students work through the exemplars, they can consult the supporting chapters in Part II when these become germane to what is happening in the methods class or in their field experiences. For example, it would be helpful for students to read Chapter 18 ("Curriculum Standards as a Teaching Resource") either before or after they review the *National Science Education Standards* and *the Benchmarks for Science Literacy*. Chapter 17 ("Evaluating Your Own Science Teaching") can be used as the basis for designing a self-assessment plan for the student teaching experience. "How Children Learn" (Chapter 13), used in conjunction with Chapter 15 ("How to Select an Elementary Science Curriculum") can set the scene for analyzing lessons or entire curricula for their developmental appropriateness. Methods students can access the information and suggestions in Chapter 16 ("Teaching in Partnership with Colleagues") as they prepare for their student teaching experience or a team-teaching venture with fellow methods students.

We have made some assumptions in our design for this book. These include:

- The elementary science methods course is campus-based and includes some classroom observations and interactions with elementary school children.

- The methods class size is no more than 30 students.

- The accommodation for the class can be arranged so that students can work comfortably in small collaborative groups, between 3 and 5 students per group, and also with furniture that can be arranged in group tables or suitable working areas.

- Students will have access to typical elementary science materials to try out lessons.

- Students will have access to the Internet, either during methods class or on their own.

- Students will have access to a curriculum library, so they can examine and compare a variety of elementary science curricula.

- Students will have had some of their basic education courses either before or during the time they are taking their elementary science methods course.

Ultimately, of course, it is up you to decide how this book fits into the syllabus of your institution. The marginal notes in the Instructor's Edition are designed to help in judging this fit. These notes reflect our own experiences as elementary teachers and teachers of elementary science methods students, as well as our experiences as curriculum developers, researchers, and inservice teacher educators. We intend that this book's exemplars and supporting chapters provide a framework to help new elementary science teachers feel a sense of comfort and confidence as they embark upon their science teaching careers.

PART

I

Ten Exemplary Lessons

LIVING

THINGS

HAVE

CERTAIN

NEEDS

1

Investigating Living Things

WHAT CHILDREN CAN LEARN FROM THIS EXEMPLAR

Children's Thinking about Life and Living: The Research Base

A group of fourth graders were given three drawings and asked to identify which of the drawings showed items that were alive. The drawings consisted of a fish, a rock, and a tree. The children were universal in their agreement that the rock was not alive, although some children mentioned fossils in rocks and wondered if that meant that the rocks were once alive. The fish was deemed alive because it moved, ate, and had baby fish. There was a discussion about how the fish got "air." Children who knew something about fish proffered information about gills and how they thought these worked to help fish breathe.

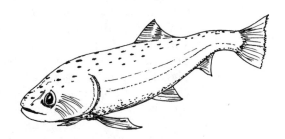

The real puzzler to the children was the tree. Most thought it was alive because it grew, but they were confused about how it got food. They also were concerned about the fact that the tree was unable to move from where it was growing. Some help was offered by one child, who said: "Trees die when they get cut down or hit by lightning. If it can die, it must have been alive." After a long discussion, the children decided that:

- The rock was not alive, because it didn't move, didn't eat, didn't have babies, and didn't breathe.
- The fish was definitely alive, because it moved, ate, had babies, and could breathe.
- The tree was alive, because it grew and needed water, but it was "less alive" than the fish, because it couldn't move under its own power and couldn't breathe.

The picture activity was just the starting point for an entire series of investigations that included: What are living things? How do we know they are alive? What do they need to live? The activity's results are interesting in another sense, because they illustrate what researchers, from Piaget to the present, have discovered about children's thinking about life and living. Piaget found that many children think of nonliving objects as living because such objects can move and seem to respond in other ways. As children get older and gain more experience of living things, their ideas about what is "living" become more sophisticated. From thinking, at ages 6 and 7, that anything that moves is alive (whether it moves by itself or something moves it), children at ages 9 through 11 think things that move under their own power are alive. These things that move under their own power, however, can include rivers and clouds. A 1981 study by Tamir found that, in a sample of Israeli pupils aged 8 to 14, the children were more ready to think of natural objects as living than they were manufactured objects. The sense of something being found in nature (even a river or cloud) makes it more likely to be thought alive by a child than would be a car or a bicycle.

Teaching Implications of the Research

It is important that you assess your children's understanding of life and living before you begin any investigations into the area. You may want to use the picture activity described at the beginning of the chapter to elicit your children's ideas about what constitutes "aliveness." If you decide to do this, be sure to keep the children's responses available throughout their investigations. It might even be useful to have them posted on chart paper so that you can revisit them periodically and make changes and additions.

You will need to be alert to some of the common informal ideas your children may have about living things. They, like the children in the picture activity, may think that movement is the key indicator of life. They may also think that, if they cannot see an object move, it is not moving at all. This is one of the main reasons that children do not consider plants to be alive, or tend to think of them as "less alive" than animals. You can help them move away from this idea by setting up an investigation in which one potted plant (such as a mature bean plant) is placed in a closet with the door open just a crack to let in the light, while a second potted bean plant is left out in the light. Given enough time (and equal amounts of water), the plant in the closet will grow toward the light (a phenomenon known as *phototropism*). If children observe these two plants every day, and make records of their observations, this will help them to see that plants do have limited movement.

For children in upper elementary grades, it is difficult to show that plants respire with hands-on investigations. There are laboratories that illustrate this, but they are best suited to upper middle school or high school level, as they involve sophisticated concepts and tools. You can, however, use the same bean plants mentioned earlier to illustrate that plants need water (just water one and don't water the other). Seed collecting and seed germinating can help children understand that plants reproduce others of their own kind. It is important that you not take your children beyond what they are ready to understand about plants. They need to have hands-on investigations—as well as field experiences, videos, and other experiences—to help them understand that plants are living things.

You may find that your children do not consider humans to be animals, even though they share the basic life requirements of other living things: movement, respiration, sensitivity, growth, reproduction, excretion, and nutrition. Many young children think of "animals" as having fur, feathers, or scales. Insects, jellyfish, starfish, worms, and other invertebrates (animals without backbones) might not be thought of as animals. You can help children to understand the needs of animals by keeping some of these in the classroom, and caring for, and observing them. Children can then compare the habits and needs of these animals with their own habits and needs. The exemplary lesson that follows is designed to help your children understand the basic needs of living things. You may want to use it as a first experience in this area, or it may come toward the middle of a series of investigations into life and living.

Science Background

Living things, also known as *organisms,* can be classified as such because they exhibit certain behaviors. They all:

* Need food to survive
* Use oxygen to release energy from food
* Give off carbon dioxide as a waste product
* Respond to stimuli
* Reproduce their own kind

Living things may show a greater or lesser tendency to respond to stimuli; this does not mean that they are more, or less, "alive." The state of being alive is an absolute: something is alive or it is not. Because there are so many different types of organisms, all the way from single-celled bacteria to flowering plants to human beings, it is sometimes difficult to detect the signs of life in all of these types. Many types of plants, for example, do not appear to respond to stimuli (touch, light, heat, chemicals, gravity) because they are rooted in the ground. Plants do, however, react to light by grow-ing toward it. Roots grow toward the center of the Earth due to the force of gravity. The leaves of some plants, such as the mimosa tree, curl up when touched; the "fly-catcher" portion of the Venus Fly Trap, a carnivorous plant; closes when an insect crawls inside.

Children who are just learning about plants will have trouble under-standing that plants make their own food, the simple sugar called *glucose,* from carbon dioxide and water in the presence of light and chlorophyll, a green pigment found within the cells of the plant. The plants do not have to be "fed" to live. What confounds understanding about plants and their food-making process (known as *photosynthesis*) is that there are commer-cial products called "plant food." Many children see such plant food and other fertilizers as "feeding" the plant through its roots. They will need a number of experiences to be able to understand that it is mostly the leaves of plants that are the manufacturing site of the food for plants. You can help children to understand how plants are able to grow without external "food" by growing cuttings of plants in water. Put some of these plants in darkness, so that your children can observe what happens in both in-stances. The plants in sunlight and water will thrive, while the cuttings in water and darkness will turn yellow and become spindly.

EXEMPLAR

LIVING THINGS HAVE CERTAIN NEEDS
Investigating Living Things

Note: The investigation is most suitable for children in grades 4 and 5.

OVERVIEW

As living things themselves, your children will be aware of many of their own needs. What they may not have thought about is that they are only one species of living thing in a huge world of life. All living things have certain elements in common. To survive, they need: a source of food, oxygen to burn up that food, water, an environment to which they are suited, and freedom from invading organisms.

Children can discover many of the needs of living things by observing them, either in the classroom or out, over an extended period. This gives them the opportunity to make observations on a regular basis, record them in a systematic fashion, and interpret what they have recorded. They can look for patterns and relationships in their records to find out what living things have in common. They can also learn to care for plants and animals, both in the classroom and in the wild. These are skills they will use throughout their lives.

KEY PEDAGOGICAL IDEAS

- Scientific investigation can start with familiar objects or events.
- Children can be immediately engaged in investigating a question that has personal significance for them.
- Scientific investigations can involve a range of associated curriculum areas, providing opportunities for children to apply and enhance their skills in a meaningful context. This applies especially to mathematics, language/communication, art and crafts, as well as other related science ideas.
- When children engage in scientific investigations, trying to find answers to their own questions, they are being scientists themselves, using scientific research processes such as observing, predicting, fair-testing, recording, and reviewing results.

KEY SCIENCE CONCEPTS

- Living things need such basics as water, food, and air, among others.
- Living things depend upon their environment for their basic needs.
- Damage to the environment can affect the well-being of living things.

SUPPORTING NATIONAL STANDARDS

National Science Education Standards

LEVEL K–4

Content Standard A: As a result of activities in grades K–4, all students should develop:

- Abilities necessary to do scientific inquiry
- Understanding about scientific inquiry

Content Standard C: As a result of activities in grades K–4, all students should develop an understanding of:

- The characteristics of organisms
- Organisms and environments

Benchmarks for Science Literacy

By the end of the 5th grade, students should know that

- For any particular environment, some kinds of plants and animals survive well, some survive less well, and some cannot survive at all.
- Insects and various other organisms depend on dead plant and animal material for food.
- Organisms interact with one another in various ways besides providing food. Many plants depend on animals for carrying their pollen to other plants or for dispersing their seeds.
- Changes in an organism's habitat are sometimes beneficial to it and sometimes harmful.

BEFORE YOU BEGIN

Technology Connection

Collect resources on animals, such as trade books, videos, charts, CD-ROMs, or magazines. Use a search engine to locate safe Web sites about animals that your children could access. Some of these include the Web site for the National Geographic Society (www.nationalgeographic.com), the National Wildlife Federation (www.nwf.org), and the National Zoo in Washington, D.C. (www.si.edu/natzoo/). *National Geographic* has an extensive catalog of nature films that you may want to use as introductions or follow-ups to this lesson. A number of them are particularly well suited to a younger audience.

Linking to the Community

Arrange for a classroom visit from a veterinarian, professional from the humane society, or horticulturist, so that your children can learn about the proper care of living things in the classroom. Arrange for a field trip to a zoo, farm, nature center, park, or aquarium, so that children can apply what they have learned about living things to new situations.

Preparing Materials

Scout out the areas beyond your classroom to discover what living things are nearby. Arrange to have plants and animals in your classroom that students will find interesting to observe over time. Discuss your plant and animal needs with adult classroom volunteers, as well as your district science supervisor, so that you can get the help you need in procuring, sheltering, and caring for the living things with which your children will be working.

A NOTE ABOUT SAFETY!   Science investigations should be safe. Ensure that students are not exposed to any hazards or dangers while they are engaged in investigations. Draw their attention to the need to observe safety procedures at all times, especially when handling animals in the classroom. Be sure that students wash their hands after handling plants or animals. Go to the Internet at www.nsta.org for the National Science Teachers Associations' *Guidelines for Responsible Use of Animals in the Classroom.*

ASSESSING PRIOR KNOWLEDGE

Investigating Living Things: Getting Things Going! (15 min)

It is important to establish first what the term *living things* actually means to your children. Ask them to draw three pictures of living things that they know about, making them large enough so that everyone can see them from a distance. (Using markers or dark crayons will increase visibility.) Post these on the bulletin board.

Note: See if any of your children have drawn plants. Often these living things get left off the list because children, especially very young ones, equate "living things" with animals.

Ask your children to look at the collection of drawings, and introduce these questions:

> How do we know that these are living?
>
> How are all of these living things alike?
>
> What are ways in which these living things are different?
>
> What do these living things need to stay alive?
>
> What other living things are there that you haven't drawn?

EXPLORING CONCEPTS

Agreeing about What Living Things Are and What They Need to Survive (10 min)

Hold an open discussion using the posted drawings as a resource. List the children's ideas about living things and what they need. You may want to do this using an overhead transparency, poster paper, or the board.

> What needs do living things have that we can all agree upon?
>
> If your children have trouble with this task, you could ask them to focus on themselves as living things. They will know that they need:

- Food
- Water
- Shelter (clothes and buildings)
- Air
- Freedom from disease and predators (safety and health)

Note: Include only those items that your children contribute and agree upon. Be sure to leave space for later additions to the list.

Alongside the list *What Living Things Need*, set up another list called *Key Questions to Ask about Living Things and What They Need*. Explain that, to investigate in an organized way, we need to find good questions to ask about what living things need:

> What important questions can you think of to ask about living things and what they need?

Help your students to formulate useful questions and list them. The box shows an example of this.

> **QUESTIONS TO INVESTIGATE**
> * Do all living things have the same needs?
> * How can we find out if all living things have the same needs?
> * How do living things get what they need?
> * What happens to living things if they don't get what they need to live?
> * What living things could we observe in and around our classrooms?

As a class, your students will be investigating the question: What do different living things need to survive?

If this question does not arise from your children's thinking and discussions, add it to the list yourself. Explain to your children that they will be investigating the question as a class, and that the investigation will take place over a long period of time (several weeks). Tell them that they will have the opportunity to investigate their own questions about living things.

FOCUSING ON AND EXPLAINING CONCEPTS

How Do We Go About Observing Living Things? (10 min)

Have available a large insect, such as a grasshopper or a big beetle, in a large glass jar with holes punched in the lid. You will also need to have a medium-size potted plant, such as Swedish ivy, to show your children.

Note: Be sure that all children can see both the insect and the plant clearly from where they are sitting.

Ask the children how they know that both the insect and the plant are living things. Ask them to list ways in which these two living things are alike.

> Ask the children if the insect has everything in the jar that it needs to live.
>
> What does the insect have in this jar to help it live? What does it still need?

Have children volunteer what they think the insect has and what it still needs. Ask them what they noticed (observed) about the insect that helped them with their answers. Ask them what they already knew about insects that helped them.

Finally, ask your children how they could learn more about the needs of the insect. Where could they find this information?

Repeat these questions for the plant. Does it have everything it needs to survive? How could they find out more about the needs of the plant?

Note: This section is the lead-in to the idea of a long-term investigation—a longitudinal study.

How Do Scientists Find Out about Living Things? (5 min)

Show a natural science video that illustrates how field biologists go about studying living things. The Jane Goodall films about her work with primates are some of the best. (*Among the Wild Chimps* is one of these; you can get the Goodall films through the National Geographic Society film collection.)

Before you show the video, alert your children to the fact that they will be watching a field biologist (a scientist who studies living things in the wild) at work. Ask them to watch how the biologist studies the living things. They may want to write down their ideas as they watch the video.

When you have finished showing the video (and you may want to show more than one), ask your students to volunteer what they think are the important things to remember when studying living things (especially in the wild). List these on the board or on paper chart.

Some items that your children may list could include:

- Find one place to study and stay there.
- Move with the animals if they migrate.
- Keep accurate records (both written and pictorial).
- Learn as much as possible about the living things before you set out to observe them.
- Don't disturb or hurt the living things.
- Get as close as is safe to what you are studying.
- Keep a regular schedule when you make your observations.

Discuss their suggestions and add them to the list as appropriate. Then ask the children:

> How would you go about studying plants and animals that live close to where you live?

What would be a good plan for studying those living things to find out what they need?

Part 1: How Can I Study Living Things? (30 min)

Revisit the list of questions your children generated about studying the needs of living things. Ask each group of children to specialize in one question and to make a plan for how they would investigate that question by studying living things. (See important **Note** that follows before you start this.)

The questions that were generated originally included:

- Do all living things have the same needs?
- How can we find out if all living things have the same needs?
- How do living things get what they need?
- What happens to living things if they don't get what they need to live?
- What living things could we observe in and around our classrooms?

Give the children time to draft their investigation plans, keeping in mind what field biologists do to observe living things.

Note: You may find that your children, depending upon their developmental readiness, need to investigate simpler, more direct and more specific questions than those above. An example of these could be:

- Do squirrels and blue jays have the same needs?
- Do pet animals and wild animals living around here have the same needs?
- How do pet animals get what they need to live?
- How do I know that my pet animal is not getting everything it needs to live?
- How can we find out if Swedish ivy and the class gerbil need the same things to survive?
- How does the Swedish ivy get what it needs to live?
- How does the squirrel in the schoolyard get what it needs to live?
- What happens to the Swedish ivy if it doesn't get what it needs?
- What living things are in our classroom that we could study?
- What living things can we study right around the school?

Ask your children to share their draft plans with the class. They will be testing their plans in Part 2 of this investigation.

Part 2: Observing Living Things in the Wild (30 min)

In this part of the overall investigation into the needs of living things, your students go outdoors with you to test their plans, taking their plans and record books with them. You need to discuss proper outdoor behavior in advance, being sure that each group knows its task: to try out its observation plan in the wild. You will need about 30 minutes outside for your children to find an area to observe, make their observations, and, perhaps, move to another area if the first one doesn't work out.

Before you go outside, discuss with your children how they will be using their senses to make observations. (See the section below on Using Senses to Make Observations). The boxes list materials you may need and ways of using senses while observing.

MATERIALS NEEDED
- Clipboards and paper or hard-cover notebooks
- Pens to record observations
- Magnifiers to observe small plants and animals
- Space outdoors to observe living things in the wild
- Classroom pets and plants
- Classroom resources about living things and their needs
- Videos showing field biologists at work

USING SENSES TO MAKE OBSERVATIONS
- Look at living things as closely as is safe to see details (using magnifiers if necessary).
- Feel the texture of selected living things and describe this texture (bark, leaves, fur).
- Hear the sounds produced by different living things (bird calls, chirps, barks).
- Smell **safely** to find any odor that a living thing gives off.

Scientific observations must be made in an organized way. This is an opportunity to introduce methods of recording data. Ask your students to think about the best way of recording their observations outdoors:

How could you best record your observations?

How can you do this so others can see and understand your recordings?

Here is a useful method to which you could alert your children if they have difficulty designing their own:

OBSERVATION DATA CHART		
DATE	PLACE	TIME OF DAY
Names of living things		
Observations of them and where they live		

Take the class outdoors, and give them time to try out their plans and make their observations. When each group has made its observations and recorded them so that others can see and understand them, go back inside and ask the groups to look over their observations.

Ask your children to think about these questions:

How well did your group's plan work?

How could you improve your plan to give you more useful information?

How could you change your original question to help you learn more about the needs of living things?

When your children have analyzed their plans and observations, ask them to share their thoughts with the rest of the class. Encourage children to alter plans and/or questions, depending on what they learn from other groups.

Designing and Carrying Out a Long-Term Study of Living Things (60 min for design; several weeks for investigation)

It is important for your children to understand that, to learn about many living things—especially those that, like plants, change slowly—scientists must observe, systematically, over a very long time. What your children need to do next is decide on a question about the needs of living things that they really want to investigate and make a plan for how to do this over several weeks. Points that they will need to decide include:

- Where, close by, are the living things I want to investigate?
- How often can I observe these living things to find out what they need?
- What evidence am I looking for that will help show the needs of these living things?
- Where can I find out about these living things ahead of time, so that I know something about them before I start?

Ask your children to think carefully about how they could design their **long-term study** to investigate their own research question about living things:

How could you find some of the answers to your question about the needs of the living things you are studying?

ABOUT LONG-TERM STUDIES

Long-term studies help scientists answer questions about things and events that change over time. A long-term study is set up so that the observer can keep some things constant while other things change. (For example, the *place* might stay constant, but the *things that live there* might change. Another example could be that the same living thing is observed, but it might change over time with age or some other factor.)

The long-term study that your children design can focus on a specific area outside the school, a classroom or home pet, a classroom or home plant, zoo animals, or park animals or plants. What is important is that your children make an observational record of the living thing *over time,* so that they can note changes or growth patterns. Remind them that they are studying these living things to find out what they need to live. They will need to collect observational evidence to back up their conclusions about what the living things need. The following is a format that may help children with their study design.

OUR STUDY DESIGN
Our research question
Where we will make our observations
What we hope to observe
What we plan to record each time we observe
What we hope to learn from our investigation
How we plan to share what we have found with others

Your children will need several weeks to carry out their investigations. It is up to you and to them to decide the frequency of their observations (daily, every other day, weekly). They may want to take photographs of what they are observing, or make drawings. It is important to stress to your children that, at the end of their investigation, they will be sharing their results with others. They should be thinking from the beginning about the way they will want to do that. Let them know when the end of the investigation will be, when the presentation time is, and how they will be evaluated on what they have done.

Reviewing the Results (15 min)

This is a very important part of the investigation. Here, the results of each group's investigation are shared and reviewed by everyone. Your children may have chosen to present their data with photographs, as a bulletin board, as a poster, or by some other method. Let each group have enough time to show what they found and describe how they went about the task.

Your role is to act as a moderator:

Now, tell us, why did you decide to carry out your investigation that way?

Did the results surprise you? Why?

What was the most interesting thing you learned about living things and what they need to survive?

Note: The ways in which your children consider these questions may be a key learning moment for some of them, so be alert to their ideas.

Encourage children to ask questions in an organized and sensible way. Look out for any misunderstandings that individual children may have and try to clarify any points that do not seem clear.

Making Thoughtful Connections (15 min)

To put everyone's investigations into context, it is now very important that you allow your children to reflect on their findings and the findings of other groups. Ask them to think about what the investigations have revealed about what living things need to survive:

> What have we discovered about living things and what they need?
>
> Let's look back over our first ideas about living things and what we thought they needed to survive. Which of our ideas changed? What did you learn that changed your first ideas?
>
> What role do people seem to play in helping other living things to get what they need?
>
> In what ways might people keep other living things from getting what they need?
>
> What do you think might happen on the planet if all living things had everything they needed to live?

EXPANDING CONCEPTS

Drawing Conclusions (5 min)

To put the whole investigation into perspective and relate it to the wider issues of life on the Earth, ask your children what other questions they would like to investigate about living things:

> What other questions do you think would be worth investigating?
>
> How would you use what you now know about long-term studies to investigate the question(s)?

Note: This is a logical extension to this module, and you can follow the same general structure.

Some children may enjoy investigating other questions at home and reporting their results.

Take some time to reflect carefully on your experience with this investigation and use this sheet to record your evaluations. This will help you consolidate your ideas and provide a useful set of reference notes when you use the investigation in the future. Add more pages if you need to.

WORKING IN METHODS CLASS

What was the most important learning experience for you?

What experiences do you think will be important to remember when you do this activity with children in school?

What would you change in this activity for use with children?

What concerns do you have about using this activity with children?

(continued)

What do you need to know more about before you use this activity with children?

Points to discuss with faculty and colleagues:

WORKING WITH CHILDREN IN SCHOOL

What happened in the way you expected?

What happened that you had not expected?

What would you change when repeating this activity with children?

What did you learn about the children by doing this activity?

What did you learn about yourself as a teacher from this activity?

Points to discuss with faculty and colleagues:

PARTS OF LIVING THINGS HAVE CERTAIN FUNCTIONS

2 Investigating the Way Animals' Body Parts Work

WHAT CHILDREN CAN LEARN FROM THIS EXEMPLAR

Children's Thinking about Body Parts: The Research Base

Animals are adapted to their environments through their anatomical and physiological features. Certain body parts enable animals to get food. A bird's bill is a clue to the particular type of food it eats. Birds like toucans, which eat relatively large fruits, have large bills that open wide. The bills of swallows and martins, birds that catch insects while flying, open wide so they can "scoop" for insects as they soar through the sky. Flesh-eating birds like eagles, hawks, ospreys, and owls have hooked bills for tearing.

It is important for children to understand that the body parts of animals help to suit the animals to their particular habitats. Children frequently assume that animals have made conscious decisions in developing their body parts. This is a common informal idea even among many adults, who are often surprised to discover that the ideas of such scientists as Lamarck are not accurate. It was Charles Darwin who put forth the theory of natural selection—that living things best suited to their habitats survive to reproduce, thus passing their favorable characteristics on to their offspring.

Teaching Implications of the Research

The preassessment activity at the beginning of this chapter's investigation is designed to help children discover that a particular body part—the human hand, in this instance—helps humans to survive in their environment. Through the use of our hands, we are able to find and grow food, build shelters, obtain water, and do all the other things that help us to survive as a species.

It is important that you use this initial activity to determine what your children think about body parts and their role in animals' adaptation to their environment. The questions in the preassessment will help you to draw out these ideas. Be sure to keep a record of what your children think for later comparison.

Activities in the investigation that follow the preassessment help children to build their understanding of adaptation and body parts. The children observe other animals to discover what body parts suit these animals to their environments. For example, adaptations such as hollow bones and feathers as covering make birds light enough to fly successfully. A thick layer of fat keeps marine mammals warm enough to survive in icy oceans. Flippers, fins, and streamlined shapes make it easy for aquatic animals to move in the water. Turtles are protected from predators by hard shells, whereas animals such as chameleons and many insects depend upon camouflage. Providing your children with many examples of animals in their habitats will help them to make the connection between body parts and the suitability of animals to their environments.

Science Background

The anatomy (structure) and physiology (life processes) of an organism are closely linked to the organism's habitat and lifestyle. Through the process of natural selection, the organism that is best suited to the habitat survives to reproduce. Those organisms that are less well suited to the habitat may not be able to find food or shelter, or may become a food source of other organisms. For example, a large bird with long slender legs and a long bill is better suited to finding fish in a marshy area than a bird with short legs and a short bill. A plant that can tolerate shade is better suited to growing on the floor of a forest than a sun-loving plant such as a sunflower or corn plant. A lizard with a mottled tan skin is well-suited to blending in on a sandy desert, just as a snowshoe rabbit is protected by its white coat in the winter.

To help understand how living things are adapted to their habitats and lifestyles, imagine what would happen to specific living things in environments for which they are *not* suited. For example, imagine what would happen to:

- An alligator on an ice floe in the Arctic Ocean
- A polar bear in an Everglades swamp
- A penguin in a city park
- A robin in the Sahara desert
- A camel in the Canadian tundra
- An iguana on the South Pole
- A palm tree in Finland in the winter
- A sagebrush in the Brazilian rainforest

For each of these examples, think of what it is about the organism that ill suits it to the habitat mentioned. What would have to happen to each organism to suit it more closely to the habitat? (Think about both the structure of the organism and its life processes.) Here's one example of how to do this.

ALLIGATOR ON AN ICE FLOE IN THE ARCTIC OCEAN

Problem
Alligators, being reptiles, are cold-blooded. This means that they control their body temperature through external means, such as lying in the sun to get warm or burrowing into the mud to cool down. They eat other animals—fish, small mammals, frogs—and are good swimmers.

Solution
For alligators to survive in the cold of the Arctic Ocean, they would need to be able to control their body temperature internally, as do birds and mammals. For insulation, they would also need a thick layer of fat under their skin and fur on the outside. Polar bears, which *do* live on ice floes in the Arctic Ocean, have thick layers of blubber under their skins and heavy coats of fur. Polar bears and alligators are similar, however, in that they are carnivores, armed with sharp teeth and great strength. They are also good swimmers, which enables them to go after their prey.

It is important to help your children understand that an organism's anatomy and physiology determine that the organisms can live in a certain way in a particular habitat. It is not that the organisms *choose* to grow long legs or sharp teeth, rather that these enable them to survive to reproduce more of their own kind. This is the process of *natural selection.*

EXEMPLAR   **PARTS OF LIVING THINGS HAVE CERTAIN FUNCTIONS**
Investigating the Way Animals' Body Parts Work

Note: This investigation is most suitable for children in grades 1 and 2.

OVERVIEW

As living things themselves, your children will be aware of many of their own needs. What they may not have thought about is that they are only one species of living thing in a huge world of life. All living things have elements in common. To survive, they need a source of food, oxygen to burn up that food, water, an environment to which they are suited, and freedom from invading organisms.

Your children can discover many of the needs of living things by observing them, either in the classroom or elsewhere, over an extended period. This gives your children the opportunity to make observations on a regular basis, record them in a systematic fashion, and interpret what they have recorded. They can look for patterns and relationships in their record to find out what living things have in common. They can also learn to care for plants and animals, both in the classroom and in the wild. These are skills they will use throughout their lives.

KEY PEDAGOGICAL IDEAS

- Scientific investigation can start with familiar objects or events.
- Children can be immediately engaged in investigating a question that has personal significance for them.
- Scientific investigations can involve a range of associated curriculum areas—especially mathematics, language/communication, art and crafts, as well as other related science ideas—providing opportunities for children to apply and enhance their skills in a meaningful context.
- When children engage in scientific investigations, trying to find answers to their own questions, they are being scientists themselves using scientific research processes such as observing, predicting, fair-testing, recording, and reviewing results.

KEY SCIENCE CONCEPTS

- Animals' body parts have certain functions.
- Animals' body parts are designed to suit the functions of those parts.

SUPPORTING NATIONAL STANDARDS

National Science Education Standards

LEVEL K–4

Content Standard A: As a result of activities in grades K–4, all students should develop:

- Abilities necessary to do scientific inquiry
- Understanding about scientific inquiry

Content Standard C: As a result of activities in grades K–4, all students should develop an understanding of:

- The characteristics of organisms
- Organisms and environments

Benchmarks for Science Literacy

By the end of the 2nd grade, students should know that

- Some animals and plants are alike in the way they look and in the things they do, and others are very different from one another.
- Plants and animals have features that help them live in different environments.

BEFORE YOU BEGIN

Technology Connection

Collect resources on animals—trade books, videos, charts, CD-ROMs, or magazines. Use a search engine to locate safe Web sites about animals that your children could access. Some of these include the Web site for the National Geographic Society (www.nationalgeographic.com), the National Wildlife Federation (www.nwf.org), and the National Zoo in Washington, D.C. (www.si.edu/natzoo). *National Geographic* has an extensive catalog of nature films that you may want to use as introductions or follow-ups to this lesson. The National Zoo Web site has a photo gallery of animal pictures that you might find very useful as your children investigate animal features.

Linking to the Community

Visit a local zoo, nature center, natural history museum, aquarium or farm to find out what animals are there for your children to observe, and what information the place has about its inhabitants. Also, find out what the arrangements are for your children to visit the facility. Survey your children's parents or guardians to find out if there are any parents knowledgeable about animals, their anatomy, and their care, who might be willing to work with your class.

Preparing Materials

Find out if you can obtain several sets of rubber animal feet for your children to use in the assessment portion of this investigation. Read over the investigation and prepare handouts, cutouts, and whatever else you will need for the activities.

A NOTE ABOUT SAFETY! Science investigations should be safe. Ensure that students are not exposed to hazards while they are engaged in investigations. Explain that they need to observe safety procedures at all times, both when handling animals in the classroom and while observing animals in the wild or in captivity. Make sure that children wash their hands after handling animals. Go to the Internet at www.nsta.org for the National Science Teachers Association's *Guidelines for Responsible Use of Animals in the Classroom* for more information.

ASSESSING PRIOR KNOWLEDGE

Investigating the Way Animals' Body Parts Work: Getting Things Going! (15 min)

It is important to acquaint your children with the functions of some of their own body parts. They are animals, too! Hang a large poster-board cutout of a "generic" person, in everyday clothes, on your board or bulletin board. (Make sure that the person has hair, eyes, nose, mouth, hands, ears, and feet showing and labeled.) If it is feasible, ask your students to do the artwork for this. Give students index cards or large sticky notes, and ask them to write down a few words in response to the following:

> Our person has lots of body parts, but to get us thinking we're going to work with just a few. Choose two of the labeled body parts on our person. What is just one thing that we use each of those body parts for? For each body part with which you are working, list one thing on a card and be sure to print large enough for everyone to see from a distance.

Give the students time to do this on their own or in pairs. When they have finished, provide tape (if you are using cards, rather than sticky notes), and ask the students to take turns posting, on each of their body parts, what it is used for.

When this is finished, you should have a large display of the children's ideas about each of the body parts. Review their ideas about what each of the body parts does. Look for both sophisticated and less-sophisticated ideas about the function of each of the body parts. Things that your students might come up with can include:

Hands: grasping, waving, poking, pushing, scratching, feeling

Eyes: seeing, crying, sensing touch, keeping out dirt, expressing feelings

Nose: smelling, filtering out pollen and dust, letting air in, letting waste (mucus) out, working with the tongue so we can taste things better

Mouth: tasting, licking, chewing, letting air in and out, filtering out bad things, expressing emotions; making words

Ears: hearing, filtering out impurities, helping us to balance

Legs: walking, running, helping us to sit, kicking (defense), swimming

Feet: walking, running, pushing, balancing, grasping, swimming

Hair: keeping head warm, keeping out unwanted insects, covering ears

This first activity is a lead-in to the next one, in which your children will be specialists in examining the design of a certain body part in terms of how the form and the function work together.

EXPLORING CONCEPTS

Investigating the Design of Body Parts (20 min)

In this investigation, your children will be focusing on just one body part per pair or small group. To get them started, take one body part from your generic person as an example, and model how your children can match the design, or *form,* of a body part, to its *function* or job for the animal (person).

Ask everyone to look at their hands. Bend them, wave them; examine the skin, nails, and joints. Ask your students to think about how their hands are designed to do what hands do (refer to the sticky notes on the generic person for this). How, for example, are hands designed so that we can grasp objects? (Many joints, flexible skin, muscles under the skin, different-sized fingers that work together, thumb that works in an opposite direction to the fingers.)

Ask each group of students to do the same task with a body part that they choose or you assign. They might want to draw a diagram of their body parts on a large piece of paper, then use arrows to show how the design helps the body part to do its job.

Labeled Hand

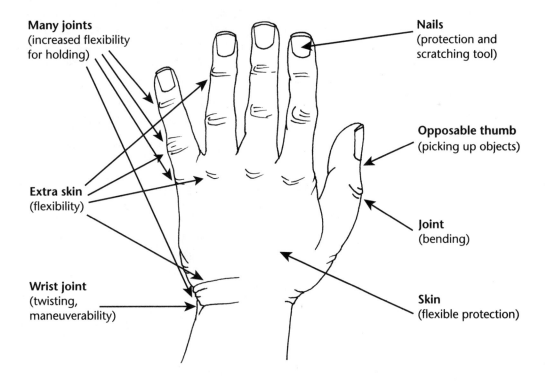

Give your children time to work on this, then ask each group or pair to share what they have discovered with the entire class. Be sure that your children are focusing on *how the design of the body part helps the part to do its job.* Encourage other children to ask questions as each group presents.

To get the children thinking even more about the functions of their body parts, ask them:

How would your life change if you didn't have hands [or the use of your eyes, ears, etc.]?

How do people manage who don't have the use of all their body parts? How could you find this out?

Note: You could wind this discussion up (or begin it) by playing a recording of Cat Stevens' song "Moon Shadow." This song describes what someone would do if he lost the use of his hands or eyes, for example.

Post all of the body parts with their form and function analyses. These will be an excellent in-class reference for the rest of this investigation.

FOCUSING ON AND EXPLAINING CONCEPTS

How Are Other Animals' Body Parts the Same or Different from Humans'? (20 min)

In this part of the investigation, your children will extend their specialization into one body part by comparing it to similar body parts in other animals. Show your children a video of a variety of animals in the wild (check with your school media center to find *National Geographic* videos or those made by wildlife agencies. Remember that the National Geographic Society Web site lists all their nature videos. Before you show the video, ask your students to focus on the body parts of the animals shown that are similar to the body parts in the human that they have just studied.

Ask your students to think about these questions as they watch the video:

How are the animals' body parts the same as those in humans?

How are the animals' body parts different from those in humans?

How do the animals' body parts help them to survive in their surroundings?

Note: You may want to make a record sheet ahead of time, to help your children focus on these key questions as they watch the video.

RECORD SHEET FOR OBSERVING BODY PARTS
Our key body part:
Similar body parts in other animals:
Ways that the other animals' body parts are different from ours:

(continued)

RECORD SHEET FOR OBSERVING BODY PARTS *(continued)*

Ways that the other animals' body parts are similar to ours:

How I think that the body part helps the animals fit in their surroundings:

Before you show the video, make sure that all of your children are clear on what they are supposed to be looking for. Review which body parts each group of children is specializing in. Show the video (perhaps more than once), and give your children time to discuss and record their ideas about the body parts of other animals. Ask them to share their observations and thoughts with the rest of the class. Here is an example of what one group of students might find.

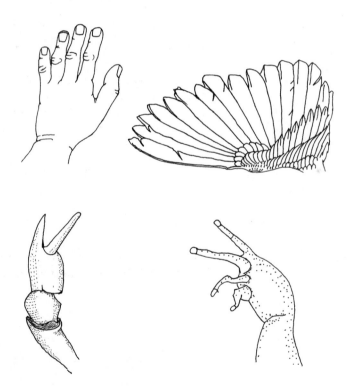

HUMAN HANDS

- Similar parts in other animals: bird's wing, frog's forefoot, lobster's claw
- How the parts are the same as humans': help to grasp, in a similar part of the body, help to propel, help to run, can be used for defense
- How the parts are different from the human equivalent: shape, scales and feathers rather than just skin, some don't have fingers, some help the animal to propel itself, some look very different from human hands

- How the parts help the animal to survive in its surroundings: The frog's hands are designed to grasp branches so the frog can climb. The bird's wing is very light in weight, and the bones are spread widely. This helps to catch more air with the feathered surface of the wing, so the bird can fly.

Give your children the opportunity to do more research on the body parts of different animals. They can use textbooks, CD-ROM encyclopedias, videos, charts, library books, and the Internet. When they finish their research (which may take several days), ask each group to make a display showing how body parts differ from animal to animal, and how the design is uniquely suited to the animal in its environment. Small murals would work well for this display, or even clay models set up on the side of the room.

Give each student group a chance to discuss with the entire class what they have found. Ask them, too, what questions arose as they studied the different animals' body parts? List these on chart paper for further investigation.

APPLYING CONCEPTS

Studying Animals and Their Body Parts (25 min)

In this last part of the investigation, your children will be taking their knowledge of animals and their body parts and applying it to observing live animals in a zoo, nature center, aquarium, or farm. You will have arranged for a trip to one of these settings ahead of time.

Explain to your children that they will once more be specialists in animal body parts on this trip (as they were with the human and other animal activities), but this time they will be specializing in one animal, seeing how its key body parts help it to survive best in its surroundings.

Let the children know in advance what types of animals they can see where you will be traveling. Each group should choose a different type of animal, as they will be spending most of their time observing that animal. (This will reduce crowding, and result in a really diverse set of observations.) Encourage students who have cameras (and adult permission) to bring these along to take pictures of their specialist animal in action.

Describe the observation task to your children, and then give them a handout to refer to on their trip. Their job, working as a group, is to:

1. Observe their chosen animal in its habitat, and describe how its body parts are adapted to its surroundings.

2. Write down their observations in a record book or on a record sheet.

3. Take or draw pictures of their animal, showing how it uses its body parts to get around, obtain food, communicate with other animals, defend itself, care for offspring, stay out of danger.

4. Describe, in writing, what the animal's surroundings are like.

Before you go on the trip, discuss with your children how they will be using their senses to make observations. (See the upcoming box on Using Senses to Make Observations).

MATERIALS NEEDED

Clipboards and paper or hard-cover notebooks

Pens to record observations

Cameras (if permitted by the place you are visiting)

USING SENSES TO MAKE OBSERVATIONS

- Look at living things as close as is safe to see details.
- Hear the sounds produced by living things (bird calls, chirps, barks, etc.)
- Smell (**safely**) to find any odor that a living thing gives off.

Scientific observations have to be made in an organized way. This is an opportunity to introduce methods of recording data. Ask your students to think about the best way of recording their observations in their record books or record sheets:

How could you best record your observations?

How can you do this so others can see and understand what you record?

The following chart presents a useful method of recording to which you could alert your students if they have difficulty in designing their own.

OBSERVATION DATA CHART		
DATE	PLACE	TIME OF DAY

Name of our animal:

Description of the key body parts we are observing in our animal:

Description of the surroundings of our animal:

Ways in which our animal's body parts help it to survive in its surroundings:

Take the class on the field trip, allowing enough time for each group to make as complete an observation data set as possible. You might find it useful to have a short discussion about their discoveries before you come home from the trip, since your children might forget an observation if they do not have the chance to capture it before they leave for home.

SHORT-TERM FIELD STUDIES

Short-term field studies are useful in finding out about things that are already there when you show up. (In other words, what you have come to observe is not dependent upon changes over time.) A short-term field study requires a subject or subjects, clear questions to ask about the subject, a well-prepared and nonintrusive observer, and a good record-keeping strategy.

This short-term field study follows a pattern that children can use when doing work such as analyzing form vs. function, seeing what lives in a pond or woods, and observing and analyzing many other biological phenomena.

Displaying and Reviewing the Results (30 min)

Back in your classroom, ask your children to create a poster display showing what they have discovered about their animal and its body parts. Give them enough time, and a variety of display materials, so that they do a thorough and informative job. Set aside time for a whole class sharing session. This is a very important part of the investigation. Here the results of each group's investigation are shared and reviewed by everyone.

Your students may have chosen to present their data with photographs, as a bulletin board or poster, or in some other way. Let each group have enough time to show what they found out and describe how they went about the task. Your role is to act as a moderator:

What did you find out about your animal that really surprised you?

What was the most interesting thing you learned about how your animal's special body parts suited it to its surroundings?

Note: The ways in which your students consider these questions may be a key learning moment for some of them, so be alert to their ideas.

Encourage students to ask questions, but in an organized and sensible way. Look out for any misunderstandings that individual students may have and try to clarify any points that do not seem clear.

Reflect and Connect (15 min)

To put everyone's investigations into context, it is now essential that you allow your students to reflect on their findings and the findings of other groups. Ask them to think about what the investigations have revealed about *how animals' body parts work:*

What have we found out about animals and their body parts?

How does the design of body parts help the body part to work in a certain way?

How do specially adapted body parts help animals to survive where they live?

EXTENDING CONCEPTS

Drawing Conclusions (5 min)

To put the whole investigation into perspective and to relate it to the wider issues of life on the Earth, ask your students what other questions they would like to investigate about animals and how they are adapted to their surroundings.

What questions do you think would be worth investigating next about animals and their surroundings?

How would you use what you now know about field studies to investigate the question(s)?

Note: This is a logical extension to this module, and you can follow the same general structure.

Some students may enjoy investigating other questions, in other settings, and reporting their results to the class.

Take some time to reflect carefully on your experience with this investigation and use this sheet to record your evaluations. This will help you consolidate your ideas and provide a useful set of reference notes when you use the investigation in the future. Add more pages if you need to.

WORKING IN METHODS CLASS

What was the most important learning experience for you?

What experiences do you think will be important to remember when you do this activity with children in school?

What would you change in this activity for use with children?

What concerns do you have about using this activity with children?

(continued)

What do you need to know more about before you use this activity with children?

Points to discuss with faculty and colleagues:

WORKING WITH CHILDREN IN SCHOOL

What happened in the way you expected?

What happened that you had not expected?

What would you change when repeating this activity with children?

What did you learn about the children by doing this activity?

What did you learn about yourself as a teacher from this activity?

Points to discuss with faculty and colleagues:

THE
PROPERTIES
OF
MATERIALS

3 Investigating Containers

WHAT CHILDREN CAN LEARN FROM THIS EXEMPLAR

Children's Thinking about Materials: The Research Base

Children have difficulty distinguishing between a material and the object made from that material. Activities that help move children toward an understanding of the differences between objects and materials can include breaking apart an object and asking students:

1. Has the material (wood, metal, plastic) changed? How has it changed? Is it still (wood, metal, plastic)?

2. Has the object (popsicle stick, plastic soda bottle, paper bag) changed? How has it changed?

Another way of helping children to distinguish between materials and objects is by having a scavenger hunt so that they can find objects made of a particular kind of material. Once these objects are collected, the children can be asked to describe the objects' physical properties (color, shape, shine, odor, hardness). The converse of the scavenger hunt would be to have children collect a number of the same objects made from different materials. Such objects could include buttons (wood, plastic, metal); cups (plastic, glass, ceramic, wood, metal, paper); bags (cloth, paper, plastic); or spoons (wood, silver, stainless steel, plastic). Children could then group together all of the objects made from the same type of material, and look for similarities in the properties of the material:

Plastic: spoon, button, cup, bag

Properties: bendable, somewhat shiny, can be broken or torn

Wood: spoon, button, cup

Properties: hard, doesn't bend easily, hard to break, not as shiny as plastic, has lines in it, feels strong

Paper: bag, cup

Properties: very bendable (sometimes more than plastic; easy to tear; falls apart when it gets wet, not as strong as plastic)

Children also often ascribe the properties of a material or substance to the particles (atoms or molecules) that make up that substance (Ben-Zvi, Eylon, & Silberstein, 1986). Atoms of gold, for example, are thought of as shiny and yellow. For young children, this informal idea is not much of a problem, since they are not yet developmentally ready to work with such abstract ideas as particles. It becomes an issue for much older children, however, when they are formally operational and ready to begin thinking about the nature of matter.

Teaching Implications of the Research

It is important that you assess your children's understanding of materials and objects before you begin any investigations into the area. You may want to use the scavenger hunt, described later in this chapter, to do this. If you do, keep a record of children's responses for later comparison.

The investigation in this chapter is useful in helping children to distinguish between objects (containers) and the materials used to make them (plastic, metal, glass, paper and cardboard, ceramic, wood, metal). Before you begin the investigation, ask your children to describe the material from which a set of containers is made. Revisit this activity when you complete the investigation.

Science Background

Containers are designed to hold a variety of materials that might be solids, liquids, gases, or a combination of these three states of matter. The containers must be designed to complement the materials they contain. For example, a plastic bottle is well suited to hold dishwashing liquid, but a cardboard box would not be suited for this product because the detergent would leak out. Containers can be made of **metals, polymers,** or **ceramics.** Each of these types of materials has special properties (characteristics) that suit it to its contents.

Metal containers, such as aluminum cans for carbonated beverages and steel cans for gasoline, match the requirements of their contents very well. A carbonated beverage, for example, must come out of its can:

* Fizzy

* Fresh

* Cold

* Wet

- With an expected taste and level of sweetness
- With an expected color

The properties of the aluminum metal soda can allow the manufacturer to:

- Seal it to retain the "fizz" (carbon dioxide)
- Seal it to keep out contaminants (freshness and flavor)
- Seal it to prevent loss of product through evaporation (wet)
- Keep out light (maintain color—and sweetness, if an artificial sweetener is used)
- Chill and warm the product in the can to facilitate packaging and serving.

A **ceramic** container (such as one made from tempered glass or pottery) has heat-resistant properties. Such containers are good for cooking because they allow the contents of the container to be cooked without breaking or shattering the container itself. Ceramic containers are strong and can be shaped when heated to high temperatures, but they are brittle and will break relatively easily when dropped.

Polymeric containers can be of two types: natural or synthetic. Polymers, which are long chain molecules of many smaller repeating molecules, can come from nature, or can be made in laboratories. The word *poly* means "many" and *mer* means "unit." Paper containers, which come originally from wood pulp, are mostly composed of fibers of the natural polymer *cellulose*. Cellulose's interlocking fibers give the paper flexibility and dry strength. Paper containers also let air in, and absorb moisture. Paper containers are best for dry products such as cereal, rice, and unbuttered popcorn.

An example of a synthetic polymer is polyethylene, a common plastic. Polyethylene is used for shopping bags and many other products. It has stretch, elasticity, and strength. It is also resistant to moisture, so that it can be used for "juicy" products. The molecule polyethylene is made of repeating units of ethylene, a petroleum-derived molecule.

It is important, in teaching about containers, that children match the properties of the container to the properties of the contents of the container. They may need help in coming up with familiar words to describe the properties, so you may need to help them with that.

EXEMPLAR

THE PROPERTIES OF MATERIALS
Investigating Containers

Note: This investigation is most suitable for children in grade 3.

OVERVIEW

Your children are no strangers to containers. From their earliest moments, they have been surrounded by a vast range of examples, and they use containers every day for a variety of purposes: drinking, transporting materials, storing, eating, preserving, and much more. However, your children probably take containers for granted and have rarely studied them closely for their design and materials.

Many different materials are used to make containers. Exploring various examples of containers provides a rich way of helping children to understand many of the *properties of materials*. Exploring containers also offers opportunities for children to develop a broad range of scientific understanding.

KEY PEDAGOGICAL IDEAS

- Scientific investigation can start with familiar objects or events.
- Children can be immediately engaged in investigating a question that has personal significance for them.
- Everyday materials can be used to teach science.

Scientific investigations can involve a range of associated curriculum areas—especially mathematics, language/communications, art and crafts, as well as other related science ideas—providing opportunities for children to apply and enhance their skills in a meaningful context.

- When children engage in scientific investigations, trying to find answers to their own questions, they are being scientists themselves using scientific research processes such as observing, predicting, fair-testing, recording, and reviewing results.

KEY SCIENCE CONCEPTS

- Containers are made from specific materials to hold other materials that have certain properties.
- The properties of the materials from which containers are made determine the most effective use of the container.

SUPPORTING NATIONAL STANDARDS

National Science Educational Standards

LEVEL K–4

Content Standard A: As a result of activities in grades K–4, all students should develop:

- Abilities necessary to do scientific inquiry
- Understanding about scientific inquiry

Content Standard B: As a result of activities in grades K–4, all students should develop an understanding of:

- Properties of objects and materials

Content Standard E: As a result of activities in grades K–4, all students should develop:

- Abilities of technological design
- Understanding about science and technology

BENCHMARKS FOR SCIENCE LITERACY

By the end of the 5th grade, students should know that

- Naturally occurring materials such as wood, clay, cotton, and animal skins may be processed or combined with other materials to change their properties.
- Through science and technology, a wide variety of materials that do not appear in nature at all have become available, ranging from steel to nylon to liquid crystals.

BEFORE YOU BEGIN

Technology Connection

Collect as many print, video, and electronic resources about modern technology and containers as you can. Also, search the Web for useful, technology-related Web sites. Discuss the technology investigation with your school's media center manager so that technology resources can be pulled when your children are ready for them. You may want to check the technology education standards at Web site www.iteawww.org/TAA/TAA.html.

Linking to the Community

Survey parents to find out if anyone in your community is involved in the production or distribution of containers. This could be someone who provides aluminum cans to beverage makers or someone who sells plastic storage containers.

Preparing Materials

- Arrange the classroom furniture so that children can work in small groups.
- Set up your materials center.
- Have plenty of examples of containers handy but hidden from view.

A NOTE ABOUT SAFETY!   Science investigations should be safe. Ensure that children are not exposed to any hazards while they are engaged in investigations. Remind them to observe safety procedures at all times. Monitor your children as they use tools. Make sure that, if an investigation requires it, they wear safety goggles and aprons.

ASSESSING PRIOR KNOWLEDGE

Investigating Containers: Getting Things Going! (10 min)

It is important to begin by establishing what the term *containers* means to your children. Ask them to make up a sunburst diagram, either individually or in their groups.

Container Sunburst (empty)

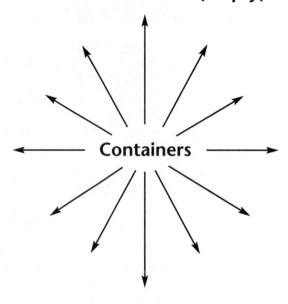

Note: It may be useful to ask the children to do this on large sheets of paper so that they can be posted for comparison. Ask them to draw their sunburst diagrams in ways that others can see and understand.

Make sure that your children clearly understand the task. Explain that this is a *brainstorming session* and that they should try to put down all the different things they think of when they see the word *containers,* even if other members of their group have different ideas.

Container Sunburst (filled in)

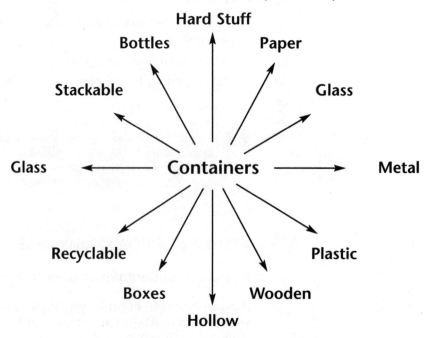

Note: If some groups finish before others, have them draw some illustrations on their diagrams to make them more easily understood by others.

Post the completed sunburst diagrams so that everyone can see them. Ask your children to look at all of the diagrams:

> How are they different?
>
> How are they similar?

EXPLORING CONCEPTS

Agreeing about Uses for Containers (5 min)

Hold an open discussion using the posted sunburst diagrams as a resource:

> Can we find some things that are common to all containers?
>
> What are the main things that containers do?

Try to steer your children gently toward some of these categories:

> What reasons can we all agree upon?

On a chalkboard, or its equivalent (poster board, overhead transparency, flip chart), make a list entitled *Key Points about Containers*.

Note: Include only those items that your children contribute and agree upon. Be sure to leave space for later addition to the list.

> **SOME USES FOR CONTAINERS**
> - To hold materials
> - To organize materials
> - To protect materials from damage
> - To help store materials
> - To help carry materials from one place to another
> - To make materials easy to use
> - *Note:* There may be other reasons.

Next to the list *Some Uses for Containers* set up another list called *Key Questions to Ask about Containers*. Explain that, to investigate in an organized way, we need to find good questions to ask about containers:

> What important questions can you think of to ask about containers?

Help your children to formulate useful questions and list them. The box shows some possible items.

QUESTIONS TO INVESTIGATE

- What materials are used for containers?
- What happens to containers after they are thrown away?
- Which containers can hold liquids? Why is that?
- What kinds of containers are best if we want to see what is inside?
- What kinds of containers are best for dangerous materials?
- What are important parts of containers?

As a class, your children will be investigating:

How can we test the properties of materials used to make containers?

If this question does not arise from your children's thinking, add it yourself. Tell them that they will have the opportunity to investigate their own questions afterwards. Explain that this is because the whole-class investigation will help them to learn the steps of exploring questions scientifically.

FOCUSING ON AND EXPLAINING CONCEPTS

What Containers Do We Use Every Day? (10 min)

Ask your children to bring in one or two containers (with permission from the adults at home) for the next day. *The containers should be for safe items.* (Do not ask for aerosol cans.) On the day of this activity, have children arrange their containers on a big table. Add any containers that you may have brought.

Ask each group of children to examine the variety of containers in the classroom collection:

How are they similar?

How are they different?

Let them look closely at the *materials* that were used to make the containers:

How many different materials can you find in your collection?

Encourage them to notice the *design* of the containers:

What have the containers been designed to do?

Ask the children to study their containers to see how the combination of *materials* and *design* enables a container to do the tasks it is supposed to do:

How do materials and design work together to make a useful container?

Finally, ask each group to select just one of their containers that they think shows good use of *materials* and *design* and prepare to tell others why they think this is so.

What Have We Found Out about Containers So Far? (5 min)

Have one member of each group, in turn, hold up the container he or she has selected as making good use of both material and design, and explain the reasons for the choice. When all groups have reported their findings, revisit *Key Points about Containers* and *Key Questions to Ask about Containers*. Help the children see any connections. Ask them if any further points or questions could now be added:

What other points about containers should we add to the list?

What other questions about containers can we add?

Discuss their suggestions and add them to the lists as appropriate. Then ask:

What materials seem to be useful for containers?

What Materials Are Useful for Containers? (20 min)

Ask your children to offer suggestions for materials they think could be useful for containers and list them. Next, have one member of each group come up to the Material Center and collect the five sample materials.

MATERIALS NEEDED
Each group should have samples of:

- Corrugated cardboard
- Lid from plastic delicatessen container
- Aluminum foil
- Watch glass
- Brown paper (from grocery bag)
- Plastic foam (meat tray, washed)

Ask each group to study the six materials closely for similarities and differences:

How are the six materials the same?

How are they different?

Encourage them to observe each material closely, using their senses, and make a note of each observation.

USING THE SENSES TO MAKE OBSERVATIONS

- **Looking** at objects or materials closely and seeing small details (using magnifiers if necessary)
- **Feeling** for the texture of the surface (and edges) of objects or materials and describing them
- **Hearing** the sounds that can be produced from objects or materials when they are tapped gently
- **Smelling** (safely!) to find any odor that an object or material is emitting.

A NOTE ABOUT SAFETY!   🛈   As a general scientific rule, **tasting should be avoided** except in very special circumstances.

Note: Observe smell by gently wafting the odor towards the nose.

Scientific observations have to be made in an organized way. This is an opportunity to introduce methods of recording data. Ask your children to think about the best way of recording their observations:

How could you best record your observations?

How can you do this so others can see and understand your recordings?

The following form presents a useful method your children could use if they have difficulty in designing their own.

OBSERVATION DATA CHART				
MATERIAL	SIGHT	TOUCH	SOUND	SMELL
Cardboard				

(continued)

OBSERVATION DATA CHART *(continued)*				
MATERIAL	SIGHT	TOUCH	SOUND	SMELL
Plastic				
Aluminum				
Paper				
Glass				
Foam				

When each group has made its observations and recorded them so that others can see and understand them, have them share their findings. This can be done by posting their results, or by having each group in turn present its findings. Ask everyone to think about how the similarities and differences in these materials that make them useful for containers:

What kind of product might be best contained in this material?

How is the container designed to hold certain materials?

Note: You need to help your children understand that it is the different characteristics (properties) of these materials that make them useful for different containers.

Together with the whole class, build up a chart that shows what kinds of products various containers are used for, and possible reasons.

Note: This is where your collection of containers will come in useful. Be sure to have them handy.

Here is a sample chart that you and your children could use to record their ideas.

CHART OF CONTAINER MATERIALS		
MATERIAL	USEFUL FOR	REASONS
Cardboard		

(continued)

CHART OF CONTAINER MATERIALS *(continued)*		
MATERIAL	USEFUL FOR	REASONS
Plastic		
Aluminum		
Paper		
Plastic foam		

Thinking about Other Properties
These Materials Have (5 min)

It is helpful for your children to understand that scientists use the word *properties* to describe characteristics that materials can have. This is an opportunity to introduce the term in a natural way. Spend some time discussing this with them. Ask them what *properties of materials* they have identified so far, using their observations. Ask them if they can think of other different *properties* the sample materials may have:

> What else might be different about the materials?

> What tests could we do to find out if there are differences?

The box lists some other properties that they may mention.

OTHER MATERIAL PROPERTIES
- **Water-resistance.** Can the material keep contents dry?
- **Stretch.** Can the material stretch?
- **Elasticity.** Can the material stretch and return to its original shape?
- **Tear resistance.** If designed to tear, how easily does the material do this?
- **Density.** Does the material float or sink in water?
- **Moldability.** Can the material be easily formed into different shapes?

Ask your children to think about how they could design a *fair test* to investigate each of these properties:

How could you test each of the materials for differences in some of these things?

Tell each group that each group is going to design a *fair test* for a particular *property* of the materials. Help everyone to understand what is meant by *fair testing* in an investigation.

FAIR TESTING

The idea of a test being FAIR is an important one in science investigations. A FAIR TEST is one in which the design of the testing procedure does not allow anything to distort the results of the test. Often this means:

- following the exact same procedure each time the test is done
- repeating the tests several times to check that the results are accurate and reliable.

Designing a Fair Test (15 min)

Now, allocate one property to each group. For example:

Group 1   Water resistance

Group 2   Stretch

Group 3   Elasticity

Group 4   Tear resistance

Group 5   Density

Group 6   Moldability

Help each group to follow the investigation procedure shown in the following box.

INVESTIGATION PROCEDURE
Each group should:

1. **Discuss possible test designs** and then pick the one that seems the most fair.
2. **Check the design** with you (the teacher), giving you a chance to help refine it if necessary.
3. **Think about and decide** what they are going to use as a measurement for their test.
4. **Prepare a good method of recording** the test results (data chart, table, pictorial representation, number).
5. **Gather materials** they need for the test.
6. **Predict the most likely results** of the test ahead of time and record them along with the reasons for the prediction.

ABOUT PREDICTING

- Making a sensible prediction of the most likely results of a test is an important scientific skill. Here it helps children to focus on the key points of the test they are designing.

- Predictions should be made on the basis of what children already know about the materials (not a simple guess).

- Writing down the predictions before testing helps children to think about them clearly and provides a basis for comparison to the actual results.

- Giving reasons for the prediction encourages children to think about the fairness of the test and gives them a basis for reflection when the actual results do not correspond to their original expectations.

When you are sure that everyone understands the important ideas about designing a *fair test,* ask each group to discuss possible designs for testing the property they have been allocated (water resistance, tear resistance). It is important that they first *brainstorm* possible designs, and then decide which to develop. Remind your children that they will have to submit their proposed design to you for approval before they begin to assemble materials for the actual test.

Ensure that each group's *fair test proposal* includes the items in the box that follows.

FAIR TEST PROPOSAL
Items to be included:

1. **A drawing or diagram** showing the test design and how it will work

2. **A list of materials and equipment** needed for the test

3. **The question** the test is designed to answer (this should be written out carefully)

4. **The method for recording** the results of the test
5. **A prediction** of the most likely result of the test
6. **Reasons** for the prediction
7. **How the results** of the test will be reviewed and analyzed
8. **How the findings** of the test will be displayed for others to see and understand

Note: It may be helpful to have these points displayed for each group to see while they are planning.

As the groups are engaged in this design task, move from group to group offering help and advice. It will help if you ask them about their designs:

How can you be sure that your test is fair?

Can you think of anything that might make your test unfair?

How can you best record your results?

Can you improve the question that you are testing?

Is your prediction sensible?

Approving and Conducting the Tests (20 min)

This is a crucial part of the activity. Here, you are trying to help your children to see that sensible standards of investigating are important. Your role is not to be "judge and jury," however; rather you need to be a facilitator in helping children do the best they can with their tests.

As you move among the groups, help them to get to the point where you feel they are ready to proceed with their tests:

If you can just think of another method of recording results, you'll be ready to start!

Is there anything else you need to think about before you begin testing?

You seem to have thought everything out, so now you can get the materials and get started!

Try to get the best out of each group without being overbearing. Have groups start testing as soon as you feel they are adequately prepared.

ABOUT MANAGING TIME

Inevitably, some groups (and individual children) will work more quickly than others. It can sometimes be difficult to manage time in a way that works for everyone. It will help if:

- You set a clear amount of time for the testing: "You must complete this by _____."
- You have an extension activity for those groups who finish the task ahead of others. For example, ask them to design a better way of doing the same test in the light of their results: "How could you improve the design of your test to give better results?"
- Remind everyone about time passing: "You have about 10 minutes left!" "I think you could speed that up if. . . ."

When you feel that everyone is close to being finished, encourage the children to share their work in progress:

> We need to have you report some of your findings. Don't worry if you haven't quite finished. We'll look at the results you already have.

Now, ask each group to spend five minutes to make final preparations.

Reviewing the Results (15 min)

This is a very important part of the investigation. Here the procedures and findings for each group are shared and reviewed by everyone. It will help if the presenting group stays at its station, and other groups gather around. If this is not possible, have each group in turn come to the front of class to give its presentation. Your role is to act as a moderator:

> Now tell us, why did you decide to do it that way?
>
> Did the results surprise you? Why?

Be sure to have each group show its test *predictions* and also their *reasons for the predictions*:

> Was your prediction correct?
>
> Do you think this confirms your reasoning?
>
> If what you predicted didn't happen, can you find the reason?
>
> Do you need to revise your reasoning from the test results?

Note: The ways in which your children consider these questions may be a key learning moment for some of them, so be alert to their ideas.

Encourage children to ask questions in an organized and sensible way. Look out for any misunderstandings that individual children may have and try to clarify any points that do not seem clear.

Making Thoughtful Connections (15 min)

To put everyone's investigations into context, it is now essential that you allow your children to reflect on their findings, and the findings of other groups. Ask them to think about what the investigations have revealed about the *properties* of the materials tested and how these might relate to their usefulness for *containers:*

> What have we discovered about the materials?
>
> How can these properties be useful for containers?
>
> What properties will suit what kind of containers?

MATERIALS USED FOR CONTAINERS		
MATERIAL	USEFUL FOR	REASONS
Cardboard		

(continued)

MATERIALS USED FOR CONTAINERS *(continued)*		
MATERIAL	USEFUL FOR	REASONS
Plastic		
Aluminum		
Paper		
Plastic foam		

Note: It will be helpful to revisit this chart and build a new version based on everyone's findings.

Drawing Conclusions (5 min)

To put the whole investigation into perspective and to relate it to the wider issues of *containers*, spend some time re-visiting the *Key Points about Containers* list and ask your children how their investigations have helped their understanding about containers.

APPLYING AND EXPANDING CONCEPTS

You can also revisit the *Key Questions to Ask about Containers* list. Ask your children which other questions they would find useful to investigate and how they might design *fair tests* to do this:

What questions do you think would be interesting to investigate next?

How would you use what you know about fair testing to investigate the question(s)?

Note: This is a logical extension to this module, and you can follow the same general structure.

Some children may enjoy investigating other questions at home and reporting their results.

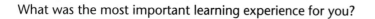

Take some time to reflect carefully on your experience with this investigation and use this sheet to record your evaluations. This will help you consolidate your ideas and provide a useful set of reference notes when you use the investigation in the future. Add more pages if you need to.

WORKING IN METHODS CLASS

What was the most important learning experience for you?

What experiences do you think will be important to remember when you do this activity with children in school?

What would you change in this activity for use with children?

What concerns do you have about using this activity with children?

What do you need to know more about before you use this activity with children?

Points to discuss with faculty and colleagues:

WORKING WITH CHILDREN IN SCHOOL

What happened in the way you expected?

What happened that you had not expected?

(continued)

What would you change when repeating this activity with children?

What did you learn about the children by doing this activity?

What did you learn about yourself as a teacher from this activity?

Points to discuss with faculty and colleagues:

FORCES

AND

MOTION

4 Investigating What Causes Things to Move

WHAT CHILDREN CAN LEARN FROM THIS EXEMPLAR

Children's Thinking about Forces: The Research Base

Research into the cognitive psychology of younger learners (7- to 9-year-olds) has revealed that many children equate a force with strength (Duit, 1984). Even if they have a more sophisticated view, many children tend to believe that force can only have one characteristic at a time and do not think in terms of forces occurring in pairs (pushes and pulls). The way in which the word *force* is used in conversation can lead to confusion. People "force" other people to do things. "May the Force be with you" is a statement that equates force with energy. Children may perceive forces as causing things to move, but not as being involved in objects that are not moving (Driver, 1984).

Teaching Implications of the Research

It is important that you assess your children's understanding of force before you begin any investigations into the area. An example of how to do this is given at the beginning of the Exemplar in this chapter. Be sure to save your children's responses for comparison at the end of the investigation.

Children have difficulty in understanding forces because forces can only be observed by their effects. Forces may be perceived as magic by children.

Understanding that forces work in pairs is particularly difficult. The authors of one study into children's understanding of forces and motion (Erickson & Hobbs, 1978) suggest that children can be helped to understand that forces act in pairs by presenting a series of events (such as people interacting with playground equipment—this chapter's Exemplar), and asking these questions:

What is pulling?

What is pushing?

We also suggest providing children with some examples involving motion and some involving nonmotion. Moving objects can include:

- Ball rolling down a ramp
- Person swinging on a swing set
- Person blowing up a balloon and letting it go
- Two people on a seesaw going up and down

Stationary (nonmotion) situations can include:

- Book resting on a table
- Person sitting on a chair
- Two playing cards, resting against one another in the shape of a tent
- Tug of war when both sides are equal
- Two people on a seesaw perfectly balanced

The investigation in this chapter will help children to understand that:

- Forces act in pairs.
- Forces are invisible.
- When forces are balanced, there is no motion.
- When forces are unbalanced, there is motion.
- Some forces are greater than others.

Science Background

Forces are that which cause motion. Since forces are invisible, we can only observe the results of the forces, not the forces themselves. There are gravitational forces and electromagnetic forces. Gravity is the attraction between all matter. Gravity decreases with distance and increases with mass. That means that the farther an object is from something else, the less is its gravitational attraction; the more mass something has, the greater its gravitational attraction. The relatively great mass of the Earth, for example, pulls on the relatively smaller mass of everything on the planet's surface, keeping everything on the surface.

The effect of gravity is most easily seen by dropping something. It falls down, not up. Children have a great deal of direct experience with gravity, but may not understand that gravity is a force that exists between all matter, not just between the Earth and what is on its surface. They may also not know that gravity varies according to distance and mass. Pictures of astronauts making great leaps on the moon help children to build the concept that gravity can be less in other situations than it is on the Earth. Footage of astronauts floating around in the microgravity of outer space can also help to build this understanding.

Electromagnetic forces may be more alien to your children. They will have experienced the effects of static electricity when they get a shock from touching metal on a dry day, but may not understand how the charge built up. You can help them to understand by giving them experiences such as rubbing a balloon against someone's sweater and holding the balloon next to someone's long hair. The electrostatic effect will pull the hair toward the balloon. Help them to build the idea that an electrostatic force gets smaller with distance by trying the balloon investigation at greater and greater distances from the hair. Your children can also use the balloon to observe the effects of a lesser force (couple of rubs on the sweater in the same direction) to a greater force (many rubs on the sweater in the same direction).

Children will probably have had experience with magnets because refrigerator magnets are so common. Although magnets work by pushing and pulling (*like* charges push each other and *unlike* charges pull), children may have the idea that the magnets are "sticking" to the surface of the refrigerator. You can help them to build their understanding of how magnets work by giving them bar magnets with the poles marked on the ends. Let the children experiment with the magnets to find out what the different poles do to each other. Also let them work with magnets that are not in bar shape to build the idea that all magnets have poles, no matter what their shape. Magnets of varying strengths can help children to understand that it is possible to increase a magnetic force. Another way of increasing the effect of the magnetic force is to put magnets closer to one another.

Overall, it is important for your children to understand that forces are behind motion. When forces are unbalanced (the push is stronger than the pull, or vice versa), there is motion. When the forces are balanced (the push is as strong as the pull), motion stops.

EXEMPLAR

FORCES AND MOTION:
Investigating What Causes Things to Move

Note: This investigation is most suitable for children in grades 3–5.

OVERVIEW

Your children are surrounded by a world of motion. Things fall, rotate, slide, run, jump, spin, and wave. Your children themselves are usually moving in one respect or another. In fact, if you watch them on the playground at lunch or recess, you will see that they seem to revel in movement! They may not, however, have ever thought about how motion starts, and how it stops.

This series of investigations will help them to understand that unbalanced forces, as a rule, result in motion. When those forces are balanced, the motion stops. Forces can usually be described as "pushes" or "pulls" (the "pull of gravity" for example). Your children will be using their school's playground as their "forces and motion laboratory." Many pieces of playground equipment illustrate the principles of forces and motion in a fairly straightforward, yet interesting, way.

KEY PEDAGOGICAL IDEAS

- This investigation is an example of a short-term experiment using your school as a laboratory. It is important for your students to understand the key science and technology concepts listed below through this investigation in an "outdoor laboratory."

KEY SCIENCE CONCEPTS

- Some science investigations take a short time; others take a much longer time.
- Things move when the forces acting on them are unbalanced.
- When forces acting on an object are balanced, motion stops.
- Forces can be described in terms of pushes and pulls.
- Making and recording accurate observations is one of the most important parts of investigating a science question.

SUPPORTING NATIONAL STANDARDS

National Science Education Standards

LEVELS K–4 AND 5–8

Content Standard A: As a result of activities in grades K–4 and 5–8, all students should develop:

- Abilities necessary to do scientific inquiry
- Understanding about scientific inquiry

Content Standard B: As a result of activities in grades K–4, all students should develop an understanding of:

- Position and motion of objects

Content Standard B: As a result of activities in grades 5–8, all students should develop an understanding of:

- Motions and forces

Content Standard E: As a result of activities in grades K–4, and 5–8, all students should develop an understanding of:

- Abilities of technological design
- Understanding about science and technology

BENCHMARKS FOR SCIENCE LITERACY

By the end of the 5th grade, students should know that

- The earth's gravity pulls any object toward it without touching it.
- Without touching them, a magnet pulls on all things made of iron and either pushes or pulls on other magnets.
- Without touching them, material that has been electrically charged pulls on all other materials and may either push or pull other charged materials.

BEFORE YOU BEGIN

Technology Connection

Collect as many print, video, and electronic resources about forces, motion, and machines as you can. Also, search the Internet for sites relating to forces and motion. You may find it useful to check the NASA Web site (www.nasa.gov) because overcoming a force (gravity) to get objects into space is one of their major goals. The Society of Automotive Engineers (SAE) has a program called World in Motion that you and your students might find interesting. They can be contacted at: www.sae.org/students/awimcurr.htm.

Linking to the Community

Anyone in your community who works in transportation may be interested in visiting your classroom to discuss how various methods of transport must withstand and overcome forces to get from one place to another. A train or subway driver, for example, knows how brakes must be powerful enough to overcome the momentum of a moving train. A pilot knows that the design and speed of the plane must be able to create enough lift to overcome the force of gravity and wind resistance.

Preparing Materials

This investigation will be pleasant to do in warm weather because much of the observing will be outdoors. If you do choose to do this in cooler weather, be sure that all of your children are warmly dressed.

You will need to survey your school's playground to see what equipment is there and what type of motion it undergoes. Equipment that will be most useful will be slides, swings, seesaws, and roundabouts. Check with your colleagues to make sure that your examining the play equipment doesn't interfere with someone else's recess or outdoor investigation.

Note: Some of the terms used in this investigation may be new to your children. You may wish to discuss their understanding of gravity (pulling force) and friction (slowing force that results when two surfaces are moving against each other). Give them as many examples as possible before they start. While they may not have a clear understanding of the terms, your children will have practical knowledge of how these forces act to start or stop motion.

A NOTE ABOUT SAFETY!   Science investigations should be safe. Ensure that students are not exposed to any hazards while they are engaged in investigations. Remind them to observe safety procedures at all times, especially when outdoors working with playground equipment.

ASSESSING PRIOR KNOWLEDGE

Investigating the Way Things Move: Getting Things Going! (15 min)

It is important to establish your children's initial level of understanding about forces and motion. Ask them to think about what makes things move and to write down (or draw pictures of) as many examples as possible. You may want to have them do this using carbonless paper, so that they and you both have copies of their ideas for later assessment purposes. Ideas that they may come up with can include:

- Wind blows them.
- They move on their own.
- They fall down.
- Engines make them go.
- They slide down a hill.
- Someone turns them on.
- Someone winds them up.
- They have batteries.
- They sink through water.
- Someone spins them.
- Someone pulls them on a string.
- Someone pushes them along.
- Something runs into them and makes them move.
- They fall into a hole.
- They get moved by an escalator or elevator.

Ask your children to share their drawings and ideas with others in their group, discussing their ideas about what makes things move. When they have done this, ask the groups, one by one, to share their thoughts with the entire class. Make a record of what they say on the board or on chart paper.

*Note: As you write down what your children are saying, look for examples of pushes and pulls. (Anything that falls, for example, is **pulled** by gravity. Turning wheels **push** against the ground to move things. Fingers **push** against a top to make it spin, and the top **pushes** against the air and the surface as it moves.)*

EXPLORING CONCEPTS

When your children finish volunteering their ideas, ask them to sort the whole class list into motion caused by a push and motion caused by a pull. They will probably have trouble with this, since many types of motion result from a combination of forces. To help them with their ideas, spin a simple top on a table. What force caused the top to move in the first place? What force caused it to stop moving?

Another easy demonstration is to start a rocking chair rocking with a push. What type of force started it moving? What causes it to eventually stop moving? The top and rocking chair demonstrations will be connectors between thinking about how motion starts, and thinking about how it stops.

FOCUSING ON AND EXPLAINING CONCEPTS

Agreeing on the Way Motion Starts and Ways in Which It Stops (10 min)

Give each group of four children one of a set of simple objects that have the potential of moving. These can include:

- Pendulum (washer on a string)
- Yoyo
- Small toy car
- Pull toy on a string
- Rubber ball
- Wooden block on a ramp
- Set of dominoes

Ask each group to cause their object to move in a way that seems logical. Ask them to look for the following when they are making their objects move:

What started them moving? Was it a push or a pull?

In which direction(s) did the objects move?

What stopped the objects from moving? Was the "stopper" a push or a pull? How do you know?

Draw a picture of your objects showing in which direction they moved.

The objects probably moved in the following ways:

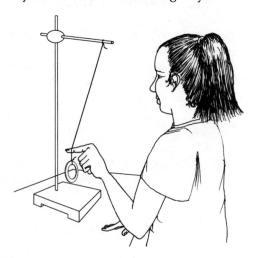

* *Pendulum* (washer on a string): Child pulled back on the washer and let it go (pull to start the motion). The pull of gravity and the air's push against the string and washer eventually made it stop moving. The motion is out and back.

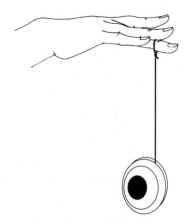

* *Yoyo:* Child pulled up on the string loop, then pushed the yoyo to get it going. The yoyo moves downward due to gravity and up due to the momentum of the initial push. If no more pushes and pulls are put into the yoyo from the child, it will eventually stop moving at the end of its string due to the pull of gravity and the pushes from air and string friction. The motion's direction is up and down.

* *Small toy car:* Child pushes the car to make it go along a linear path. The car slows down and stops due to air and surface friction plus the friction from the internal parts of the car acting against the wheels.

* *Pull toy on a string:* Child pulls on the string to make the toy move along a linear path. The toy stops when the child stops pulling on it. It also slows down due to surface and air friction (pushes).

* *Rubber ball:* Child drops the ball (pull of gravity), but the ball pushes against the ground when it hits and bounces back up. The bounces become less and less in height due to air friction (push), the pull of gravity, and loss of energy due to collisions with the ground (pushes).

* *Wooden block on a ramp:* Child slides the block down the ramp. Block begins to move due to the pull of gravity, but comes to a halt due to

the push of friction (ramp and air), as well as the collision with the ending surface (another push).

- *Set of dominoes:* Children stack up the dominoes on end so that they are close together but not touching. A push on the end domino starts the motion. Collisions with other dominoes and with the surface (pushes), as well as air friction and the pull of gravity stop the motion.

This exercise will give your children a sense of the role of forces in starting and stopping motion. Help them to describe the motion in terms of its causes and its direction.

What Happens When Forces Are Balanced and Unbalanced? (10 min)

Go outside the school to try a tug of war with a small group of children. To do this, you will need a rope and an area where no one will get hurt by a fall. Try to select about four children for each side of the rope who are relatively equal in size. Let them know that this tug of war is not for the purpose of winning, but to show how pulls and pushes can start and stop motion.

Set up the children on each side of the tug of war area with the rope. Ask the other children in the class to observe what happens with each round. To begin, ask the children on your right to pretend to be very weak, and the children on your left to be the stronger ones. At your signal, both sides begin pulling on the rope. The children on the right should be pulled right across the central area of the tug of war, and should continue to move as long as the children on the left are pulling. Ask the children:

Was the pulling force balanced (both sides equally strong) or unbalanced (one side stronger than the other)? How could you tell?

Was there motion as a result of the forces? What eventually stopped the motion?

Now, try the tug of war again, but this time ask both groups of children to try to balance the force with which they are pulling on the rope. If the pulls are equally balanced, there should be no motion toward each other from either side of the rope. Ask the children:

What happened this time? Were the pulls equal (balanced) or not equal (unbalanced)?

What happened to the motion when the forces (pulls) were balanced?

Ask the children to think about other examples of times when they saw motion stop as a result of balanced forces (gymnast doing a handstand; ice skater lifting another skater; bird trying to pull a worm out of the ground).

APPLYING CONCEPTS

How Do Forces Make Motion on the Playground? (30 min)

In this part of the investigation, your children will be going out onto the playground to analyze how forces make playground equipment start and stop, in different directions and different ways. Be sure to clear your use of the playground with your colleagues ahead of time. The following box shows what you will need to have ready for this part of the activity.

MATERIALS NEEDED

- Clipboards, pencils, and record sheets for each group of four children
- Access to playground equipment
- Cameras (optional)

Give each group of children in your class a clipboard with record sheet. Explain in advance what each group is to do, and assign each group of children to a particular piece of equipment on the playground. The directions:

We will be going onto the playground for about half an hour. During that time, you will be Motion Specialists for one piece of playground equipment. Your job is to make the piece of equipment move in the way it is designed to move, then write down the forces (pushes or pulls) that made the equipment start moving, and eventually made it stop moving. You will need to make a diagram of your piece of equipment showing the direction of movement.

This will probably work best if one person in the group is the recorder and the rest make the piece of equipment move. It is important that you do this scientifically: Do more than one trial, work safely, and make accurate observations and diagrams. Remember that you are looking for forces that start the motion, and forces that stop the motion. You may also want to investigate what happens when a large force acts on the equipment, and what happens when a small force acts in the same direction and way.

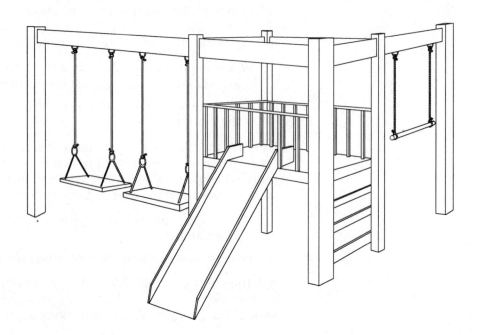

Assign each group to their equipment piece and go outdoors for the investigation. Your role is to monitor the activity for safety and understanding. You are also listening to your children's conversation, trying to pinpoint both complete and incomplete understandings of forces and motion. Give the children about 30 minutes to investigate their piece of equipment.

Note: Scientific observations have to be made in an organized way. This investigation can be used as an opportunity to introduce methods of recording data. Ask your students to think about the best way of recording their observations:

How could you best record your observations?

How can you do this so others can see and understand your recordings?

The following chart could help your students if they have difficulty in designing their own recording method.

OBSERVATION DATA CHART
Name of equipment piece
Forces that started the motion
Forces that stopped the motion
Diagram of equipment showing the direction of the motion

When your children finish their observations, while still outdoors, ask each group to show the rest of the class what they have discovered about their piece of equipment. Ask other groups to contribute their ideas about forces, motion, and the equipment itself after each group presents. At the end of the playground time, ask the students to save their data sheets and diagrams for the next day.

Reviewing the Results (15 min)

This is a very important part of the investigation. Here, the data collected by each group are analyzed by the entire class. Ask your children to make large drawings of their piece of play equipment, labeling it with the direction of movement and type of force that starts it and stops it. Post all of these drawings so that everyone in the class can see them at once. Your role is to act as a moderator in the discussion of the drawings:

What similarities do you see in all of these drawings?

Encourage children to discuss their thoughts in an organized way. Watch for any misunderstandings that individual students may have and try to clarify any points that do not seem clear.

Making Thoughtful Connections (15 min)

To put everyone's investigations into context, it is now very important that you allow your children to reflect on their findings, and the findings of other groups. Ask them to think about what the investigations have revealed about *how forces make objects move:*

> What have we discovered about how things move and stop moving?
>
> How can this help us in learning about how all things move in the world?

EXPANDING CONCEPTS

Drawing Conclusions (5 min)

To put the whole investigation into perspective and relate it to the wider issues of forces and motion, ask your children to think about other, related things that they would like to investigate:

> What other questions do you think would be worth investigating about forces and motion next?
>
> How would you use what you now know about forces and motion to plan your investigation?

Questions your children might enjoy investigating can include:

> Are all forces pushes and pulls? How could I find this out?
>
> What forces make the Earth move?
>
> What might happen if we didn't have the force of gravity?
>
> What might happen if we could make a surface with almost no friction?
>
> How do we reduce friction on a surface?

Some students may enjoy investigating other questions at home and reporting their results.

Take some time to reflect carefully on your experience with this investigation and use this sheet to record your evaluations. This will help you consolidate your ideas and provide a useful set of reference notes when you use the investigation in the future. Add more pages if you need to.

WORKING IN METHODS CLASS

What was the most important learning experience for you?

What experiences do you think will be important to remember when you do this activity with children in school?

What would you change in this activity for use with children?

What concerns do you have about using this activity with children?

(continued)

What do you need to know more about before you use this activity with children?

Points to discuss with faculty and colleagues:

WORKING WITH CHILDREN IN SCHOOL

What happened in the way you expected?

What happened that you had not expected?

What would you change when repeating this activity with children?

What did you learn about the children by doing this activity?

What did you learn about yourself as a teacher from this activity?

Points to discuss with faculty and colleagues:

CHEMICAL REACTIONS FORM NEW SUBSTANCES

5 Investigating Chemical Reactions

WHAT CHILDREN CAN LEARN FROM THIS EXEMPLAR

Children's Thinking about Chemical Reactions: The Research Base

Children thinking at the concrete operational level usually have quite a bit of trouble with the concept of chemical reactions—that substances with certain specific properties can combine to form new substances with different properties. Children often think that any change in a material or substance, whether physical or chemical, is a chemical change (Briggs & Holding, 1986). For example, children who have been taught that a color change is an indicator of a chemical change may understandably think that combining blue water and yellow water to make green water constitutes a chemical change.

In the same vein, children who may have learned that the release of a gas is an indicator of a chemical change may believe that the formation of water vapor from liquid water is a chemical change. Stavridou and Solomonidou (1989) found, in working with children aged 8–17, that the children who understood the concept of reversability did better in differentiating between physical and chemical changes than those children who did not have this understanding.

To help children understand what a chemical change actually is, first find out what they think the word *substance* means (Bouma, Brandt, & Sutton, 1990). Many children have a nonscientific definition of the word *substance*.

To them, a substance is any material, whether composed of one type of particle or many different types of particles. Sometimes children think that if a substance is in another state it is a completely different substance. This is understandable. Ice, for example, has notably different properties from liquid water: it is hard, it has a definite shape, it can be broken, it is very cold, and so on. It takes many experiences with many different types of examples for children to be able to build a correct concept of what a substance actually is.

Andersson (1990) and Pfundt's (1981) research into children's understanding of a chemical change has resulted in the following series of children's beliefs:

- Some children have no concept at all of a chemical change, and no explanation for it.
- Some children believe that some matter involved in chemical reactions just disappears.
- Some children understand that new materials result from a chemical reaction.

Teaching Implications of the Research

The preassessment activity at the beginning of the Exemplar in this chapter will help you discover what your children's ideas and attitudes are about the general concept of chemistry. You may find that a number of your children have quite negative feelings about chemistry, equating it with "poison," "pollution," or "explosions." Hands-on experiences with safe chemistry can often help children achieve a more balanced and informed view about chemistry in general and chemical reactions in particular.

In teaching about chemical reactions, it is important to give your children many examples of reactions. Ask them to make observations about the properties of the substances before and after combining them. If children are old enough to understand density (mass per unit volume), you might want to do "before and after" densities with them to establish that a new substance has been formed.

Allow your children to observe many examples of physical changes to establish that a physical change does not result in the formation of a new substance. You may want to ask them, after the change, if the substances involved could go back to their original forms. For example, cut-up paper could be pulped and rolled out to make another sheet. Ice can be melted to liquid water, which can then be frozen to ice again. A ball of clay can be made into many shapes, but it is still clay. Table salt can be dissolved in water, but when the water evaporates, the salt is left behind.

The investigations in this chapter give children the opportunity to observe the properties of substances before and after they undergo any change. Emphasize to children that a chemical change results in a new substance but physical change does not.

Science Background

Chemical reactions are defined as the formation of one or more new substances (products) from the combination of other substances (reactants). The atoms in the reactants recombine in new ways to form the products. No matter is lost in the reaction (the Law of Conservation of Matter). Some reactions occur spontaneously, while others need energy added to make them occur. Chemists use chemical equations to predict what will happen in a chemical reaction, and to keep track of how the atoms recombine into new substances. Generally, atoms join together to form new molecules, although there are exceptions.

One of the simplest chemical reactions is the formation of a water molecule (H_2O) from hydrogen (H_2) and oxygen (O_2). This is a reaction that needs energy to make it go. The equation for the reaction looks like this:

$$2H_2 + O_2 \rightarrow 2H_2O$$

The reaction must be balanced (conservation of matter: what goes in must come out), so it takes two molecules of hydrogen combined with one molecule of oxygen to make two molecules of water. If you add up the atoms, there are four hydrogens on both the left and the right of the arrow and two oxygens on both sides.

It is not important for your children to be able to balance equations. What they should know, however, is that the amount of matter in the universe is finite. We can't make more of it. What we can do, however, is recombine the matter to make new things.

Some of your children will have trouble distinguishing between physical changes and chemical changes in matter. An ice cube melting, for example, is a physical change. The ice and the water both have the chemical formula H_2O. If someone runs an electric current through a sample of water, however, the current will be able to split the water molecule back into hydrogen and oxygen. This is a chemical change. Stress to your children that, if the substance remains the same, a physical change is taking place. If the substance changes to something new, a chemical change has occurred.

Common chemical reactions with which your children may be familiar include:

* Rusting of iron
* Souring of milk
* Tarnishing of silver
* Rotting of fruit
* Baking of cookies
* Cars burning gasoline
* Burning of a match
* Mixing vinegar and baking soda
* Color change of litmus paper

EXEMPLAR

CHEMICAL REACTIONS FORM NEW SUBSTANCES
Investigating Chemical Reactions

Note: This investigation is most suitable for children in grades 4–5.

OVERVIEW

Chemical reactions are an important part of our lives, although your children may never have thought about this. They may have no ideas at all about chemical reactions, other than that when two substances react, something "blows up." This incomplete understanding of what happens in chemical reactions can lead to a fear of chemistry and an unwillingness to explore chemical interactions. These investigations are designed to help your children understand that substances can react chemically to produce a new substance or substances quite different from the raw materials that formed it.

Some common examples of chemical reactions with which your children may be familiar are: rust forming; silver tarnishing; baking soda mixing with vinegar to make a gas; a candle burning; milk souring, and so on. This investigation series starts with such everyday reactions and moves toward letting your children have the opportunity to try some chemical reactions themselves. For them to gain a working knowledge of how chemical reactions can produce new materials, they will need to focus on the properties of the raw materials in the reactions, then compare these to the properties of the new substance formed by the reaction.

KEY PEDAGOGICAL IDEAS

This investigation is an example of a classroom-based laboratory activity. It is important for your students to understand the key science concepts listed below through their investigations.

KEY SCIENCE CONCEPTS

- Matter can neither be created nor destroyed.
- In a chemical reaction, substances react to form new substances with new properties.
- Chemical reactions are key to life on Earth.
- We are surrounded by chemical reactions every day, but may not be aware of what they are or what they can do.
- Matter can be changed into energy and vice versa.

SUPPORTING NATIONAL STANDARDS

National Science Education Standards

LEVELS K–4 AND 5–8

Content Standard A: As a result of activities in grades K–4 and 5–8, all students should develop:

- Abilities necessary to do scientific inquiry
- Understanding about scientific inquiry

Content Standard B: As a result of activities in grades K–4, all students should develop an understanding of:

- Properties of objects and materials

Content Standard B: As a result of activities in grades 5–8, all students should develop an understanding of:

- Properties and changes of properties in matter

BENCHMARKS FOR SCIENCE LITERACY

By the end of the 5th grade, students should know that

- Heating and cooling cause changes in the properties of materials. Many kinds of changes occur faster under hotter conditions.

- When a new material is made by combining two or more others, it has properties that are different from the original materials. For that reason, a lot of different materials can be made from a small number of basic kinds of materials.

BEFORE YOU BEGIN

Technology Connection

Collect as many print, video, and electronic resources about chemical reactions as you can. Contact the American Chemical Society through their Web site (www.acs.org) for information on educational resources.

Linking to the Community

Arrange for a classroom visit from someone who works in the chemical industry, or a chemistry-related industry, so that your children can learn about what chemists, chemical engineers, and chemical technicians do. Arrange for a field trip to a site where chemistry is used (wastewater treatment plant, water treatment facility, carbonated beverage bottling facility, chemical plant).

Preparing Materials

Borrow a science supply catalog from a middle or high school science teacher, if your school doesn't have one. You may wish to order some special supplies for some of the optional activities in this investigation series.

A NOTE ABOUT SAFETY!   Science investigations should be safe. Ensure that students are not exposed to any hazards while they are engaged in investigations. Remind them to observe safety procedures at all times, especially when handling chemicals and glassware. Make sure that you have a pair of properly fitting safety goggles with side shields for each of your students. While the reactions in this series are not hazardous, even vinegar in the eyes can cause problems.

ASSESSING PRIOR KNOWLEDGE

Investigating Ideas about Chemical Reactions: Getting Things Going! (15 min)

It is important to establish your children's understanding and attitudes about chemistry before you begin this investigation series. You can do this using a free association technique. Put one big word—CHEMISTRY—on a piece of chart paper posted where everyone can see it. Ask your children to call out the first word that comes into their minds when they see this.

Write down what they say in a "sunburst" format around the focus word. Be sure to give your children time to think of several responses, but monitor the feedback session so that everyone gets a chance to contribute.

Review the words your children produced in the sunburst. Look for words that reflect knowledge, attitudes, and, perhaps, chemistry-related skills that your children may have. Examples of such words would be:

- **Knowledge:** Acids, acid rain, reactions, chemicals, chemists, color changes, making things, geology, energy, density
- **Attitudes:** Explosions, pollution, harmful, hard, dangerous, smelly
- **Skills:** Chemistry set, mixing, measuring, experiments, science equipment

Hold a general discussion about chemistry and ask your children why they think chemistry is important to their lives. Ask them if they know about any chemical discoveries that have contributed to our lives. (They may not know much about this at all. You may need to steer them toward some ideas.) Tell them that chemistry has produced, among many other things:

medicines

plastics

ceramics

fibers

coatings

paint

tests for monitoring water quality

cosmetics

foods (substitutes, additives)

soaps and detergents

polishes

fertilizers

pesticides

synthetic rubber

Give your children time to conduct research about the contributions of chemistry in general and chemical reactions in particular. They can access the Web, CD-ROM encyclopedias, the school and community libraries, or other resources. You might want to give them a weekend to do this and ask them to bring what they have discovered to class.

EXPLORING CONCEPTS

Finding Out about Chemistry and Chemical Reactions (15 min)

Hold an open discussion of what the different groups have to share about chemistry and chemical reactions. List what they have found on the board or chart paper:

How does chemistry contribute to our lives?

List these ideas on the board or chart paper as children name them. Explain that they will be investigating how chemical substances combine to form new materials. They will need to be careful observers and experimenters throughout. They will also need to be careful about safety when doing their experiments. Show your children how to wear their goggles and stress the importance of wearing them when it is required. Review general safety procedures with them. Emphasize that, if an accident does occur, you need to be the first one to know about it.

Observing Properties of Materials (30 min)

In this first part of the investigation, your children will be observing the properties of many substances. This is important to establishing that the properties of substances change when they undergo a chemical reaction. For scientists to be able to establish that a reaction has occurred, they need to note carefully the difference between a substance's properties before and after a reaction.

A NOTE ABOUT SAFETY!   It is important that your children wear their goggles when working with the substances in this part of the investigation, even though the substances are benign.

For this part of the investigation, you will need to have the materials listed in the following box.

> **MATERIALS NEEDED**
> vinegar
> baking soda
> white glue
> laundry starch
> zippered plastic bags
> red cabbage juice (grind cabbage with hot water, pour off colored water)
> nonfat dry milk
> candle
> lemon juice
> water
> plastic cups (4–8 oz)
> stirring sticks
> plastic spoons
> safety goggles
> colored rubber balls (one per pair or per group)

Set the materials up in different stations, as follows:

Station 1: Vinegar, baking soda, plastic spoons, and cups

Station 2: White glue, laundry starch, plastic spoons, and cups

Station 3: Red cabbage juice, lemon juice, baking soda, plastic spoons, and cups

Station 4: Candle

Station 5: Nonfat dry milk, water, vinegar, cups, plastic spoons, and cups

Before your children begin working at the stations, you must establish what you mean by *physical properties* of materials. Demonstrate this by giving each group or pair of children a colored rubber ball. Ask the children what words they would use to describe the ball. Encourage the children to use all their senses (except taste) when making their observations about the rubber ball. They then jot down their observations in a journal or record sheet. Take their observations and write them on the board. Words that they might use can include:

- Red (or whatever color the ball is)
- Round (or spherical)
- Smells like rubber
- Bounces
- Can be squeezed
- Is a solid
- Is about 10 cm around (or whatever it is)
- Is harder than a foam ball, but not as hard as a steel ball
- Feels smooth
- Has a ridge around it
- Makes a noise when bounced on a surface

FOCUSING ON AND EXPLAINING A CONCEPT

Explain to the children that the characteristics they have observed about the rubber ball are that ball's physical properties. Group the children's observations according to the sense they used to make them. These include:

Sight: Color, shape, size, unusual appearance (ridges)

Sound: Noise the ball made when bouncing

Touch: Resilience of the ball, texture of the surface, comparison of hardness with other objects

Smell: Smell of the material from which the ball was made

Let the children know that it is important that they be able to describe the properties of substances or objects, so that they can tell later if the substance or object has changed. They will go from station to station, observing and recording the physical properties of the substances at the stations. The children may write their observations in a notebook or journal, or you may wish to provide them with a record sheet.

This will take quite a while to do, and the children will need your help and guidance as they go through the process. Some of the stations have a few of the same materials as other stations, and your children will need to observe and record their properties only once. When they have recorded the properties of these substances, they will be prepared to track the properties after the substances react with one another. You might find that a chart like the following is useful in helping them to record their observations.

SUBSTANCE	PROPERTIES			
	SIGHT	SMELL	TOUCH	HEARING
Baking soda				
Vinegar				
White glue				
Laundry detergent				
Candle				
Dry milk				
Water				
Red cabbage juice				
Lemon juice				

OBSERVATION DATA CHART

APPLYING CONCEPTS

Investigating Evidence of Chemical Reactions (60 min)

In this part of the investigation, your children will be making new substances from the ones whose properties they have just observed. It is important that the children wear their safety goggles for these reactions, and that they follow the directions at each station very carefully. It is also important that they make accurate observations, and record these with care.

For this part of the investigation, you will need the materials listed in the following box.

MATERIALS NEEDED
vinegar
baking soda
empty 16-oz soda bottles
large round balloons
white glue
laundry starch
zipper plastic bags
red cabbage juice
nonfat dry milk
birthday candle in holder
matches
measuring spoons
lemon juice
plastic cups (4–8 oz)
stirring sticks
water
plastic spoons
safety goggles
plastic funnel
paper towels

Organize your class so that small groups of children have a set amount of time (say, 10 min) to work through a station. The set-up for each station is as follows:

Station 1: Vinegar, baking soda, measuring spoons, plastic spoons, balloon, 16 oz bottle, paper towels, plastic funnel, and cups

Station 2: White glue, laundry starch, plastic spoons, measuring spoons, paper towels, and cups

Station 3: Red cabbage juice, lemon juice, baking soda, water, plastic spoons, paper towels, waterproof marker, and cups

Station 4: Candle in candleholder and matches (you may prefer to do this one as a demonstration)

Station 5: Nonfat dry milk, water, vinegar, cups, plastic spoons, measuring spoons, baking soda, paper towels, and cups

What the children need do at each station should be described on an index card taped to the table or counter. The directions for each station are as follows.

Station 1: Put 2 tablespoons of baking soda in the bottle, using the funnel provided. Now, pour 2 tablespoons of vinegar into the mouth of the balloon. Attach the balloon to the bottle, and let the balloon hang down over the side. Now, lift up the balloon and let the vinegar flow into the bottle. Observe what happens when you do this. Are any new products formed? What ideas do you have about what they might be? How have the raw materials changed? How could you find out?

Station 2: Mix 2 tablespoons of white glue with 2 teaspoons of laundry starch in a cup. Stir the mixture very well. You may take it out of the cup to make your observations. Are any new products formed? What ideas do you have about what they might be? How have the raw materials changed? How could you find out?

Station 3: Put about 4 tablespoons of red cabbage juice into each of three plastic cups. Leave the first cup alone, and label it *Control*. Label the second cup *Acid* and the third cup *Base*. Record the color of the cabbage juice in the first cup. Add a teaspoon of lemon juice to the second cup. What happens? Record your observations. Add ½ teaspoon of baking soda to the third cup, and stir. What happens? Record these observations also. Are any new products formed? What ideas do you have about what they might be? How have the raw materials changed? How could you find out?

Station 4: This may be a station, or your teacher may do it as a demonstration because it involves fire. Light the candle with the match. Allow the candle to burn for a couple of minutes. What do you observe? Are any new products formed? What ideas do you have about what they might be? How have the raw materials changed? How could you find out? Be sure to blow the candle out when you have finished with your observations.

Station 5: Read the package directions, and make up ½ cup of milk with hot water. To this, add 2 tablespoons of vinegar, and stir. Pour off the liquids, and keep the solids in the cup. Add ½ teaspoon of baking soda to the solids in the cup and stir. Are any new products formed? What ideas do you have about what they might be? How have the raw materials changed? How could you find out? Write down your observations of this reaction.

Be sure to give your children enough time to do each station, think about what is happening, and discuss their thoughts and observations. This will probably take two days (one hour total). When they have finished all of the stations, engage the whole class in discussion. Ask your children to share their thoughts about the stations they have completed and the evidence for any chemical reactions they observed. Your role in the discussion is as a moderator. It is important that you help your children, through their investigations and their discussions, to understand the key concepts for this activity series.

The fundamental idea you really want them to understand is that chemical reactions result in products that have properties that are usually quite different from the properties of the raw materials. For example, the nonfat milk in Station 5 started out (after it had been mixed up) as a white liquid that flowed very much like water. It probably smelled like milk, and felt like milk. The baking soda started out as a white powdery solid, with a salty smell and a gritty feel. The vinegar started out as a clear liquid with a sour smell. When these three materials were combined, they resulted in a product that was a white, sticky, semi-solid, with a bumpy texture and distinctive odor (glue). The final product shared some of the properties of the reacting materials, but had other properties that were different.

In the case of Station 1, the vinegar (a weak acid) reacted with baking soda (a mild base) to produce carbon dioxide gas and a salt (sodium acetate). Although one of the reacting materials was a liquid with a strong odor and the other was a white, gritty, powdery solid, the product of reacting these two was a colorless gas (heavier than air, if the balloon was tied off and dropped), and a white solid in the bottle of the reacting bottle.

In Station 2, a sticky white semi-liquid reacted with a blue, viscous liquid to make a semi-solid, stretchy substance, somewhat like Silly Putty®. In this reaction, your children were able to change glue, a polymer (a long-chain molecule of repeating units) so that its properties became quite different. Slime, with which many of your children will be familiar, is made in a very similar way.

In Station 3, a liquid (red cabbage juice) with a distinctive color and odor reacts with vinegar in one case and baking soda in the other to change color. Red cabbage juice is one of a group of plant extracts known as "natural indicators," because they react with acids and bases to produce a color change.

Station 4 can be done as a station or a demonstration, if you are concerned about your children working with lighted candles. This is an example of a combustion reaction. The fuel in the candle (wax) is heated and combined with the oxygen in the air. The result is water, carbon dioxide, and other byproducts. You may find that many of your children think that it is only the wick of the candle that is burning, and that the wax is merely there to "hold the wick up." It is important to their understanding of combustion in general that they know that the wax (which, if paraffin-based, came from fossil fuels) is the fuel.

Ask your children to focus in on their evidence for a chemical reaction. You will be discussing this in the next segment.

Reviewing the Results (15 min)

This is a very important part of the investigation. Here the work done by each group is shared and reviewed by everyone. Ask students to share their observations of the chemical reactions. Your role is to act as a moderator:

> What sorts of things happened when one material reacted with another?
>
> What evidence did you find that new materials were formed as a result of the chemical reactions?

Evidence that your children may note about chemical reactions can include:

- Color changes
- Gas released
- Change of texture
- Different odor produced
- Liquid changing to a solid material, or producing a solid material
- Heat given off
- Heat absorbed

Note: The ways in which your children consider these questions may be a key learning moment for some of them, so be alive to their ideas. Look out for any misunderstandings that individual children may have and try to clarify any points that do not seem clear.

Making Thoughtful Connections (15 min)

To put everyone's investigations into context, it is now very important that you allow your children to reflect on their own and others' observations about chemical reactions. Ask them to think about what the investigations have revealed about *chemical reactions:*

> What have we discovered about how chemical reactions can produce new materials?
>
> How can this help us in learning about the way the chemical world works?

EXPANDING CONCEPTS

Drawing Conclusions (5 min)

To put the whole investigation into perspective and relate it to the wider issues of chemical reactions, ask your children to think about other, related things that they would like to investigate:

What other chemical reactions do you know about?

What questions about these reactions do you think would be worth investigating next?

How would you use what you now know about chemical reactions to plan your investigation?

Note: This is a logical extension to this module, and you can follow the same general structure.

Some students may enjoy investigating other questions at home and reporting their results.

Take some time to reflect carefully on your experience with this investigation and use this sheet to record your evaluations. This will help you consolidate your ideas and provide a useful set of reference notes when you use the investigation in the future. Add more pages if you need to.

WORKING IN METHODS CLASS

What was the most important learning experience for you?

What experiences do you think will be important to remember when you do this activity with children in school?

What would you change in this activity for use with children?

What concerns do you have about using this activity with children?

(continued)

What do you need to know more about before you use this activity with children?

Points to discuss with faculty and colleagues:

WORKING WITH CHILDREN IN SCHOOL

What happened in the way you expected?

What happened that you had not expected?

What would you change when repeating this activity with children?

What did you learn about the children by doing this activity?

What did you learn about yourself as a teacher from this activity?

Points to discuss with faculty and colleagues:

LIVING

THINGS

REPRODUCE

6 Investigating the Way Seeds Become Adult Plants

WHAT CHILDREN CAN LEARN FROM THIS EXEMPLAR

Children's Thinking about Seeds and Plants: The Research Base

Quite a bit of research work has been done into children's thinking about seeds and their relationship to adult plants. One common idea children have about seeds is that they are not alive (Tamir, Gal-Chappin, & Nussnovitz, 1981). They can become alive, however, when they are planted in the ground, where they can get energy, water, and food from the soil. This idea of "food from the soil" and "plants use water as food" extends to some children's thinking about adult plants. Even older children, with extensive experience in life science classes and instruction on photosynthesis, do not understand that plants make their own food—that they do not get "food from water" or "food from soil nutrients" (Parker, 1985).

An explanation for the pervasiveness of informal ideas about plants and seeds is suggested by one study into children's interest in plant reproduction. Compared to interest in the reproduction of animals, interest in the reproduction of plants is very low. A number of the children studied did not believe plants reproduce either sexually or asexually. Mating was considered essential for sexual reproduction, therefore plants (even flowering plants) could not reproduce in this way.

Another informal idea that children had about seeds and plants is that everything a plant needs to grow is contained within the seed. There was no idea or explanation of generating more "stuff" in the growth and development process of plants (Tamir et al., 1981).

Teaching Implications of the Research

In helping children understand the role of seeds in producing new plants, it is important that you give them as many experiences as possible in observing the series of events that result in a seed. These can entail:

- Germinating a seed
- Planting the sprouted seed
- Providing the plant with what it needs to survive and thrive (sunlight, water, air)
- Making observations of the plant as it grows and recording those observations
- Noting the production of flowers and identifying the male and female parts of the flowers
- Nurturing the plants all the way through seed production
- Harvesting the seeds and dissecting a few to observe the embryo, food, and protective covering
- Planting the harvested seeds and repeating the cycle

Although this is time-consuming, if children are engaged in the process of seed production all the way through, they can make connections between the seed, the plant resulting from the seed, the reproductive process of the plant, and the new seeds produced by the plant. It is important to select plants that grow rapidly and produce flowers with easily observable male and female parts. Bean plants may be one possibility.

Science Background

Living things are able to make more of their own kind. Depending upon their species, living things reproduce in a variety of ways. Some very simple organisms, such as the one-celled amoeba (found in pond water), simply make copies of themselves and divide into two. Some sponges are able to enclose bits of their tissue in capsules (called *gemmules*) when conditions are too dry for the sponge to survive. When the water level rises again, the gemmules are able to grow into mature sponges.

More sophisticated organisms also have various ways of reproducing. Some plants can reproduce asexually through what is known as "vegetative reproduction." If you have ever taken a cutting from a plant and put it into water to root, you have witnessed this type of reproduction. Plants that produce runners (such as strawberries) are also reproducing vegetatively.

Sexual reproduction is the joining of two cells (one male sperm, one female egg) to produce a fertilized egg. That egg then divides repeatedly to form many more cells with the exact genetic makeup of the original fertilized egg. Eventually, the new cells begin to specialize (differentiate) to become tissues.

Plants that reproduce through seeds undergo sexual reproduction. The flower of the plant can produce both sperm (found in pollen grains) and eggs (found in the base of the flower). The diagram of the flower at the top of page 95 will illustrate what parts produce what sex cells.

When a pollen grain falls on top of the pistil of the flower, the pollen grain begins to grow a tube down the center of the pistil. When this tube reaches the ovary (where the eggs reside), the sperm cells in the pollen

Flower Cross Section

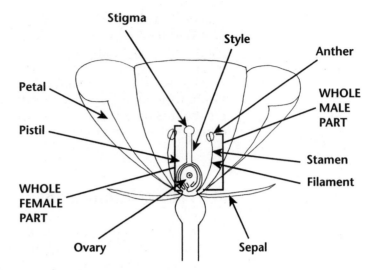

travel down the tube to join with the eggs. The fertilized eggs eventually become the seeds of the plant. The ovule of the flower becomes fleshy and develops into the fruit.

Different seed-producing plants produce different kinds of fruit. Your children will be familiar with many kinds—but they may not know that some of what they consider vegetables are actually fruits. You may want them to examine a wide variety of fruits and nonfruits to help them build this concept. Encourage your children to look for the seeds in the fruits. Examples include:

FRUITS
- Tomatoes
- Peaches
- Apples
- Bananas
- Peppers
- Rose hips

NONFRUITS
- Carrots
- Potatoes
- Broccoli
- Asparagus
- Artichoke
- Spinach

EXEMPLAR

LIVING THINGS REPRODUCE
Investigating the Way Seeds Become Adult Plants

Note: This investigation is most suitable for children in grades 1–3.

OVERVIEW

One of the characteristics of living things is that they make more of their own kind (*reproduce*). You can introduce this idea to your children through plants and their seeds. Not all plants reproduce by seeds; ferns and many other simple plants reproduce by spores, and cone-bearing plants produce "naked seeds" in their cones. (This is where they get their name *gymnosperm*, which means "naked seeds.") For the sake of familiarity and simplicity, this investigation will examine how some common plants make others of their own kind through seeds.

KEY PEDAGOGICAL IDEAS

- This investigation is an example of a long-term experiment using your classroom as a laboratory. It is important for your students to understand the key science concepts through this investigation. (See next section.)

- When doing a long-term science investigation with young children, it is important that everyone have a task to do, and know when it is to be done. A calendar with names and tasks is useful to help organize this and to keep interest alive.

KEY SCIENCE CONCEPTS

- Sometimes science investigations take place over time, so that we can observe and record changes in things.

- Living things make more of their own kind through a variety of processes. One of these processes is the production of seeds by flowering plants.

- Making and recording accurate observations are important parts of investigating a science question.

SUPPORTING NATIONAL STANDARDS

National Science Education Standards

LEVEL K–4

Content Standard A: As a result of activities in grades K–4, all students should develop:

- Abilities necessary to do scientific inquiry
- Understanding about scientific inquiry

Content Standard C: As a result of activities in grades K–4, all students should develop an understanding of:

- The characteristics of organisms
- Organisms and environments

BENCHMARKS FOR SCIENCE LITERACY

By the end of the 2nd grade, students should know that

- Some animals and plants are alike in the way they look and in the things they do, and others are very different from one another.
- Plants and animals have features that help them live in different environments.

By the end of the 2nd grade, students should know that

- There is variation among individuals of one kind within a population.
- Offspring are very much, but not exactly, like their parents and like one another.

BEFORE YOU BEGIN

Technology Connection

Collect resources on plants, such as trade books, videos, charts, CD-ROMs, or magazines. Use a search engine to find Web sites on plants. You may want to locate the Web site of the National Arboretum (www.ars-grin.gov/ars/Beltsville/na/) or the American Horticultural Society (www.ahs.org).

Linking to the Community

Arrange for a classroom visit from a local horticulturist, gardener, or landscaper so that your children can learn about the proper care of plants in their classroom. Arrange for a field trip to a local gardening center, arboretum, or nature center, so that children can observe plants growing and producing seeds in a variety of settings.

Preparing Materials

For this investigation to work well, it will be important that you have space and light in your classroom to grow plants. If you do not have windows, you may need to set up a plant light, plant stand, and shelves to accommodate the plants in pots. If you do not have this setup available, check with a local middle school or high school science teacher to see if you can borrow a plant stand with shelves and light.

Buy seeds (or have them donated) that germinate quickly to produce shoots and roots. Beans work very well for this, as do radishes. Bean seeds are large, while radish seeds are very tiny. You will also need to make a collection of a variety of seeds, both wild and commercial, for your children to examine. The best time to do this is in the fall.

Collect small pots for planting. You will also need about 10 lb of potting soil and a small shovel or trowel for each group of children.

A NOTE ABOUT SAFETY! Science investigations should be safe. Ensure that students are not exposed to any hazards while they are engaged in investigations. Remind them to observe safety procedures at all times, especially when handling soil and planting tools in the classroom. Children should wash their hands after they finish working with soil or plant materials.

ASSESSING PRIOR KNOWLEDGE

Investigating the Way Seeds Become Plants: Getting Things Going! (15 min)

It is important to establish what your children's understanding is about how flowering plants reproduce through seeds. Ask your children to make a series of drawings, or write a series of short sentences, explaining how they think a common plant like a sunflower (or other readily recognizable plant common to your area) starts out. You may want to draw a sunflower on the board for a prompt, or distribute a handout with a picture of a sunflower, including its roots. Before they get started, ask them to think about these questions:

How did the sunflower grow to be so tall?

How did the sunflower start its life?

If you have ever grown sunflowers (or other flowers), how did you grow them?

How long do sunflowers usually last?

What happens to sunflowers at the end of their growing season?

Ask your children to share their drawings and sentences with others in their group and discuss their ideas about where the sunflower comes from. When they have done this, ask the groups, one by one, to share their thoughts with the entire class.

Note: Some of your children may have drawn pictures that indicate religious or mythical causes behind the growth of the sunflower. At the beginning of this investigation, you are accepting the ideas the children already have about where plants come from. It is important to be sensitive to ideas as they arise, and to let children make their own observations and conclusions as the investigation progresses. Your job is to facilitate scientific investigation, moderate discussions of findings, and create an atmosphere in your classroom where children can discover how the natural world works.

EXPLORING CONCEPTS

Agreeing about the Way Flowering Plants Start Out (10 min)

Hold an open discussion of what the different groups have to say about the sunflower. List their ideas on the board or chart paper:

What ideas can we all agree upon about how the sunflower starts out?

List these on the board or chart as they come up. Some of your children may think the sunflower starts as a small plant and grows to a bigger one.

Many children, especially those with yards and gardens, will have had experience with planting seeds. What they may not know is that seeds are specific for each type of plant. Sunflower seeds, which are produced by the flower part of the sunflower at the end of the growing season, will only produce a sunflower, and not a string bean or a radish.

Note: Include only those items that your children contribute and agree upon. Be sure to leave space for later additions to the list.

Explain that, to investigate exactly how flowering plants start out from seeds, we need to come up with clear questions to investigate:

> What important questions can you think of that will help us to understand how different types of flowering plants grow from seeds?

Help your students to formulate useful questions and list them in a way similar to the following box.

QUESTIONS TO INVESTIGATE

- What parts of the plant produce seeds?
- How can we find out how seeds grow into new plants?
- What plants (and their seeds) would be good examples for us to investigate, and why?
- Whom could we ask to find out more about how plants make more of their own kind?
- Do all seeds grow into plants in the same way?
- How are seeds different from each other?

> As a class, your students will be investigating:

> How do seeds become adult plants?

If this question does not arise from your students' thinking, add it yourself. Explain to your students that they will be investigating the question as a class, and that the investigation will take place over a long period of time (several weeks). Tell them that they will have the opportunity to investigate their own questions about flowering plants and seeds.

FOCUSING ON AND EXPLAINING CONCEPTS

How Do We Go About Observing Seeds? (10 min)

Go outdoors to see what seeds are available to be collected. Obviously, this works best in the autumn. If you choose to do this activity at another season, you will need to have a seed collection available for your students to examine. You can do this by collecting and storing the seeds yourself in the fall, or you can buy seeds from a gardening center and use those.

Note: You will need to have enough seeds of different varieties so that your children can observe a number of characteristics. Seeds such as acorns, sweet gum seeds, burrs, dandelion puffs, milkweed pods (with seeds inside), radish seeds, beans, flower seeds (especially sunflower seeds), and pumpkin seeds, would make a good collection.

Give each group a collection of seeds to examine. Ask the group to observe the seeds carefully, and write down their observations and thoughts in response to these questions:

What do all of these seeds have in common?

What are the differences that you observe between the seeds?

What types of plants do you think made these seeds? How can you tell?

What ideas do you have about what has to happen to these seeds for them to become adult plants?

The children may write their thoughts and ideas in a notebook or journal, or you may wish to provide them with a record sheet. Encourage them to make drawings of the seeds and describe them as best they can. You may also want your children to group the seeds according to characteristics they find to be similar (large, round, fleshy seeds could be in one group; thread-like seeds could be in another; and tiny, round seeds in a third).

When the groups have finished their observations, ask each group to share what it has discovered about its seeds. Focus the class on the similarities in seeds: area for stored food; methods of dispersal; part that could grow into the plant; and so on. They will be working more with these ideas in the next part of this investigation. Before you move on, take time to show your children pictures of a wide variety of flowering plants (use plant charts, videos, trade books). Ask them:

Are all of these plants alike? In what ways are they different?

Would you expect all of them to produce the same kinds of seeds? Why or why not?

How can seeds give us a clue to the plants that made them?

What's in a Seed That Can Grow into a Plant?
(10 min to set up; 2 weeks to germinate)

In this part of the investigation, your children will be examining a particular seed, a lima bean, to find out about the parts of a seed. Lima beans are good choices because they are large and easy to see and they germinate readily in the right conditions. The following box lists materials needed for this investigation.

MATERIALS NEEDED

- Whole, pre-soaked lima beans (3 whole ones plus 1 cut lengthwise for each pair of children)
- Magnifiers for each child
- Supply of paper towels
- Drawing paper and pencils
- Handout showing labeled drawing of a whole and split lima bean seed
- Zipper plastic bags (pint size)
- Masking tape and markers to label the bags

Give each pair of children one whole lima bean seed and one that has been cut in half lengthwise. These can be on a paper towel. Children will also need to have magnifiers.

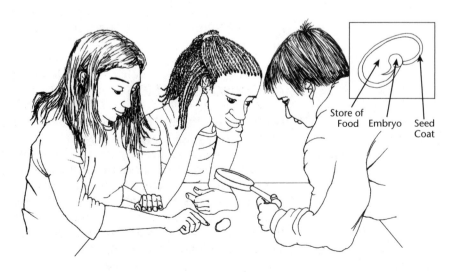

Store of
Food   Embryo   Seed
Coat

Ask the children to look carefully at the beans, both with the naked eye and through the magnifiers. Ask them to draw the whole bean and the inside of the cut bean.

Make and distribute a copy of the diagram of a lima bean seed with the parts labeled (page 101). Ask children to compare their drawings of the lima bean with the handout. They can also label their own drawings (as best they can) using the handout. Explain to your children what the different parts of the seed are for:

- Embryo: Grows to be the new plant (from the fertilized egg in the flower). The embryo will give rise to the new plant's roots and shoots.
- Stored food: Feeds the embryo until the embryo can develop leaves and roots to feed itself.
- Seed coat: Protective covering of the seed. It is usually tough.

Your children can then put one of their soaked lima beans by itself in a zipper plastic bag and zip the bag shut. They can put a second lima, on a dampened paper towel, into another zipper plastic bag and zip that shut. Both bags should be labeled with the date that they were put into the bag, as well as the names of the children in the group.

Have children put the bags in a dark place (such as a cupboard) and check them every day to see what happens. Ask the children to write down their observations about the appearance of the lima bean (and the bag itself) every day. You may want to give them a data chart to use for this, or have them construct a chart for themselves.

Let the seeds stay in the closet for two weeks, reminding the children to check them each day. At the end of that period, ask your children to look over their data, and think about these questions:

What happened to the seeds in the first few days? Why do you think this happened?

What part of the seed produced shoots? Roots?

What differences (if any) did you notice about the bean with the damp paper towel, and the bean without?

What did this investigation help you to understand about how plants grow from seeds?

What part of the seed do you think resulted in the parts of the plants you saw at the end of the two weeks? What is your evidence for that?

Ask the children to save their seedlings to plant in soil for the next investigation.

APPLYING CONCEPTS

How Does a Plant Grow from a Seed?
(20 min to plant seeds; 3 weeks to grow plants)

In this last part of the investigation, children plant their germinated lima beans (as well as a selection of other fast-growing seeds) to find out how the seed changes as it germinates and grows into an adult plant. This gives your students a chance to carry out a long-term investigation in the classroom, and to make careful records of observations over a long period of time. For the investigation, each group or pair will need to have the materials listed in the following box.

MATERIALS NEEDED

- Selection of fast-growing seeds (radish, grass, limas, sweet peas)
- One pot for each type of seed
- Water supply
- Tape and markers to label pots
- Potting soil
- Access to sunlight or plant light
- Plain envelopes
- Metric ruler
- Journals or data sheets

Distribute materials to each group of children so that they have a total of at least three kinds of seeds to plant per group (including their germinated lima beans). Demonstrate to your children how to plant the seeds in potting soil according to the directions on the seed packets. Show the children how to water the planted seeds and how to label the pots, using masking tape and markers, with the name of the plant and the names of the children in the group.

Give the children time to plant their seeds, according to your instructions, and label their pots. They need to keep some seeds in labeled plain envelopes so that they can compare the plant, as it grows, to the seed that produced it. Ask the children to put the potted plants into the plant stand or on the windowsill. It is important that they check the pots each day to make sure that they stay moist, but not too wet.

At this point, you may want your children to make predictions about what will happen with their seeds, based on their prior knowledge and their recent experience with the lima bean.

ABOUT PREDICTING

- Making a sensible prediction of the most likely results of an investigation is an important scientific skill. It helps students to focus on the key point of the investigation they are doing. Predictions should be made on the basis of what students already know about the seeds (not a simple guess).
- Writing down the predictions before the investigation helps students to think about them accurately and provides a basis for comparison to the actual results.
- Giving reasons for the prediction encourages students to think about the fairness of the investigation and gives them a basis for reflection when the actual results do not correspond to their original expectations.
- The children should observe the pots every day, writing down their observations of how the plant develops from the seed. They will probably find it useful to make drawings of their plants as they grow. Read over the ideas that follow on using their senses to make observations and share this with your students.

USING SENSES TO MAKE PREDICTIONS

- Looking at objects or materials closely and seeing small details (using magnifiers if necessary)
- Feeling for the texture of the seeds and plants and describing them
- Smelling (**safely**) to find any odor that an object or material is emitting.

Scientific observations have to be made in an organized way. This is an opportunity to introduce methods of recording data. Ask your students to think about the best way of recording their observations:

How could you best record your observations?

How can you do this so others can see and understand your recordings?

The following is a useful chart your students could use if they have difficulty designing their own recording method.

OBSERVATION DATA CHART

Name of plant

Date planted

Drawing of seed

Day 1 observations (drawing of plant, measurement of height)

Day 2 observations

Day 3 observations

Each group makes its observations over three weeks. When they have completed the entire recording period, your children create a display showing how each of their seeds has grown into an adult plant, stage by stage. They may choose to do this on a poster, using graphs showing how their various plants have grown. This can be done by posting their results, or by having each group in turn present its findings.

Ask all the children to think about how the different seeds grew into plants:

How did the seeds change as they grew into adult plants?

What did the seeds need to grow into adult plants?

What did the plants need to grow once the seeds had sprouted?

How did the ways in which the seeds grew differ from plant to plant?

Note: You need to help your students understand that seed type and growing pattern are specific for the particular type of plant. Also, that one cannot get a carrot plant out of a radish seed, or vice versa. Important ideas that they should carry away from this investigation are shown in the following box.

IMPORTANT IDEAS ABOUT HOW SEEDS GROW

- Seeds have an embryo, which is the baby plant, stored food for the baby plant to grow roots and shoots, and a seed coat to protect the seed while it is growing.
- Each flowering plant has its own type of seed.
- Seeds can sprout in darkness, but they need moisture to do this.
- Once a seed has sprouted and grown roots, it needs water, light, and air to continue to grow.
- Plants make more seeds to keep producing their own kind.

Reviewing the Results (15 min)

This is a very important part of the investigation. Here the data collected by each group are shared and reviewed by everyone. Ask students to present their findings about their plants, one group at a time. It is important that their display be easily visible to everyone. Your role is to act as a moderator:

What do your results tell us about how different seeds grow into adult plants?

Did anything you found out surprise you? Why?

Be sure to have each group show its investigation predictions and also their *reasons for the predictions:*

Was your prediction about the seeds and plants correct?

Do you think this confirms your reasoning?

If the event you predicted didn't happen, can you find the reason?

Do you need to revise your reasoning from the investigation results?

Note: The ways in which your students consider these questions may be a key learning moment for some of them, so be alert to their ideas.

Encourage the children who are not presenting to ask questions in an organized and sensible way. Look out for any misunderstandings that individual students may have and try to clarify any points that do not seem clear.

Making Thoughtful Connections (15 min)

To put everyone's investigations into context, it is now very important that you allow your students to reflect on their own findings and the findings of other groups. Ask them to think about what the investigations have revealed about how *seeds grow into adult plants:*

> What have we discovered about how plants make more of their own kind?
>
> How can this help us in learning about how other living things make more of their own kind?

EXPANDING CONCEPTS

Drawing Conclusions (5 min)

To put the whole investigation into perspective and to relate it to the wider issues of living things reproducing, ask your children to think about other related things that they would like to investigate:

> What other questions do you think would be worth investigating next?
>
> How would you use what you now know about seeds and plants to plan your investigation?

Note: This is a logical extension to this module, and you can follow the same general structure.

Some students may enjoy investigating other questions at home and reporting their results.

Take some time to reflect carefully on your experience with this investigation and use this sheet to record your evaluations. This will help you consolidate your ideas and provide a useful set of reference notes when you use the investigation in the future. Add more pages if you need to.

WORKING IN METHODS CLASS

What was the most important learning experience for you?

What experiences do you think will be important to remember when you do this activity with children in school?

What would you change in this activity for use with children?

What concerns do you have about using this activity with children?

(continued)

What do you need to know more about before you use this activity with children?

Points to discuss with faculty and colleagues:

WORKING WITH CHILDREN IN SCHOOL

What happened in the way you expected?

What happened that you had not expected?

What would you change when repeating this activity with children?

What did you learn about the children by doing this activity?

What did you learn about yourself as a teacher from this activity?

Points to discuss with faculty and colleagues:

PEOPLE

USE

TECHNOLOGY

7 Investigating the Way to Use Technology to Solve Problems

WHAT CHILDREN CAN LEARN FROM THIS EXEMPLAR

Children's Thinking about Technology: The Research Base

Not much research has been done into children's thinking about technology in general and design in particular. Some work has been done with older children aged 11 to 14 (McCormick, Hennessy, & Murphy, 1993). In this age group it has been discovered that children are not aware of what constitutes the design process (idea generation, research, schematics and diagrams, prototypes, testing, revision, additional testing, scaling up, and so on). They also do not understand why it is important, in technology, to assess a design for flaws, efficiency, cost effectiveness, or safety, among many other things.

Another finding from research into this area has revealed that some children, when given design tasks, have difficulty using their knowledge and skills from other areas of study (McCormick et al., 1993). They do not see the job of design as being interdisciplinary. When actually engaged in considering aspects of design, children may not think that the properties of materials used in their product are functions of the particles that make up those materials. They may not have sufficient experience in design-and-make projects to know that the properties of materials determine their use in products.

Teaching Implications of the Research

To help your children understand what is involved in the design process, it would be useful to teach the process explicitly, using their own design projects (such as the ones in this chapter's investigations) as models. Have them match up what they did as they worked on a design with the steps of the design process. You can also use their own projects as source material for teaching about *evaluating* a design. Do a general design evaluation yourself, then ask them to evaluate each other's designs. Questions they should ask themselves in their evaluations include:

- Will the design make a safe product?
- Will the design make the best product for the job?
- Will the design give the best value for the money and time involved?
- Will the design still work when it is "scaled up"?
- Will the design make a product that is environmentally friendly?

To help children use their knowledge and skills from other content areas to accomplish a design task, you may want to give teams of students specific assignments, each dealing with a different subject area. For example, the tasks could be sorted like this:

- Mathematics (diagrams, measuring, scale, shapes)
- Art (drawings of prototypes, importance of color)
- Science (forces, energy sources, materials and their properties)
- Language arts (description of the design and product, rationale for patent)

Science Background

Technology is the application of science to solve problems. One of the very first uses of technology was in the invention of the wheel and axle. Until the wheel and axle, heavy loads had to be dragged or pushed. The new invention allowed carts to be built that could be used to move goods and people much more easily from place to place. The wheel and axle could not have been built without tools. Tools, too, are thus even earlier examples of technology. Tools such as knives, spears, and bows and arrows allowed early humans to protect themselves and to hunt for food.

Through the ages, as humanity faced more and more sophisticated problems, the technology to meet those problems became more sophisticated as well. After the invention of the movable sail, for example, sailors were able to range much farther from shore and journey more efficiently. Navigation was a problem until the sextant came on the horizon. Today's sailors have the huge advantage of the satellite-driven Global Positioning System (GPS), which can locate anything on the planet.

Sometimes, the very technology that is used to solve a problem can result in new and unforeseen difficulties. The gasoline-powered combustible engine, for example, has enabled humans to travel great distances quickly and comfortably. The number of cars on the road, however, has resulted in air and noise pollution, depletion of natural resources, traffic gridlock, and highway accidents. Faced with such problems, humans then develop even more technological solutions: catalytic converters on engines (to reduce pollution); alternative energy sources for cars (electric cars); public transportation systems; highway cameras to detect speeders.

It is important for your children to understand that technology uses science in practical ways to find solutions to challenges. To help them with this concept, they should work together to design ways of overcoming problems using everyday materials and common, safe, tools. You can give them examples of problems that they could solve, or challenge them to find such problems on their own. For example, let's say you have a storage problem for book bags in your classroom. Invite your students to come up with alternative ways of storing the bags. Or, you could ask them each to bring in a household problem they've observed. They could then work in groups to invent ways of solving the problems. Some ideas of household problems can include:

- Feeding pets when the family is away
- Making sure all the plants get watered
- Storing canned food
- Getting fallen leaves off the lawn
- Keeping shower supplies convenient
- Keeping track of bills and payments
- Making enough lunches for one week

E X E M P L A R   **PEOPLE USE TECHNOLOGY**
Investigating the Use of Technology to Solve Problems

Note: This investigation is most suitable for children in grades 4–5.

OVERVIEW

Our world has become increasingly more technological with time. Many homes in the United States have their own computers, voice mail, Internet connections, mobile telephones, televisions, videotape players, cameras, fax machines, and many labor-saving devices (dishwashers, clothes washers, self-cleaning ovens, blenders, automatic bread-makers).

Technology is the application of science to solve practical problems. It is important for your children, growing up in our technological Western society, to have a good working knowledge of the role of technology in their lives. To do this, they will be applying some basic scientific principles to solving a practical, everyday problem at home. This will give your children a chance to design a piece of technology, try it out, revise it, and try it again. They will also be making a working prototype that they can display and explain to others.

KEY SCIENCE CONCEPTS

This investigation is an example of a *design-and-make* activity. It is important for your children to understand several key ideas about technology through their work:

> People can design and make objects and systems for specific purposes.
>
> Sometimes science investigations involve building things, testing them, revising them, and testing them again.
>
> Technology makes practical application of science.
>
> The job of engineers and systems designers is to come up with technological solutions to practical problems.

SUPPORTING NATIONAL STANDARDS

National Science Education Standards

LEVELS K–4 AND 5–8

Content Standard A: As a result of activities in grades K–4 and 5–8, all students should develop:

- Abilities necessary to do scientific inquiry
- Understanding about scientific inquiry

Content Standard B: As a result of activities in grades K–4, all students should develop an understanding of:

- Properties of objects and materials
- Position and motion of objects

Content Standard B: As a result of activities in grades 5–8, all students should develop an understanding of:

- Properties and changes of properties in matter
- Motions and forces

Content Standard E: As a result of activities in grades K–4 and 5–8, all students should develop an understanding of:

- Abilities of technological design
- Understanding about science and technology

BENCHMARKS FOR SCIENCE LITERACY

By the end of the 5th grade, students should know that

- Naturally occurring materials such as wood, clay, cotton, and animal skins may be processed or combined with other materials to change their properties.
- Through science and technology, a wide variety of materials that do not appear in nature at all have become available, ranging from steel to nylon to liquid crystals.

By the end of the 5th grade, students should know that

- There is no perfect design. Designs that are best in one respect (safety or ease of use, for example) may be inferior in other ways (cost or appearance). Usually some features must be sacrificed to get others. How such tradeoffs are received depends upon which features are emphasized and which are downplayed.

BEFORE YOU BEGIN

Technology Connection

Collect as many print, video, and electronic resources about modern technology as you can. Also, search the Internet for useful, technology-related Web sites. Discuss the technology investigation with your school's media center person, so that technology resources can be pulled when your children are ready for them. You may want to check out the technology education standards at Web site www.iteawww.org/TAA/TAA.html.

Linking to the Community

Arrange for a classroom visit from an engineer so that your children can learn about how engineers use technology to solve problems. You may also want to arrange for a field trip to a site where technology is used to solve problems. Examples of such sites can be car repair shops, water treatment plants, power utilities, recycling plants, and telephone companies.

A NOTE ABOUT SAFETY! Science investigations should be safe. Ensure that children are not exposed to any hazards while they are engaged in investigations. Remind them to observe safety procedures at all times, especially when handling tools and using electricity in the classroom. Make sure they wear eye protection when working with tools. Remind them to wash their hands when they finish an investigation, and to put away all materials and tools, if this is appropriate for your class.

ASSESSING PRIOR KNOWLEDGE

Investigating the Way Technology Is Used to Solve Problems: Getting Things Going! (15 min for brainstorming; 30 min for home interview)

It is important to establish what your children's understanding is about technology and how it is used. Ask them to think about all of the appliances and other devices they may have at home that make life easier. You can help them with this by prompting them with these questions:

How do you get your clothes clean?

What devices are used to prepare meals?

How do your dishes get clean?

How do your floors get cleaned?

If you have a yard with trees, how do the leaves get cleaned up?

How do you get to and from school?

How do you communicate with people from a distance?

How do you find out information?

How are you entertained in your spare time?

Where does your clean water supply come from?

Where does your used water supply go?

EXPLORING A CONCEPT

After your children have thought about responses to these questions, ask them, as an at-home investigation, to interview an older person (preferably someone at least 30 years older than the child) about how technology has changed with time. The children can use the question list above, but adapt it in this way:

How did clothes get cleaned when you were my age?

Ask your children to write down the responses that the older person gives for these questions and bring the information to class the next day. Make up a large chart, on poster paper or the board, like the one that follows.

Changes in Technology

	Then (30 years ago)	*Now*
Cleaning clothes	washing machine with a wringer; hung clothes to dry	automatic washer and dryer
Cleaning dishes	washed and dried by hand in sink	automatic dishwasher
Cleaning floors	large canister vacuum cleaner	upright vacuum cleaner, small vacuums for small spaces
Communicating	telephone, letters	telephone, email, voice mail, Web pages, pagers, faxes
Entertainment	TV, sports, theater movies	TV, home videos, computer games, sports
Finding information	books, magazines, asking people	CD-ROMs, Internet, books

Making such a chart will help your children to see that, even in the last thirty years, technology has changed our lives significantly. They may be able to realize the incredibly influential role that communication advances have had on society. Many people now work from home using home computers with Internet connections and faxes. They can stay in touch with their offices and work without distraction, while avoiding the commute that contributes to air pollution in cities and large towns.

FOCUSING ON AND EXPLAINING A CONCEPT

Tracking Technology for a Century: A Timeline of Progress
(2 days for research; 1 day to make timeline)

To give your children a clearer understanding of how technology has been used to solve problems over time, they will be conducting specialist research on one particular category of technology. Their job is to find out how one problem has been addressed through technology over the past hundred years. They can conduct this research in the school and local library, through the Internet, and by using CD-ROM references. Here are examples of questions that your children can investigate (encourage them to think up some on their own, as well):

How did people communicate over long distances?

How were copies of important documents made?

How did people get from place to place as quickly as possible?

How did people get the energy they needed to heat homes, and run machines?

How were clothes made?

How was food grown?

How were houses built?

How did goods exchange hands?

How were buildings lighted?

How were people treated for disease?

Let the children work in pairs or small groups on the question of their choice. Ask them to collect or draw pictures showing how the technology related to their question has changed over the years. When they have finished their research, each group can design and make a poster or mural showing the types of technology that were representative of a particular time period.

One point the children might discover through their research is that changes in technology are increasing at a much more rapid rate over time. For example, the telephone began to be in general use from about the 1890s. However, the design of the telephone, and the technology that supported it, didn't change greatly for many years. Then technology moved from a central exchange and party-line system to the highly complex system (with fiber optics and satellites) that has come about in recent years.

When they have finished their posters or murals, ask each student group to share what it found out about technological changes with the rest of the class. Ask your children to look for patterns and trends that they see emerging over time. Some things that they might notice are:

- Technology is a response to a practical problem.
- Many technologies depend upon other technologies.
- When a new technology first comes out, it is usually quite expensive, and may be somewhat crude in materials and design. With use, research, and new materials, the technology decreases in price, and usually improves in design and materials. Computers and phones are examples of this.
- Sometimes technology that is developed to solve one problem can create new, unthought-of, problems. Cars, for example, solved the big problem of getting from place to place in a relatively short amount of time. With the great number of cars on the road, however, now there are the problems of air pollution, accidents, and traffic jams to deal with.

APPLYING A CONCEPT

Designing a Technological Response to a Practical Problem (2 hr)

While much of today's technology relies upon such sophisticated devices as semiconductors and microcircuits, your children can still get a sense of how technology works by designing and building something that uses science to solve a practical problem. In this part of the investigation, you will challenge your children to come up with an innovative way of addressing a practical household problem that uses:

- Their knowledge of how things work
- Their basic science understandings
- The contributions of all the members of the group

To do this investigation, you will need to prepare the materials listed in the following box.

MATERIALS NEEDED

- Tool kits (hammer, screwdriver, nails)
- Pieces of wood
- Simple circuit components (wires, alligator clips, battery holders, light bulbs, bulb holders, buzzers, propellers, solar cells)
- Mirrors

- Tape and glue
- Safe scissors
- Safety goggles
- Various containers (delicatessen containers, boxes)
- Poster board
- Cardboard tubes
- Boxes
- Rubber or plastic tubing
- String and rubber bands
- Markers
- Aluminum foil and plastic wrap
- Timers

You won't know everything you will need until your children show you their plans to solve their problems. You may need to enlist the help of the children themselves, or adults such as parents, guardians, and classroom volunteers, to bring in additional materials. The job of your children is:

1. Select one practical problem from the following box (or come up with their own idea).
2. Brainstorm ways in which the problem could be solved.
3. Write out a plan for designing and making the technology that would solve the problem.
4. Get your approval and advice for their plan.
5. Assemble the materials and tools they need to make their device or system.
6. Build the device or system.
7. Try out the device or system to see how well it works to solve the problem.
8. Redesign the device or system (if necessary) so it works better.
9. Make a presentation of their problem, plan, device, and the results of their trials to the rest of the class.

PRACTICAL PROBLEMS TO SOLVE WITH TECHNOLOGY
- Feeding pets when the family is away from home
- Keeping plants watered when the family is away from home
- Communicating with someone in the family without making a lot of noise
- Keeping a lunch fresh all day at school
- Getting packages off a tall shelf
- Helping an older person who has problems walking to get around the house
- Helping a young child keep toys organized and off the floor
- Seeing who is outside your door before you open it

Your children will need a good deal of guidance to do this task in a creative, safe, and useful way. Discuss the project ahead of time, and let them know that, while there are already technological solutions for a number of the problems listed, you would like them to think of fresh, yet practical, ways of using technology to help solve these problems. Give them time to think, do some research, and make plans to solve the problem. Then, discuss their plans with them, helping them to see alternatives for material or design issues when these arise.

Help your children to assemble the materials they need and monitor them as they build and try out their devices or systems. When all the plans have been implemented, and the devices or systems tried and revised, have your children prepare a presentation during which they can explain what they did to solve the problem and the role that technology played in their solution.

Reviewing the Results (15 min)

This is a very important part of the investigation. Here, the devices designed by each group, as well as the results of the trials, are reviewed by everyone. Ask your children to make their presentations to the class, showing what they did, how it works, and how they came to build it. Your role in the presentation session is to act as a moderator:

How well did your device work to solve the problem?

What could you have done to your device or system to make it work better?

Encourage the other children in the class to ask questions and make observations during the presentations. Ask the children to think about, and discuss, what science was behind each of the pieces of technology presented. Were some based on electricity? Did some work with gravity? Did some use other kinds of pushes and pulls to work? Did some work because of the properties of the materials used (flexibility, reflectiveness, water-tightness)?

Look for any misunderstandings that children might have and try to clarify any points that do not seem clear.

Making Thoughtful Connections (15 min)

To put everyone's investigations into context, it is very important that you allow your children to reflect on what they and other groups did to solve the practical problem with technology. Ask them what their investigations revealed about *how technology can be used to solve practical problems:*

> What have we discovered about how technology works to solve problems?
>
> How can what we have learned help us to make good use of technology in the future?

EXTENDING CONCEPTS

Drawing Conclusions (5 min)

To put the whole investigation into perspective and to relate it to the wider issues of technology use worldwide, ask your children to think about other, related things about technology that they would like to investigate:

> What other questions about technology would you like to investigate?
>
> How would you use what you now know about designing, making, and revising technology to help you with your new investigation?

Some children may enjoy investigating other questions at home and reporting their results.

Take some time to reflect carefully on your experience with this investigation and use this sheet to record your evaluations. This will help you consolidate your ideas and provide a useful set of reference notes when you use the investigation in the future. Add more pages if you need to.

WORKING IN METHODS CLASS

What was the most important learning experience for you?

What experiences do you think will be important to remember when you do this activity with children in school?

What would you change in this activity for use with children?

What concerns do you have about using this activity with children?

What do you need to know more about before you use this activity with children?

Points to discuss with faculty and colleagues.

WORKING WITH CHILDREN IN SCHOOL

What happened in the way you expected?

What happened that you had not expected?

(continued)

What would you change when repeating this activity with children?

What did you learn about the children by doing this activity?

What did you learn about yourself as a teacher from this activity?

Points to discuss with faculty and colleagues:

ENERGY

IS

TRANSFORMED

8 Investigating Energy and Its Transformations

WHAT CHILDREN CAN LEARN FROM THIS EXEMPLAR

Children's Thinking about Energy: The Research Base

Of all the science concepts there are for children to understand, most have the greatest difficulty with energy transformations. For many children, energy is equated to forces, movement, fuel, and food. Energy gets "used up" and has to be replenished (Solomon, 1983). Energy is also thought of as being a sort of material—something that is stored in certain places (such as batteries or electrical outlets) to be released later when it is needed to make something work or move (Watts & Gilbert, 1985). Many children also have a "fluid" concept of energy. Energy flows from one place to another. It can flow from one object into another object, resulting in the movement of the second object. Once movement of an object occurs (or, indeed, any energy event is "completed"), the energy dissipates.

Since energy, like forces, is invisible, its presence can only be determined by observing its effects. It is not surprising, therefore, that children at the concrete operational level have great problems understanding energy and energy transformations. The use of the word *energy* in everyday language also serves to foster incorrect conceptions. People speak of "having no energy" when they get up tired in the morning. When there are fuel shortages, we term it an "energy crisis." Children hear adults say things like "I need to eat this chocolate bar to get my energy level up." When working with energy ideas and children, it is best to watch how you use the word *energy* in conversation. Sentences like "Here's a peanut butter cracker to help you get your energy back" or "You'll use up all your energy if you jump around like that" reinforce incorrect ideas that energy gets lost and must be replenished.

Teaching Implications of the Research

It is important to allow children to express their ideas about energy as they conduct the investigations in this chapter. Encourage them to discuss such questions as:

What is energy?

What has energy?

Does everything have energy?

How would you use the word *energy* in a sentence?

Work with your children to build an understanding of energy as being both stored (potential) and in motion (kinetic). You can demonstrate that a book on a table has stored energy by virtue of its elevated position. A stretched rubber band has stored energy. And so does a candy bar (chemical energy).

Give children lots of examples of energy transformations to explore (as in the investigations in this chapter). Ask them to describe what happens to the energy in each step of the energy transfer. Constantly reinforce the idea that energy does not "go away," it is simply transformed to another type of energy.

Science Background

Energy cannot be made or destroyed. It can be transformed, however, from one form to another or one type to another. The forms of energy are potential (stored energy) or kinetic (energy of motion). Potential energy can be by virtue of position (the book on a table was an example of potential energy) or composition (the candy bar was an example of stored chemical energy—as is a dry cell).

Kinetic energy, on the other hand, comes in a variety of types. These include:

- Light
- Heat
- Electricity
- Nuclear
- Sound
- Mechanical (motion)

Potential energy can be changed into kinetic energy in many ways. When a dry cell is connected in a circuit to a light bulb, and the circuit is complete, the stored chemical energy in the dry cell is converted to electricity, heat, and light. When a rock falls off a cliff, the potential energy that the rock has due to its position atop the cliff is converted into mechanical energy (movement of the rock) and sound energy (sound when the rock hits the side of the cliff on its way down). The stored chemical energy in firewood is converted into heat, light, and sound when the wood burns. Our bodies convert the stored chemical energy in food to heat and mechanical energy. We also convert the stored energy in food into other forms of stored energy (fat and protein).

Almost all energy sources can be traced back to the Sun. The sun provides the light energy for plants to make food (glucose) from carbon dioxide and water. Plants are at the bottom of the food chain, thus providing the source of energy for all animals. Plant and animal remains that were deposited long ago formed the eventual basis of the petroleum and natural gas reserves that we use as a source of most of our energy. Alternative energy sources, such as wind, waves, the Sun, and hot springs (geothermal), are all either directly or indirectly dependent upon the Sun.

Energy transformations are difficult for children to understand. You can help them to build these concepts by providing them with many experiences interacting with energy transfer phenomena. You will need to give them numerous examples of how energy is transferred before they conduct their own investigations. As much as possible, try to help your children link energy transformations back to the Sun.

E X E M P L A R

ENERGY IS TRANSFORMED
Investigating Energy and Its Transformations

Note: This investigation is most suitable for children in grades 4–5.

OVERVIEW

Energy and its transformations are difficult areas for many people (not just children) to understand. Since energy occurs not just in one form, but can be changed from one form to another, understanding the concept can be tricky. One of the best ways for your children to become familiar with energy is to give them many experiences of working with it, identifying it, and tracking its transformations.

They will already have the broad general understanding that energy is needed to "make things go" or "make things happen." They will know, for example, that if they heat up an ice cube it will melt. If gasoline is put into a working car, the car will run. If plants get light, they will grow. You can build on these simple examples to help children find connections between the types and forms of energy. At the end of this investigation, your children will put their knowledge of energy to work to design a system that will move a toy car along a pathway. They will need to explain how they put the energy into the car to make it move, and where the energy "went" when the car finally stopped.

KEY SCIENCE CONCEPTS

This investigation is an example of a design-and-make activity. It is important for your students to understand several key things about energy and technology through this investigation:

- People can design and make objects and systems for specific purposes.
- Sometimes science investigations involve building things, testing them, revising them, and testing them again.
- Energy can be potential (stored) or in motion (kinetic).
- Energy can be chemical, nuclear, light, mechanical, heat, sound, and electrical.
- One form of energy can be transformed to another form, but the energy cannot be created or destroyed.
- Matter can be changed into energy and vice versa.
- We use a variety of resources to produce energy.

SUPPORTING NATIONAL STANDARDS

National Science Education Standards

LEVELS K–4 AND 5–8

Content Standard A: As a result of activities in grades K–4 and 5–8, all students should develop:

- Abilities necessary to do scientific inquiry
- Understanding about scientific inquiry

Content Standard B: As a result of activities in grades K–4, all students should develop an understanding of:

- Properties of objects and materials
- Position and motion of objects
- Light, heat, electricity, and magnetism

Content Standard B: As a result of activities in grades 5–8, all students should develop an understanding of:

- Properties and changes of properties in matter
- Motions and forces
- Transfer of energy

BENCHMARKS FOR SCIENCE LITERACY

By the end of the 5th grade, students should know that

- Moving air and water can be used to run machines.
- The sun is the main source of energy for people and they use it in various ways. The energy in fossil fuels such as oil and coal comes from the sun indirectly, because the fuels come from plants that grew long ago.

BEFORE YOU BEGIN

Technology Connection

Collect as many print, video, and electronic resources about energy as you can. Contact the U.S. Department of Energy through their Web site (www. doe.gov) for information on educational resources. Most local electric companies also have their own Web sites and free educational materials. If possible, have your children write letters or emails requesting these materials.

In addition to the Internet connections, your students will be using technology to invent a method of getting a toy car to move. Encourage them to think about how science concepts support the technology they use to get the car moving.

Linking to the Community

Arrange for a classroom visit from someone who works in the energy industry (someone from a power plant, solar energy company, or heating company) so that your children can learn about energy-related careers. If possible, ask a person whom your students might not expect in that career (female engineer, for example). Arrange for a field trip to a site where energy is produced or used in a variety of ways. Examples of such sites can be telephone companies, power companies, car repair shops, or recycling plants.

Preparing Materials

Collect or buy enough plastic toy cars (about 8 cm long) to use in the final activity. Plan to have one car for each group of 2 to 4 children. The cars should be sturdy enough so that the children can mount energy-producing devices on them.

A NOTE ABOUT SAFETY!   Science investigations should be safe. Ensure that students are not exposed to any hazards while they are engaged in investigations. Remind them to observe safety procedures at all times, especially when handling tools and using electricity. In this investigation it is important that children wear goggles when indicated (when the peanut is lighted, for example), and that they do not taste any of the materials unless directly told to do so. Children should wash their hands at the end of the investigation, and, if appropriate, put items away.

ASSESSING PRIOR KNOWLEDGE

Investigating Ideas about Energy: Getting Things Going! (15 min)

It is important to establish your children's initial understanding about energy and its forms. Ask your children to work as individuals, and to think about, then write down, all the ways that energy helps their lives. You can help them to get started by prompting them with these questions:

Where do you get energy?

How do cars get energy?

Where does energy come from?

What would we do without energy?

After your children have thought about responses to these questions, ask them to share with one other person. Together, the two can make a more complete and more accurate list of all the ways that energy helps their lives. In the last step of this activity, ask each of the pairs of children to match up with another pair and again share their lists. Monitor discussions and listen for naïve understandings and inaccurate ideas. In preparation for the next step of the activity, as you monitor, make a list of the energy-related terms your children use.

EXPLORING CONCEPTS

Finding Connections in Ideas about Energy (10 min)

Hold a whole-group discussion of the groups' comments about their energy discussions. List their ideas on the board or chart paper:

What ideas do we have about how energy helps our lives?

List the ideas on the board or chart as they come up. Ideas that your children may come up with can include:

- Energy makes us move.
- Energy makes cars move.
- Cars need gasoline and engines to make them move.
- We need food to make us move.
- Plants need light and water to grow.
- Heat makes things melt.
- Fires make heat and light.
- Fires need wood to burn.
- If I push something, it moves.

* We get energy from oil.
* The sun gives us energy (heat, light).
* Nuclear energy plants make electricity.
* Electricity can make lights light up.
* Electricity can make radios give off sound.

Explain that your children will be investigating how energy makes things work and how energy can change from one form into another. Circle key words in their list of how energy helps us (or how we use energy). Key words could include:

heat

light

sun

move

sound

electricity

nuclear energy

wood

burn

melt

gasoline

oil

engines

grow

Energy Vocabulary Web

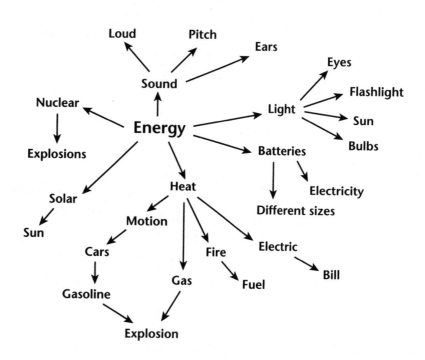

Work with your children to make a web or concept map that shows as many links as they can make between their energy words. Be sure they write the relationship between one word and another on the linking line between the words. Tell the children that they will be doing a number of energy-related investigations. You would like them to look for the connections between what makes the energy, what the energy does, and what happens to the energy after the event.

FOCUSING ON AND EXPLAINING CONCEPTS

Recognizing Types of Energy (10 min)

In this part of the investigation, you show the children how the combustion of stored energy—in a peanut—can be transformed to heat and light energy. You can do this by merely lighting a peanut with a match (with the peanut in special, safe holder).

A NOTE ABOUT SAFETY!   It is important that you wear goggles when using fire in your classroom, even as a demonstration. You should also have a glass or heavy plastic container of water under the peanut as you burn it, so that, if the burning peanut should fall out of the holder, it would fall into the water and be extinguished.

Note: You will need to make a "peanut holder" to do this demonstration. You can do this by straightening half of a large, heavy-duty paper clip and inserting the straight end of the clip into a cork. Bend the other end of the clip to make a loop. Try some peanuts in the loop to be sure that the peanut fits properly and doesn't slide through.

> **MATERIALS NEEDED**
> - Several whole peanuts, shelled
> - "Peanut holder" (big metal paper clip and cork)
> - Container of water
> - Matches
> - Goggles for all

Tell your children that you are going to show them a demonstration. You want them to watch carefully to see what happens. Focus questions for the demonstration can include:

What kinds of energy do you observe here? (stored, heat, light)

What causes the peanut to burn? (flame from the match, heat energy)

How can the peanut keep burning? (something in the peanut must fuel the fire—peanuts contain a lot of oil)

How does the peanut change as it burns? (peanut releases oil, gets smaller, becomes black; also gives off a smell)

What is left after the peanut is burned? (carbon, or charcoal; you can write on paper with the charcoal after the peanut has cooled)

The children may write their observations in a notebook or journal, or you may wish to provide them with a record sheet. Encourage them to use their eyes, ears, and noses to make the observations of the burning peanut:

Ask the children what energy the peanut started with (stored energy in the form of food; also called chemical energy)

Ask what happened to the peanut to convert the stored energy into other types of energy? (heat of the flame started the peanut burning)

Help the students to make an energy pathway showing how the stored chemical energy in the peanut was converted to heat and light.

Flame from match (heat and light) →
Fat in peanut (stored chemical energy) →
Heat and light and sound (burning peanut with crackling peanut oil) →
Charcoal remnants of peanut (stored energy; could be combusted further)

Investigating Examples of Energy Transformations (30 min)

In this part of the investigation, your children will be looking at a variety of energy transformations. They will do this in a way similar to what you did with the peanut: observing the interaction, then making an energy pathway showing what happens in the interaction. It would work best to set up stations, so that children can spend time working in small groups. They should discuss the role of energy in each interaction. You will need to have ready for this part of the activity:

MATERIALS NEEDED
- Wooden ramp
- Toy car or truck
- Small candies
- Wind-up toy
- Small book to drop from a table
- Circuit with switch that, when closed, rings a bell
- Lamp
- Hand-held fan, sailboat, and tub of water
- Distilled vinegar
- Baking soda
- Clean 16-oz soda bottle
- Large round balloon
- Plastic funnel
- Tablespoon measure
- Ruler
- Coin
- Small block of wood (about 2 cm x 2 cm x 4 cm)

Set up the stations as follows:

Station 1: Car to roll down a ramp

Station 2: Small pieces of candy on a paper plate

Station 3: Toy to wind up

Station 4: Book to drop on the floor

Station 5: Circuit with a switch that, when closed, rings a bell

Station 6: Lamp to turn on

Station 7: Sailboat to move with fan

Station 8: Baking soda in the bottle (about 2 tablespoons); Vinegar goes into the balloon, which is attached to the mouth of the bottle. When the vinegar flows into the bottle, the balloon inflates with the gas produced.

Station 9: Ruler, block of wood, coin

Organize your class so that small groups of children have a set amount of time (say, 10 min) to work through a station. An index card at each station describes what they should do. The directions for each station are as follows.

Station 1: Roll the car down the ramp. Where did the energy come from for the action you observed? Make an energy pathway showing where the energy came from to start the action and how you think the energy has been transferred.

Station 2: Eat a piece of candy. What form of energy is the candy? What happens to the energy in the candy after you eat it?

Station 3: Wind up the toy and let it go. Where did the energy come from for the action you observed? Make an energy pathway showing where the energy came from to start the action and how you think the energy has been transferred.

Station 4: Drop the book (carefully!) onto the floor. Where did the energy come from for the action you observed? Make an energy pathway showing where the energy came from to start the action and how you think the energy has been transferred.

Station 5: Close the switch on the circuit. Where did the energy come from for what you observed? Make an energy pathway showing where the energy came from to start the action and how you think the energy has been transferred.

Station 6: Turn on the lamp. Where did the energy come from for what you observed? Make an energy pathway showing where the energy came from to start the action and how you think the energy has been transferred.

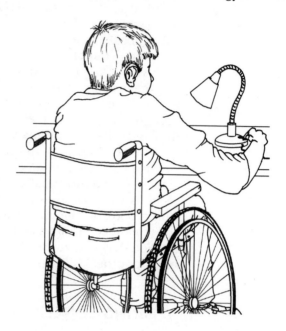

Station 7: Make the sailboat move by using the fan. Where did the energy come from for the action you observed? Make an energy pathway showing where the energy came from to start the action and how you think the energy has been transferred.

Station 8: Put two tablespoons of baking soda in the bottle, using the funnel provided. Now, pour 2 tablespoons of vinegar into the mouth of the balloon. Attach the balloon to the bottle, and let the balloon hang down over the side. Now, lift up the balloon and let the vinegar flow into the bottle. Where did the energy come from for what you observed? Make an energy pathway showing where the energy came from to start the action and how you think the energy has been transferred.

Station 9: Set up the ruler and block of wood as shown (like a seesaw). Put the coin on one end. Lightly hit the other end of the ruler. Where did the energy come from for the action you observed? Make an energy pathway for the coin.

Be sure to give your children enough time to do each station, think about what is happening, and make any energy pathways that help to explain what they have observed, and what they think is happening. This will probably take several days.

When your children have finished all the stations, hold a whole-class discussion. Ask your children to share their thoughts about the stations they have completed and the energy pathways they have made. Your role in the discussion is as moderator. It is important that you help your children, through their investigations, and through their discussions, to understand the key concepts for this activity series.

The one idea that you really want the children to understand is that *energy can be transformed, but not created or destroyed.* This is a difficult idea, since energy transformations from a single event can go in a number of directions and take a number of forms. Even for an event as simple as dropping a book on the floor, the energy put into the book by its position on the table gets transformed to both motion and sound.

You may find it useful to ask your children to post their energy pathways for other children to review and comment upon.

APPLYING CONCEPTS

Designing and Using an Energy System (2 days)

In this last part of the investigation, your children will be putting their knowledge of energy and energy transformations to work. Their job is to work together in small teams to find a way of producing enough energy to move a plastic car along a straight path. You will need to encourage them to be as creative as possible in this endeavor because, of course, the simplest way of getting the car to move is to push it. Have available some of the same energy-producing materials that your students used in the stations, with the addition of a few more items, as noted in the following box.

MATERIALS NEEDED
- Wooden ramp
- Plastic toy cars
- Circuit with switch that, when closed, rings a bell
- Hand-held fan
- Distilled vinegar
- Baking soda
- Clean, 16 oz soda bottle
- Large round balloon
- Plastic funnel
- Tablespoon measure
- Rubber bands

- Small motors
- Propellers
- Wires
- Alligator clips
- Poster board
- String
- Tape
- Glue

Explain the task to your children so that they know that they have to design an energy system to move their car along a straight path for a short distance (1 meter, for example). Give them time to look over all of the materials on the supply table before they begin. After they have seen the materials, and they have their cars, ask the children to make a plan for how they could get their cars to move at least 1 meter along a straight path. Give them time to plan, and to try out their plans with the materials. They may find that they have an idea that requires materials from home. Check to be sure that these are safe before children bring them in.

When they have finished designing, making, and testing their system to move the car, ask each group of children to make an energy pathway for their car. This will be part of their presentation when the "car-moving systems" are tried out.

Set up a time and place so that all of your children can demonstrate their car-moving systems to the rest of the class. Each group should explain what they did, why they did it, and what they predict will happen to their car. Run all of the cars, one after the other, then ask your children to think about which of the car-moving systems seem to be most effective—and most predictable.

Reviewing the Results (15 min)

This is a very important part of the investigation. Here the work done by each group is shared and reviewed by everyone. Ask students to discuss the results of the car trials. Your role is to act as a moderator:

How was energy put into the car moving systems?

Which methods seemed to work best in moving the cars along a straight line?

What are your reasons for thinking that?

What energy transformations happened during the car trials?

Note: The ways in which your children consider these questions may be a key learning moment for some of them, so be alert to their ideas. Look out for any misunderstandings that individual children may have and try to clarify any points that do not seem clear.

Making Thoughtful Connections (15 min)

To put everyone's investigations into context, it is now essential that you allow your children to reflect on their own observations about energy, and on the observations of other groups. Ask them to think about what the investigations have revealed about how *energy is transformed*:

> What have we discovered about how energy can change from one form to another?
>
> How can this help us in learning about what energy does?

EXTENDING CONCEPTS

Drawing Conclusions (5 min)

To put the whole investigation into perspective, and to relate it to the wider issues of energy transformations, ask your children to think about other, related things that they would like to investigate:

> What other questions do you think would be worth investigating next?
>
> How would you use what you now know about energy to plan your investigation?

Note: This is a logical extension to the module, and you can follow the same general structure.

Some students may enjoy investigating other questions at home and reporting their results.

Take some time to reflect carefully on your experience with this investigation and use this sheet to record your evaluations. This will help you consolidate your ideas and provide a useful set of reference notes when you use the investigation in the future. Add more pages if you need to.

WORKING IN METHODS CLASS

What was the most important learning experience for you?

What experiences do you think will be important to remember when you do this activity with children in school?

What would you change in this activity for use with children?

What concerns do you have about using this activity with children?

(continued)

What do you need to know more about before you use this activity with children?

Points to discuss with faculty and colleagues:

WORKING WITH CHILDREN IN CLASS

What happened in the way you expected?

What happened that you had not expected?

What would you change when repeating this activity with children?

What did you learn about the children by doing this activity?

What did you learn about yourself as a teacher from this activity?

Points to discuss with faculty and colleagues:

EARTH

SYSTEMS

CHANGE

9 Investigating Weather Patterns

WHAT CHILDREN CAN LEARN FROM THIS EXEMPLAR

Children's Thinking about Weather: The Research Base

Research into children's understanding about weather phenomena has revealed many interesting informal ideas about clouds, wind, air pressure, and precipitation. Ideas about clouds and rain are particularly varied. Children in grades 1 and 2, for example, have been found to believe that clouds hold water like containers—when clouds bump into each other or "split apart," rain falls. Slightly older children have revealed that they believe that clouds go to the oceans, pick up water, and take it to other parts of the world, where they let it fall as rain. Ideas from intermediate-level children include clouds acting like sponges that soak up, then release, rain (Bar, 1986).

Children's ideas about air pressure and winds are also rather curious. Air is not perceived as exerting pressure unless it is in the form of wind. Wind, say children of many ages, can be caused by moving objects. The concept of air pressure differences resulting in winds is not an idea commonly held by children (Moyle, 1980).

Teaching Implications of the Research

Young children tend to have many of the same informal ideas about the weather as did adults in early cultures. Weather is so "big" and so changeable that it is a more comfortable concept to ascribe supernatural causes to the weather (God makes it rain), or to use teleological explanations (the clouds want it to rain), rather than to try to understand the complex interactions between heat and water that drive the weather.

An understanding of the water cycle and the properties of air are both essential to a thorough understanding of weather. Young children can begin this process by making daily observations of weather and keeping a record of these observations. You can help them to build their understanding by asking them to give reasons for changes in weather from day to day. For example:

Why do you think today is rainy, when yesterday we had only a few clouds in the sky?

Why is today so much warmer than yesterday?

What do you think happened to the clouds that we saw yesterday?

How were the colors of the clouds today different from yesterday? What might that mean?

Where did the high winds come from that we have today? Why do you think it isn't this windy every day?

The following investigation into weather will give your children the opportunity to collect weather data. Use the data they collect as the basis for the questions just cited, or for others like them. Help children to discover the important interactions between heat, water, air, and energy that underlie the planet's weather.

EXEMPLAR   **EARTH SYSTEMS CHANGE**
Investigating Weather Patterns

Note: This investigation is most suitable for children in grades 3–4.

OVERVIEW

The weather is an important part of the life of every creature on the planet. It affects our health, safety, comfort, food supply, method of transportation, choice of recreation, and many other aspects of our existence. For most of us, dealing with the weather is a relatively simple thing, affecting mainly our comfort and convenience. But for farmers, and others whose lives are absolutely dependent upon weather patterns, the weather can sometimes mean success or failure—even life or death.

It is important for your children to become aware of the patterns in the weather they experience, and to understand how we measure, track, and predict aspects of the weather. They will be doing this through commercially produced weather reports, weather information on the Web, and through using their own school-based weather station.

KEY PEDAGOGICAL IDEAS

- Scientific investigation can start with familiar objects or events.
- Children can be immediately engaged in investigating a question that has personal significance for them.
- When children engage in scientific investigations, trying to find answers to their own questions, they are being scientists themselves using scientific research processes such as observing, predicting, fair-testing, recording, and reviewing results.

KEY SCIENCE CONCEPTS

- The Earth is made up of a series of interconnected systems.
- Earth systems change over time.
- Weather involves the interaction between water and heat energy.
- Weather indicators can be measured and weather patterns tracked.
- Meteorologists (scientists who study weather) use tools and technology to observe, record, and predict the weather.

SUPPORTING NATIONAL STANDARDS

National Science Education Standards

LEVEL K–4

Content Standard A: As a result of activities in grades K–4 and 5–8, all students should develop:

- Abilities necessary to do scientific inquiry
- Understanding about scientific inquiry

Content Standard D: As a result of activities in grades K–4, all students should develop an understanding of:

- Objects in the sky
- Changes in earth and sky

BENCHMARKS FOR SCIENCE LITERACY

By the end of the 5th grade, students should know that

- When liquid water disappears, it turns into a gas (vapor) in the air and can reappear as a liquid when cooled, or as a solid if cooled below the freezing point of water. Clouds and fog are made of tiny droplets of water.
- Air is a substance that surrounds us, takes up space, and whose movement we feel as wind.

BEFORE YOU BEGIN

Technology Connection

Check weather-related Web sites. One that you might want to try is http://www.weather.noaa.gov (National Oceanographic and Atmospheric Administration). Other Web sites are those for the Weather Channel and for various television stations' and newspapers' weather broadcasts. A particularly good Web site, which has links to many other weather-related sites, is www.howtheweatherworks.com.

Linking to the Community

Find out if there is a local weather station in your area, and whether your children can visit it. Check with the local cable station to find out the source of their weather information. Survey your children to find out if any adults they know would be willing to work with your class to build a housing for your weather station.

Preparing Materials

Collect newspapers that have good weather maps and information from a wide variety of sources. Check to see what weather instrumentation is available in your school (thermometers, sling psychrometers, barometers, rain gauges, anemometers).

A NOTE ABOUT SAFETY!   Science investigations should be safe. Ensure that students are not exposed to any hazards while they are engaged in investigations. Draw their attention to the need to observe safety procedures at all times, particularly when making weather measurements outdoors and when working with tools.

ASSESSING PRIOR KNOWLEDGE

How Does Weather Affect Our Everyday Lives? (20 min)

Ask your children to think about all the different kinds of weather they experience. As the children volunteer information, list items on the board. Now, ask the children to think of as many ways as they can that weather has an effect on their lives. For example:

How do you plan your day, depending on what the weather is like?

What are certain activities that you only do in warm weather? In cold weather?

When does the weather keep you from doing things?

Make a "weatherburst" on a large piece of poster board or chart paper, showing ways in which people's lives are affected by weather. Items that your children may come up with include:

- Clothing
- Sports

- Outdoor activities (picnics, swimming, sledding, ice skating)
- Food that is available at certain seasons, not available at others
- Where people live (some people move to where the air is drier, or the weather warmer)
- Avoiding hazards (people avoid certain behaviors during thunder-storms, for example, or hurricanes)
- Sanitation (floods can result in impure water supplies)
- Type of transportation (airports shut down in bad storms, as do trains at times)
- Use of energy resources (need to heat homes in cold weather and cool homes in very hot weather)
- Food supply (droughts and freezing result in a reduced food supply)

Ask your children why they think it is important to monitor weather patterns:

> Why do we need to know what the weather is going to be like days in advance?

> How can we know what the weather is like in advance?

EXPLORING CONCEPTS

Investigating Weather Indicators (at least 2 days)

In this investigation, your children will be learning about indicators that we use to track weather patterns. Eventually, they will be using this information as they design and build their own weather station for the school.

For this investigation to be successful, your children will need to have the cooperation of the school's administration, as well as other teachers and school personnel. Discuss the weather station concept with your administrators before you begin. To do this investigation with your children, you will need the materials presented in the following box.

> **MATERIALS NEEDED**
> - Indoor/outdoor thermometer
> - Weather reports from newspapers (showing weather maps); 1 for every 2 children
> - Barometer
> - Anemometer
> - Wind sock
> - Sling psychrometer (optional)

In the first part of the investigation, ask your children to work in pairs or groups as they examine a copy of the newspaper weather report and weather map. Ask them to find out:

What kind of information about the weather can you find in the weather report? Write these things down.

What sort of symbols are used in the weather map to show different information? Make a record of these symbols for later on.

Note: Your children will be using this information later when they make their own weather map and record information from their school weather station.

Show the children each of the weather instruments, demonstrate how to use each one, and explain what each instrument measures.

- *Thermometer:* Measures air temperature in degrees Celsius or degrees Fahrenheit (place in the air, out of direct sunlight, and read level of alcohol in the glass tube).
- *Barometer:* Measures atmospheric pressure (place in the air, and read dial in millimeters or inches of mercury).
- *Sling psychrometer:* Measures relative humidity (wet the "wet bulb" in the instrument and swing it outside for the amount of time given in the instructions). Take the difference between the wet bulb and dry bulb readings. This will give you a percent relative humidity, or the percentage of water vapor in the atmosphere).
- *Anemometer:* Measures wind speed in miles or kilometers per hour (most anemometers have meters that give the wind speed).
- *Wind sock:* Indicates wind direction (sock blows in the direction opposite to that in which the wind originates).
- *Rain gauge:* Measures inches of precipitation (graduated container stays outside in an open area to collect precipitation.)

Let the children try each one of the instruments in turn, so that they learn how to use and read each one. You may want to do this by setting up the instruments as stations around the room; or, even better, take them outdoors. Be sure to post the directions for each instrument close by. Ask the children to record the reading they get for each instrument in their notebooks or journals. This will give them a one-experience "snapshot" of how to take weather readings.

FOCUSING ON AND EXPLAINING CONCEPTS

Modeling the Way Weather Works (20 min)

In this part of the investigation, your children make a solar still. This simple device will help them to understand that water changes to vapor (evaporation) when enough heat energy is added. Water vapor then condenses back to liquid water when heat energy is removed. This is the *water cycle,* the "engine" that powers the "weather machine." To do this investigation, you will need:

heavy-duty plastic wrap

clear plastic tape

heavy coins

water supply

blue food color

small, heavy ceramic dish

large plastic bowl

access to a sunny window

measuring cups

measuring spoons

Note: You may want to do this as a whole class (just one or two solar stills), or you might want to have quartets of children setting up individual stills. You must have enough space to put the stills in direct sunlight or the process won't work well.

Give each group of children the materials for the solar still setup (bowl, ceramic container, coin, plastic wrap, tape, food color). Here's how the still is set up:

Solar Still Assembly

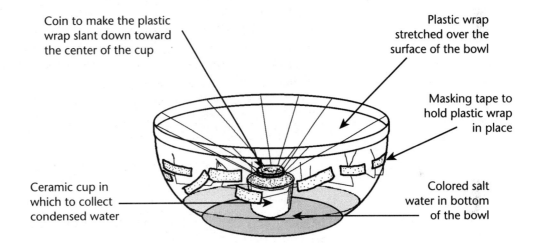

Coin to make the plastic wrap slant down toward the center of the cup

Plastic wrap stretched over the surface of the bowl

Masking tape to hold plastic wrap in place

Ceramic cup in which to collect condensed water

Colored salt water in bottom of the bowl

1. Mix about 5 drops of food color into 2 cups of water in the large bowl.

2. Place the ceramic container in the center bottom of the bowl. (Be sure that the level of the blue water is below the edge of the container. There should be nothing in the ceramic container at this point.)

3. Cover the bowl with plastic wrap, fairly tightly. Tape down the edges of the plastic wrap to the bowl.

4. Place the heavy coin on the top of the plastic wrap, directly above the ceramic container.

5. Carefully place the entire setup in direct sunlight and leave it there for at least two days.

6. Observe what is happening in the container on the underside of the plastic wrap directly under the coin.

7. At the end of several days, check the ceramic container to see what is in it.

Note: The water from the solution of food color and water evaporates in the sunlight, then condenses on the underside of the plastic wrap. The pure water then drips into the ceramic container. One extension to this activity is to set up a still in a cool, dark place as well as warm, sunny places. This will help your children to understand more about the role of heat energy in the water cycle.

Ask your children to make observations of their stills for several days and to record what they observe. At the conclusion of the investigation, ask them to look over their data, and to think about the following:

How did clear water get into the smaller container? See if you can describe the process that caused this to happen.

What effect did the direct sunlight have on the still? What might have happened to the still if it were in a cool, dark place rather than a warm, sunny place?

What ideas do you have about the solar still being a model for what happens with the weather?

Give each group a chance to discuss what they have discovered about how the solar still works. Gently lead them to an understanding of the water cycle: liquid water evaporates through heat energy to form water vapor. The water vapor in the atmosphere rises and cools. As it cools, it loses heat energy, and condenses back to liquid water. The liquid water eventually falls from the sky in the form of precipitation (rain, snow, sleet, or hail).

Help your children to understand that the measurements we take to track the weather are all related to this interaction between water and heat energy (temperature, relative humidity, air pressure).

APPLYING CONCEPTS

Making and Using a School Weather Station to Track Patterns (3 weeks)

In this last part of the investigation, your children will be using their knowledge of weather indicators and weather instruments to make a school weather station. They need to set up a protective container (usually a wooden box on legs) where they can keep the instruments outside, take the readings, and record the results. As listed in the following box, you will need the same instruments you used in the earlier exercise, with the addition of the wooden box to keep them in.

MATERIALS NEEDED

- Weather instruments listed above
- Wooden box with legs to store instruments
- Large, wall-sized map of the United States with a wipe-off surface
- Daily newspapers with weather maps or access to a Web site with weather map information
- Pens to record observations

Enlist the help of one of the adults associated with your children to build the box for the instruments. The following diagram shows one idea for how to set this up. You will need to get your school's permission to put the box outside. Be sure that it is in a sheltered place out of direct sunlight.

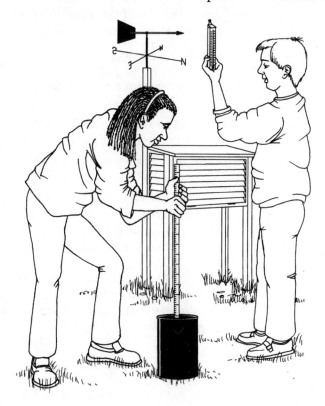

Set up a schedule so that your children are taking turns each day to record the readings from the instruments. You may want to have two groups be responsible on a particular day, so as to check each other's readings.

Set up a weather chart in the classroom so that your students can record their readings for the benefit of the entire class each day. Have a large map of the United States on your wall (preferably one with a wipe-off surface), so that your students can track the weather patterns for the entire country and see how their readings fit with the national picture. As they make their weather measurements and record their readings, ask them to look for patterns in the weather to discuss later on.

ABOUT LONG-TERM STUDIES

A long-term study allows scientists to collect data over enough time that patterns and relationships can be identified. In the case of a weather study, the data can show trends that help weather scientists (meteorologists) predict patterns in the future.

Displaying and Reviewing the Results (30 min)

After your children have collected weather data for about three weeks, take a look at the entire data set. Have your children graph the measurements for each instrument on a separate graph. This will help to highlight trends in the data. When they have finished graphing and reviewing, ask your children to think about these things:

What patterns have you noticed in the weather over the past three weeks? (All sunny days, cold followed by a warming trend, lots of rainy days one right after the other, high humidity followed by sudden thunderstorms.)

Do any of the readings seem to be related to each other in any way? How might you explain that?

Your role is to act as a moderator in the discussion of the data:

What did you find out about the weather in our area that really surprised you?

How did our local weather compare with other weather patterns in our region over the past three weeks?

Has our weather been usual or unusual for this time of year in our region? What is your evidence for saying that?

What types of things seem to influence weather in our area? (Close to a body of water; close to mountains; coastal area; latitude where you live; warm ocean currents nearby.) For this particular question, you may want your students to do some research on the Web.

Note: The ways in which your students consider these questions may be a key learning moment for some of them, so be alert to their ideas. Look out for any misunderstandings that individual students may have and try to clarify any points that do not seem clear.

Making Thoughtful Connections (15 min)

To put everyone's investigations into context, it is now very important that you allow your students to reflect on their weather data and graphs. Ask them to think about what the investigations have revealed about *weather patterns*.

What have we discovered about the way in which weather works?

How can we monitor the weather over a long period of time?

How does knowing about the weather help us to manage our lives?

EXTENDING CONCEPTS

Drawing Conclusions (5 min)

To pull the investigation into weather patterns together, ask your children to revisit their original "weatherburst" idea, but with a different focus question:

What do I now know about weather that I didn't know before?

Have each child work individually to make a "sunburst" of ideas about weather. (You may want to give them some prompts in order to get as complete a set of information as possible.) Collect these to use as an assessment of what your children think they know now about weather that is different from what they knew before their investigations. Ideas to look for in the weatherbursts include:

- An understanding of how the water cycle works
- The relationship between the water cycle and weather
- What instruments are used to measure weather indicators
- How to use the weather instruments
- How to collect data on weather
- How to graph data on weather
- How to interpret weather data
- What weather maps tell us

Take some time to reflect carefully on your experience with this investigation and use this sheet to record your evaluations. This will help you consolidate your ideas and provide a useful set of reference notes when you use the investigation in the future. Add more pages if you need to.

WORKING IN METHODS CLASS

What was the most important learning experience for you?

What experiences do you think will be important to remember when you do this activity with children in school?

What would you change in this activity for use with children?

What concerns do you have about using this activity with children?

What do you need to know more about before you use this activity with children?

Points to discuss with faculty and colleagues:

WORKING WITH CHILDREN IN SCHOOL

What happened in the way you expected?

What happened that you had not expected?

(continued)

What would you change when repeating this activity with children?

What did you learn about the children by doing this activity?

What did you learn about yourself as a teacher from this activity?

Points to discuss with faculty and colleagues:

HUMANS AFFECT THE ENVIRONMENT

10 Investigating What Recycling Does for the Environment

WHAT CHILDREN CAN LEARN FROM THIS EXEMPLAR

Children's Thinking about Recycling: The Research Base

Many children have an understanding of recycling as "good for the environment," but they often have trouble articulating exactly how recycling benefits the environment. Part of this confusion can be ascribed to children's incomplete knowledge about the environment and how it can be harmed. Among the informal beliefs that researchers have discovered about children's ideas about the environment include:

- Pollution that harms people and other animals is much more important than pollution that just harms plant life.
- Any materials that are biodegradable are more acceptable and safer for the environment than materials that are nonbiodegradable.
- "Natural" materials are not classed as pollutants.
- There is nothing environmentally harmful about disposing of solid waste in dumps. (Brody, 1992)

These ideas, and the problem that many children have with understanding the conservation of matter, provide barriers to teaching about the implications of recycling materials for the environment.

Teaching Implications of the Research

Since children have a difficult time with conservation of matter, it is not easy to help them to understand that there is a finite amount of matter on the planet. The matter can be transformed, but it does not get "used up" or go away. The more materials can be recycled, rather than put into land-fills, the smaller the landfills will be. Recycling also helps the environment by reducing human dependency of the planet's natural resources, both mined (harvested) and grown (trees, petroleum, metals).

You may find that your children haven't yet had occasion to think through the whole recycling issue. They may consider that recycling is a general solution to a number of environmental problems. It is a solution to some problems, but recycling is not a perfect process. Some plastics, for example, are not recycled at all, and in many areas paper recycling plants cannot keep pace with the incoming supply of waste paper.

Another recycling issue has to do with quality of the recycled product. Mixed plastics, for example, give a lower-grade recycled plastic than do plastics of the same source material. As a rule, paper can only be recycled about seven times before the cellulose fibers that make up the paper become too short to retain their strength. Your children will probably not know that the source material for most plastics is petroleum. Recycling plastics reduces our reliance on petroleum, a nonrenewable natural resource.

You might find it useful to work with your children to make a concept map about paper recycling. Show what the sources are for both new and recycled paper, the processes involved in both, and the environmental implications. Ask your children to think about how recycling might help such environmental problems as:

- Global warming
- Ozone depletion
- Overfishing of the oceans
- Water pollution
- Air pollution
- Soil pollution
- Natural resource depletion

This exercise will help them to understand that, while recycling can help some environmental problems, it does not help them all.

Science Background

Recycling means to put a resource back into circulation. The types of materials that are recycled most successfully are steel, aluminum, glass, plastic, and paper. The natural resources that are conserved by the recycling process are iron, aluminum, petroleum, natural gas, silicon, and wood. In the recycling process, the material is taken in its discarded form (cans, bottles, newspapers, plastics), sorted according to its properties, broken down into very small bits, and reshaped into new and useful products.

Metals are easily recyclable because they can be melted down and reshaped. Recycled metal products, such as aluminum cans, usually don't have a decrease in quality. Papers, as noted earlier, lose strength each time they are recycled because the cellulose fibers that make up the paper become shorter and shorter with each recycling process.

In recycling plastics, it is very important that the plastics be sorted according to their resin code. These resin codes, which can be found inside the recycling symbol on plastic products, indicate the type of plastic resin used to make the product. The following table shows the resin codes for recyclable plastics.

Recycling Codes for Plastics			
Plastic Type	**Abbreviation Number**	**Resin Code**	**Uses**
Polyethylene terephthalate	PETE	1	Beverage containers, boil-in food pouches, processed meat packages
High density polyethylene	HDPE	2	Milk bottles, detergent, bottles, oil bottles, toys, plastic bags
Polyvinyl chloride	PVC	3	Food wrap, blister packaging, transparent pet-food containers
Low density polyethylene	LDPE	4	Shrink-wrap, plastic bags, garment bags
Polypropylene	PP	5	Margarine and yogurt containers, caps for containers, wrapping to replace cellophane
Polystyrene	PS	6	Egg cartons, fast food trays, disposable plastic tableware
Others	OTHER	7	Multi-resin containers

Some communities only recycle certain plastics and not others, so it is especially important that the plastics get sorted when they are discarded. Mixed recycled plastics are not of as high a quality as "pure" recycled plastics, since the different plastics have different characteristics. If your school has a recycling program, you may be able to take your class to the local recycling plant to watch the process. Be aware, however, that many industrial facilities have safety concerns about visitors, and may not offer tours.

E X E M P L A R   **HUMANS AFFECT THE ENVIRONMENT**
Investigating What Recycling Does for the Environment

Note: This investigation is most suitable for children in grades 3–5.

OVERVIEW

Human beings, as a species, can have an enormous effect on the other living things on the Earth. We use the natural resources available for energy and for manufacturing; we clear the land to build; we add pollutants to the atmosphere, water, and soil; and we discard a great deal of waste into landfills and other areas. One way of controlling our effect on the environment is to manage our use of raw materials better, and to find alternatives to discarding so much waste. Recycling many materials is a way of doing both. When we recycle plastic, for example, we reduce the amount of petroleum needed as a raw material to make the plastic. We also reduce the quantity of plastic waste that ends up in landfills.

A similar situation exists with paper, aluminum, steel, and glass. For your students to understand the effect that recycling can have on both resource use and use of land for landfills, they can undergo a series of investigations that will give them hands-on experience with the science of recycling.

KEY PEDAGOGICAL IDEAS

- Scientific investigation can start with familiar objects or events.

- Children can be immediately engaged in investigating a question that has personal significance for them.

- Scientific investigations can involve a range of associated curriculum areas, providing opportunities for children to apply and enhance their skills in a meaningful context, especially mathematics, language/communication, art and crafts as well as other related science ideas.

When children engage in scientific investigations, trying to find answers to their own questions, they are being scientists themselves and using scientific research processes such as observing, predicting, fair-testing, recording, and reviewing results.

KEY SCIENCE CONCEPTS

- Recycling of certain materials reduces waste in landfills and our depletion of natural resources.

- Matter cannot be created or destroyed; it can only be transformed.

SUPPORTING NATIONAL STANDARDS

National Science Education Standards

LEVEL K–4

Content Standard A: As a result of activities in grades K–4, all students should develop:

- Abilities necessary to do scientific inquiry
- Understanding about scientific inquiry

Content Standard B: As a result of activities in grades K–4, all students should develop an understanding of:

- Properties of objects and materials

Content Standard E: As a result of activities in grades K–4, all students should develop an understanding of:

- Abilities of technological design
- Understanding about science and technology

Content Standard F: As a result of activities in grades K–4, all students should develop an understanding of:

- Types of resources

BENCHMARKS FOR SCIENCE LITERACY

By the end of the 5th grade, students should know that

- Discarded products contribute to the problem of waste disposal. Sometimes it is possible to use the materials in them to make new products, but materials differ widely in the ease with which they can be recycled.

BEFORE YOU BEGIN

Technology Connections

Collect resources on recycling such as trade books, videos, charts, CD-ROMs, and magazines. Search for Web sites using search engines (Yahoo, etc.) and key words such as *recycling; plastics; aluminum;* and *paper.* Check for safe Web sites that your children could access later. One excellent Web site is www.poly.com.

Linking to the Community

Visit a local recycling center to find out how they sort materials and what processes they use to recycle the materials. Also, find out what arrangements may be made for your children to visit the facility. Find out what potentially recyclable materials are manufactured in your area, and if your children can visit the facility. Check with the local government to find out what materials are recycled in your area, what is the pick-up arrangement, and where people can take materials to be recycled.

Preparing Materials

Find out what your school does for recycling (what materials, bins available, boxes). Read over the investigation and prepare handouts, cutouts, or whatever you will need for the activities.

A NOTE ABOUT SAFETY! Science investigations should be safe. Ensure that students are not exposed to any hazards while they are engaged in investigations. Remind them to observe safety procedures at all times, especially when handling discarded materials. Make sure that students wash their hands when they finish an investigation, and that they wear their safety goggles where indicated.

 ## ASSESSING PRIOR KNOWLEDGE

Investigating What Recycling Does for the Environment: Making a Materials Pathway (20 min)

For your children to understand that everyday objects (recyclable and non-recyclable) are made from raw materials, they can make "Materials Pathways." Children can work as individuals or in pairs. Ask each pair to choose a common object in the classroom (pencil, pen, cup, desk, chair, poster), then draw a picture of that object in the center of a large piece of paper. Ask your children to draw arrows leading to the object showing from what raw materials the object is made (wood, plastic, metal, glass, paper, etc.)

Examples of Materials Pathways

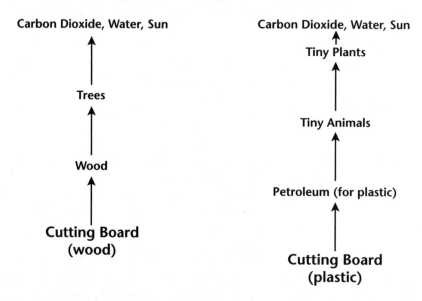

Next, ask the children to draw arrows to the raw materials to show where the raw materials came from (trees, ore, petroleum, sand). They will probably have some trouble with this part, but because this is a preassessment they need simply to do the best they can. You need to find out what they know before they begin working with recycling, and you can build on their initial ideas throughout the investigation.

Now, ask the children to draw arrows from the object showing what happens to the object when it is discarded (trash can → trash bin → garbage truck → dump or landfill → recycling plant, and so on). If the object is made out of materials that are typically recycled, ask the children what ideas they have about recycling these materials. What effect does recycling have on the whole process they have diagrammed?

When they have finished their materials pathways, ask each pair to share ideas with the other members of the class. As the moderator of this sharing session, be sure that you look for evidence of how well your children understand the following:

- Objects are made of raw materials that come from the natural world.
- The manufacture of objects can deplete our resources of raw materials.
- Recycling helps to reduce our dependence on raw materials.

When the sharing session is finished, ask your children how they could find out for sure about the effect of recycling on the use of natural resources, and the environment as a whole. They also need to find out the percentage of recyclable trash that people discard on a daily basis. This piece of information will be needed for the next part of the investigation.

Give them time to find out this information from the community, the Internet, and other resources. Later, the children present to the whole class what they have found out about the practice of recycling in general—and in their community in particular.

EXPLORING CONCEPTS

Investigating What Our School Discards (at least 2 days)

In this investigation, your children will find out how much your school discards every day, and what types of materials are discarded. This will help them, in their own "school world," to get a sense of how much waste people produce on a daily basis.

To do this investigation well, your children will need to have the cooperation of the school's administration, as well as other teachers and school personnel. Discuss this investigation with your administrators before you begin. Also, send home a letter explaining what you will be doing for the investigation and obtaining parental or caretaker permission. To do this investigation with your children, you will need the materials listed in the following box.

MATERIALS NEEDED

- Strong bathroom scales
- Kitchen-size trash bags
- Cooperation of the school's maintenance personnel
- Large chart to record the weight of the school's trash
- Disposable plastic gloves

Ask the school's custodian if he or she will work with your class to find out the weight of the trash that the school discards every day. If the trash collected from each room is put into kitchen-size trash bags, each can be weighed on a sturdy bathroom scale. If the trash from one day of the week is brought into a rather large area (common area or parking lot), your students can take turns weighing each bag and recording the weight on a large chart.

If possible, check with the custodian to see if the trash-weighing exercise can be done on two days of the week, so that you have more than one sample from which to work. (Usually, asking to do this more than two days will try the patience of your school staff.)

On a chart like the following sample you will have space to record the weight of the trash for at least two days of the week. (Consult with your custodian ahead of time to find two of the most representative trash days to do your weighing.)

OBSERVATION DATA CHART

DAY 1 (DATE:)   DAY 2 (DATE:)

Bag 1:_____pounds   Bag 1:_____pounds

Bag 2:_____pounds   Bag 2:_____pounds

Total wt:_____   Total wt:_____

Average weekly weight_____

A NOTE ABOUT SAFETY!   Be sure that you supervise the weighing process closely, in case someone has thrown away a material that could be hazardous if it comes into contact with your children while they are weighing the bags. Anyone sorting trash should wear plastic (nonlatex) gloves. Also, allot enough time for your children to wash their hands when they are finished with the weighing process.

When all of the data have been collected, ask your children to total the weight for both of the sample days and find the average daily weight of the trash produced by the school. (The more days you sample, the more representative your average weight will be. If you can negotiate more than two days with your custodian, do so.)

Now that you have the average daily weight of the trash, the next step is to find out how much of this trash is recyclable. Obviously, it would be somewhat hazardous, as well as messy, for your children to sort all of the trash in the school, but they can sample the discard bins in key areas of the school, sorting that trash into recyclable and nonrecyclable items, and finding the weights of these items. They can then compare the weights of the recyclable items to the total weight of the trash on a particular day. Again, as with the weighing exercise that preceded this, it is vital that you get the cooperation of the school staff, asking teachers, cafeteria personnel, and administrative staff to save their trash on the days that you are going to do this activity. Try to arrange to get bins from several classrooms, the cafeteria, the faculty room, the main office, the gym, and anywhere else that is a key discard area in your school.

Note: If your school already recycles, and has recycling bins, get permission to weigh the trash in each of these bins to compare to the total amount of trash your school produces on any one day.

To sort the trash (if your school does not already recycle), you will need an area with big tables so your children can pour the trash from small waste bins onto a broad surface, sort the trash into recyclable and nonrecyclable categories, and weigh each. They should wear nonlatex plastic gloves for this, and be closely supervised. The bags into which they sort recyclable and nonrecyclable items should be small trash bags of known weight. After the trash is sorted and weighed, your children can subtract the weight of the trash bag from each batch weighed.

All of this information can be recorded on another large chart similar to the one you used to weigh the total amount of trash.

Work with your children to find out the percentage of trash your school recycles on any one day. To do this, divide the weight of the recyclable items by the total amount of trash your school produces on one day. How does this percentage compare to what people recycle daily on a national basis? How well does your school measure up? Ask your children:

> What ideas do you have about how our school could improve its recycling efforts?

This question is a lead-in to the final part of the investigation into recycling.

FOCUSING ON AND EXPLAINING CONCEPTS

Sorting for Recycling (20 min)

In this part of the investigation, your children sort typically recycled materials according to the physical properties of density, magnetic attraction, and static electrical attraction. Some of these methods are used at recycling plants to sort materials. To do this investigation, you will need the materials listed in the following box.

MATERIALS NEEDED
- Baggies containing materials to sort (plastic coffee stirrers, steel paper clips, small pieces of paper, and glass marbles)
- Magnets
- Balloons (large round ones work best)
- Plastic container of water (bowl or large delicatessen container)
- Tweezers
- Sieve
- Paper towels to cover work area
- Record sheets

Give each group or pair of children a baggie with the materials. Ask them if they can identify the materials from which each of the objects is made (marbles, glass; stirrers, plastic; paper, paper or wood pulp; paper clips, steel made from iron). Ask the children for ideas about how they could separate these items, other than just picking them apart with their hands:

> What tools could you use to separate these items?
>
> How are these objects and materials different from one another?
>
> Look at some of the tools I have here. How could you use these to separate your items? Come up with a sensible plan, and we'll share our ideas.

Give your children the bowl of water, the magnets, and an inflated and tied balloon. Let them experiment with the tools and the items you have provided. Give them time to devise a plan to separate the items using the tools, then ask them to share their plans with everyone else.

After the sharing session, let your children implement their plans and separate their mixtures. One method they could use is:

1. Rub the balloon to create static. Hold the balloon over the pile of objects. The bits of paper will be attracted to the balloon and can be separated from the pile.
2. Pass the magnet over the remaining items. The paper clips will be attracted to the magnet and can be removed.
3. Put the remaining items, the plastic coffee stirrers and the marbles, into the bowl of water. The marbles, being more dense than water, will sink, and the stirrers, being less dense than water, will float.

The physical properties that can be used to separate the mixture are:

- Density (sink or float in water)
- Magnetism (attraction to a magnet)
- Static electricity (lightweight objects can be attracted by the static charge)

If you can, show your students a video about how recycling plants separate their materials, or take a field trip to your local recycling plant to see the separation process "live." Ask students at the end of this investigation:

> Why is it important to separate materials for recycling?

Let them brainstorm this question, then do research to find the answer.

APPLYING A CONCEPT

Designing a Recycling Plan for the School (25 min)

In this last part of the investigation, your children will be designing a method of improving your school's recycling efforts. If your school is already actively recycling, you may want to focus on home recycling efforts or those of the general community.

Ask students to think about what their school does well in terms of recycling, and what it could do better. Make a list of these things on a poster or chart paper. Give children time to discuss ways in which they could improve their school's recycling efforts.

One suggestion is that they could design recycling bins that are suited to the shape and properties of the materials to be recycled. For example, a recycling bin for aluminum cans could have a round hole in the top to remind people what they should put in that container. The bin could also have a magnet on the side so that people could see that their can was not steel, but aluminum.

Another suggestion would be to start a public relations/information campaign about the benefits of recycling for the school. Children could design and hang posters about recycling, or put on a skit for the school to increase overall awareness. Let the children brainstorm their ideas, then put together what seems to them a viable plan. They then present their plan for the rest of the class.

Displaying and Reviewing the Results (30 min)

When the children have finished preparing their plan for recycling in the school, they present it to their classmates. Your children may have chosen to present their data with photographs, as a bulletin board, as a poster, or in some other way. Encourage children to ask questions during the presentations in an organized and sensible way.

At the end of the sharing session, the class can decide which of the plans (perhaps all!) they can implement. Give the children time to work on their plans. Make sure that the school administration is informed about anything that involves the entire school. Your job is to act as facilitator: get permissions from the administration, find materials, and help with suggestions.

When your children have put their plans into action, monitor their progress and give them feedback. Be sure that all class members stay in touch during the process.

Making Thoughtful Connections (15 min)

After the recycling plans have been put into action, take time with your students to review what they have done and what impact (results) they think they have had on the environment. Ask them to think about what the investigations have revealed about *how humans affect the environment:*

> What have we discovered about the effect of recycling on the environment?
>
> What have we done for our school to increase the level of recycling?
>
> How can we expand our recycling plans to affect the entire community?

EXPANDING CONCEPTS

Drawing Conclusions (5 min)

To put the whole investigation into perspective and to relate it to the wider issues of the global environment, ask your students what other questions they would like to investigate about humans' effect on the environment:

> What questions do you think would be worth investigating next about the effect of people on the environment?

How would you use what you now know about designing and carrying out plans to study the effect of humans on the environment?

Note: This is a logical extension to this module, and you can follow the same general structure.

Some students may enjoy investigating other questions, in other settings, and reporting their results to the class.

Take some time to reflect carefully on your experience with this investigation and use this sheet to record your evaluations. This will help you consolidate your ideas and provide a useful set of reference notes when you use the investigation in the future. Add more pages if you need to.

WORKING IN METHODS CLASS

What was the most important learning experience for you?

What experiences do you think will be important to remember when you do this activity with children in school?

What would you change in this activity for use with children?

What concerns do you have about using this activity with children?

(continued)

What do you need to know more about before you use this activity with children?

Points to discuss with faculty and colleagues:

WORKING WITH CHILDREN IN SCHOOL

What happened in the way you expected?

What happened that you had not expected?

What would you change when repeating this activity with children?

What did you learn about the children by doing this activity?

What did you learn about yourself as a teacher from this activity?

Points to discuss with faculty and colleagues:

II

Content
and
Pedagogy

11 The Nuts and Bolts of Teaching Elementary Science

INTRODUCTION

Teaching elementary science requires a great deal of preparation: not only in designing lessons but also in setting up an inviting classroom, pulling together resources, enlisting the help of others, and finding out what resources your community (and the world at large) have available to you. This chapter presents a practical approach to the basics of preparing to teach science. These include:

- Materials (basics, procurement, management)
- Safety
- Classroom setup
- Outside resources
- Managing time and the classroom
- Using technology to teach science

Information on many of these categories is so extensive, and often so specific to where you are teaching, that discussion about them must be general. However, through numerous examples in each category we will help you make a beginning in your own teaching.

FINDING AND MANAGING MATERIALS

Much of science learning is materials-intensive. It is important for your children's development of concepts that they manipulate and examine objects as they investigate. Fortunately, the current trend in elementary science curricula is to use common materials that are readily available. It is still a challenge, however, to assemble all the things you will need to teach science. One of your first steps must be to review the curriculum you are using. This will provide guidance on what you need for each topic or lesson. Some curricula come with kits, which will make the task of assembling materials much simpler for you. You may find, however, that even kit programs need some supplementing (especially if someone has used your kits before you get them!).

The first list in the next section describes permanent equipment that is desirable in most integrated science programs. Following are lists of materials that are useful in programs focused on specific sciences. Finally, there is a list of comsumable materials that will need to be replaced from time to time, depending on the lessons being presented. Compare these lists to the materials lists in your curriculum and consult with your colleagues (to find out what is available already that you can share) before you look into procuring these materials.

Permanent Equipment (items that don't need to be replaced unless broken or lost)

GENERAL EQUIPMENT (USEFUL FOR ANY SCIENCE)

hot plate	delicatessen containers with lids
droppers	safety goggles
graduated cylinders	aprons or smocks
balances	sieves or screening with taped edges
metric rulers	magnifiers
thermometers	plastic buckets
test tubes	glass beads or small marbles
test tube racks	safety scissors
timers	big wooden spoons

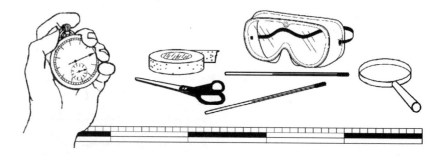

LIFE SCIENCES EQUIPMENT

aquaria	plant pots
plant stand	terraria
microscopes	

EARTH SCIENCES EQUIPMENT

barometer	small shovels	mineral collections
globes and maps	fossil collection	rock collections
stream table	fossil molds	streak plates

PHYSICAL SCIENCES EQUIPMENT

magnets	flashlight bulbs and holders
wires and alligator clips	solar cells
battery holders	motors
mirrors	propellers
lenses	switches

Consumable Items (to be replaced as used)

SUPPLIES

paper and plastic cups	aquarium filter material
baking soda (large box)	soil test kits
vinegar (gallon of white distilled)	graph paper
zipper plastic bags (various sizes)	table salt
food color	sugar
pH paper (see sources of supply below)	nontoxic markers
composition books (to record observations)	masking and plastic tape
plastic (non-latex) gloves	modeling clay
egg cartons	cornstarch
dry milk (large box)	plastic bowls
white glue	aluminum foil
plastic spoons	batteries
seeds	flashlight bulbs
soil	beral pipettes
animal feed	plaster of paris
wooden coffee stirrers	

LIVE MATERIAL

fish	anoles
plants	snails
mealworms	

PROCURING EQUIPMENT AND MATERIALS

There are essentially two ways of procuring materials: they are either purchased (by your school, your district, or another entity) or they come for free. If it is your responsibility to order materials for your science program, you will need to aware of the available sources of supply. These suppliers will provide you with catalogs depicting and describing the materials they offer. Ask your colleagues at school from which companies they typically order. If you do not have your own copy of one of the catalogs, get the toll-free number from colleagues or your school system's science specialists and order one.

Reading through a science supply catalog is an education in itself. You will be amazed at the variety of materials available. Many companies not only offer "classic" science equipment but also carry curriculum materials, videos, trade books, CD-ROMs, laser discs, and many other items. If your curriculum is kit-based, then you will most likely be ordering the kit from the company that assembled it. While this may seem obvious, there are occasions when suppliers no longer carry certain kits, and the curriculum's publishers have made a new arrangement with another supply company. The publisher will be able to inform you about any new arrangements. If you have access to the World Wide Web, you will frequently be able to order (or at least find out about) materials this way. Companies publish their Web addresses in their catalogs, or you can use a search engine on the Web to find the company in which you are interested.

You can also find many of the materials and pieces of equipment you need at retail stores of the following categories:

science stores (Nature Company, World of Science)	discount stores (WalMart, K-Mart)
science museum stores	aquarium and pet stores
hardware stores	teacher supply stores
grocery stores	drugstores
bookstores	swimming pool and spa stores
video stores	garden centers
dollar stores	

You may find it useful to have your school set up an account with certain stores so that you are not making extensive out-of-pocket purchases.

Free Materials

There are a number of sources for free materials, all of which require a bit of effort on your part. One of the first things you may want to do is get from the National Science Teachers Association (www.nsta.org) a publication called "A Guide to Free and Inexpensive Materials." This well-prepared compendium will help you to track down items from a wide variety of sources. You will find, however, that once you have established a flow of free materials to your classroom, the sources will become established and much less effort will be required on your part. There are several methods of getting free materials for your science teaching.

DONATIONS

Ask the sources listed below to send in materials, or volunteer to pick them up yourself. It is important that you know whom to contact at each of these places. To enlist the help of parents, you can send home notes with your children, request materials donations at parent/teacher meetings, or announce your needs at an open house.

When asking for donations from businesses or hospitals, try going through the human resources department (or the store manager, in the case of restaurants and hardware stores). Science-related industries and laboratories frequently donate used equipment to schools. Many hospitals have been known to donate extra (but unused) containers. Fast-food restaurants are also great sources of tiny containers.

Science-based industries and national science associations with education programs often have extensive free and low-cost educational materials that you can request. These include instructional modules, career brochures, posters, and more. A list of such organizations, with their contact information, is included in the Appendix. Most of these organizations have toll-free numbers or Web sites that you can use to procure items. The following are sources of free materials:

parents and other adults	hospitals
laboratories	utilities
national science and science education associations	fast food stores (containers)
	hardware stores (scrap wood)
industry (Dow Chemical, Merck, Lilly, Dupont, Kellogg, General Mills, McDonald's, Procter and Gamble, Johnson Wax, IBM, Monsanto, for example)	pizza places (unused pizza boxes)

SCAVENGING

You can collect a variety of materials just from scavenging. Ask other teachers, parents, and children if they have items such as the following that they would be willing to donate:

fabrics	craft supplies for displays
used packaging	pans and other containers

MANAGING MATERIALS

Once you have collected materials, you will need places to store them and methods to manage them. Some useful ways to store collections of materials include:

Tupperware® or other heavy-duty plastic bins with lids	storage boxes with lids (copier paper boxes)
shoeboxes	shopping bags
large zipper plastic bags	

It is important that you have the capacity to label the storage containers with their contents, keeping a running list taped to the outside. Many teachers prefer to sort their materials according to topic, module, activity, or some other category. If you are using a kit-based program, the containers will usually be supplied for you.

Once your materials are organized, you must find a secure place to store them that is out of the way of daily classroom life. Closets, storerooms, cupboards, and shelves all work for this. It is important that your organization of science materials be efficient, so that you don't feel overwhelmed by the amount of "stuff" that science seems to require—and, indeed, to generate. Some beginning teachers become frustrated by the demands of managing materials for their hands-on science programs. This can arise from lack of a well-thought-out materials management scheme. If you plan your materials management well, you will feel more in control of your classroom when your children are experimenting, designing, and making things.

Replacing Materials

You will find, over time, that your materials become lost, used-up, or broken and need to be replaced. Schools and school systems handle the replacement aspect in various ways. Some systems have a science supply center, usually housed at a high school or magnet school, where the high school teachers and students re-supply the needs of the middle and elementary school science teachers. Find out if your school system is set up in this way. If not, you may want to ask older children in your school (or in a local middle or high school) to help you with monitoring your materials supply. Having older children in your classroom regularly supports a cross-age approach to teaching, and your younger children will look forward to having the "big kids" in the class, especially during science time. You may also get help in re-stocking your materials from adult volunteers, college interns, and visiting scientists. Don't be afraid to ask.

Distributing and Collecting Materials

When you are preparing to teach a science lesson, you need to consider how to organize the materials for the lesson so that they get to the children and back to you in an orderly and safe manner. There are a number of ways of organizing this:

plastic trays	supply table
bins	drawers
boxes	bags

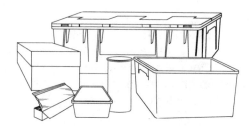

Group the materials your children will need for a particular investigation, or set up a central supply table so they can select the materials themselves. The supply table works best when you want your investigations to be as open-ended as possible. You may want to designate one child in each group as the materials "picker-upper" and another child in the group as the "putter-backer." Rotate these roles periodically so that everyone gets a turn. An alternative is to have adult or older child volunteers in the class to help with distribution and pick-up. You will have to use your judgement for this, depending upon the nature of the activity, the maturity of your children, and the time you have to do the activity. It is important always to factor in enough time at the end of a science lesson for returning materials and general cleaning up. Sometimes, this may take as long as 10 minutes, especially if you only have one sink, and there is a great deal of washing up to do.

INVESTIGATING SCIENCE SAFELY

Safety is absolutely essential in investigating science questions. You need to have a copy of your school system's safety guidelines and know the procedures to follow when accidents occur. A number of national science organizations—such as the National Science Teachers Association and the American Chemical Society—have guidelines for safety in the elementary classroom. Contact these organizations (see Appendix) for copies of their guidelines.

You will need to have the proper safety equipment for your classroom, before your children begin any investigations. This can include such items as:

eyewash	wash-up place with soap and water
correctly fitting safety goggles	fire extinguishers
aprons or smocks	first aid kit (check local policy)
gloves	emergency numbers listed

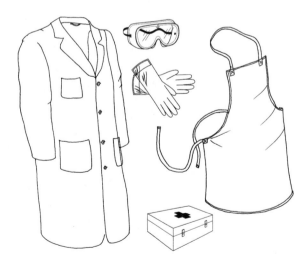

It is important that you help your children to understand and follow the safety rules. There are a number of ways in which you could do this:

- Arrange a visit by safety experts (could be a visiting scientist or someone from industry)

- Display safety posters
- Stage safety plays and skits
- Rehearse what to do in an emergency
- Reinforce informing you if there is an accident
- Review the safety rules before each activity

If an accident does happen during science investigations, you need to act quickly, and according to the safety guidelines of your school systems. The following can help:

- Be sure that you are clear on the school/county/district policy on accidents
- Establish a way of contacting the school administration quickly
- Have a method set up for having your class covered if you have to leave it with a child
- Have permission slips for certain activities on file
- Have copies of child emergency numbers (with emergency information such as allergies)
- Have fire department, hospital, and poison control hot line numbers handy

SETTING UP THE CLASSROOM FOR SCIENCE

The way your classroom is set up for science can be a determining factor in whether or not your children become excited and involved with their science investigations. You need to take a number of things into account:

- The physical setup of your room
- How you use your wall space
- What happens with your floors and ceilings
- What's going on at your windows (if you have any)
- How you use display space
- If and where you have science centers

Consider the following when arranging your classroom:

- Children need flat surfaces on which to work.
- The room should be flexible to allow for children to work alone, as pairs, trios, or quartets.
- The room arrangement needs to suit the nature of the activity.
- Work stations can be set up with this in mind:

  They can be free-standing tables with chair or chairs.

  Electricity should be close by, if needed for the investigation.

  Computers can be included as part of stations.
- Water supply may need to be handy. Ideally,

  Several sinks should be in each room.

  Sinks should be in good working order.

If there's a problem with sinks, investigate a portable lab unit or switching with another teacher for science time.

A good supply of paper towels should be on hand.

Your tap water should be tested for hardness and pH; lab results may be different from what you expected.

- Electrical supply might be needed for the activities. If so,

  Make sure your electrical supply is grounded.

  Use a surge protector with your computer.

  Have an electrician check to be sure that your outlets are safe and working.

  Check into heavy-duty extension cords (audiovisual carts are useful for this) to maximize your electrical capability.

- Arrange for space for trying out fair tests, if needed. This can involve:

  Hallways (check with administration first)

  Playground

  Fields around the school

  Cafeteria

  Gym

  Common areas (centers of pods or quads, for example)

  Safe areas in parking lots

  Wooded areas around school (be sure that you know where the school's property lines are so you don't trespass)

- Deal with disposal issues:

  Know the procedures on disposing what chemicals you use (check with the science supervisor or a knowledgeable high school science teacher for help).

  Know where your wastewater goes, so that you are not disposing of a substance down the sink that could cause problems in the watershed.

- Set up areas to keep plants and animals:

  Terraria

  Cages

  Greenhouses

  Plant stands

  Window space

  Aquaria

Using Displays in Science Teaching

Displays are an important part of learning and teaching science in the elementary classroom. You can use displays to inform your children, to remind them about safety procedures, or as a way of allowing them to share their work with others. Here are some specific suggestions for what you can do with science displays in your teaching:

- Bulletin boards

  Child work (investigation results)

Concept map as a introduction to a topic

Evolving displays (changes over time, perhaps reflecting changes in the moon, or the seasons)

3-D board using a variety of art forms

- Display cases

Child-made artifacts or prototypes

Child inventions

Photographic display showing children investigating outdoors

- Murals

Good for showing longitudinal concepts (time, distance, depth)

Post either at eye level or high in the room

Use a variety of media (including paper sculpture)

Make sure that the mural is connected by a theme

- Mobiles and stabiles

Use when motion is an important part of the display (for mobiles)

Use inexpensive materials (coat hangers, yarn, string)

Hang where they won't get bumped into

Make sure that the mobile has a theme

A special type of display is the science project display. You can help your children create informative displays for their project work if they follow these guidelines:

- Follow a set method (see Appendix for: Investigative question, resources, procedure, data, data analysis, conclusions)
- Go from left to right on the display
- Use particle board or foam board
- Use computer graphics or stencils for easy readability
- Use color wisely and effectively
- Display artifacts that illustrate the experiment
- Post photographs that show procedure and results

Constructing Science Learning Centers

Science learning centers are excellent ways of engaging your children in science investigations while other children in the class are involved in different activities. You can either construct the centers yourself, or ask an adult volunteer or older child to help you. The important thing to remember in designing and making a science learning center is to keep the focus narrow: stick with one topic or concept that the child can explore in a relatively short amount of time. For example, in a center children can explore magnets and their interactions with materials, or hook up a simple circuit, or build a kaleidoscope. The directions for what to do in the center must be absolutely clear, or the purpose of the center—independent learning—is defeated. If your children are early readers, you can dictate directions into a tape recorder, and have the tape player and headphones available at the center. The following points are suggestions to keep in mind when making your centers:

- Make a center free-standing with foam board or particle board.
- Hang a center on the wall or use a bulletin board to free up table or counter space.
- Develop your center around one particular concept or theme.
- Design the center so that it works for single children or small groups.
- Have directions for what to do clearly printed and posted at the center.
- Have hands-on components in the centers, if possible.
- Set up centers so they are easy to redo for the next children.
- Use computers in the centers where possible and appropriate.
- Incorporate an assessment component into the centers.
- Make centers colorful and engaging to do.

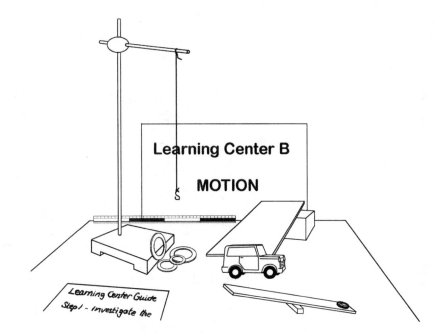

CLASSROOM SCIENCE INFORMATION RESOURCES

Modern science is changing faster than any curriculum can track. Every day, it seems, there are discoveries that turn longstanding "facts" on their heads. Therefore, it is virtually impossible for any print-based elementary science curriculum to contain the most up-to-date science information. One way of helping your children to stay current with what is happening in science is to establish an extensive science resource center, either through your school's media center or in your own classroom. Such a center needs to include print, as well as electronic and video, resources. Not only will this help your science be current but it will also encourage your children to explore science using the communications technology that scientists use. Some of the items that will help you to do this include:

- Reference books (atlases, dictionaries of science, almanacs, encyclopedias)
- Trade books on science
- Field guides
- Science activity books

- "Talking" books and a tape player
- Science-related storybooks
- Science textbooks as references
- Classroom computer
    - With CD-ROM player for encyclopedias and other software
    - Access to Internet and Web
    - Science software (simulations, etc.)
- Audiovisual resources

VCR and monitor	Audiotape player and recorder
DVD player and monitor	Camera
Laser disc player and monitor	Videotape camera
Overhead projector	CD player
Computer projector	

- Useful charts, maps, and posters

World map	Safety posters
Ocean floor maps	Science process posters
U.S. map	Local plant identification chart
Topographic maps (local, state, country)	Cloud type chart
	Visible light spectrum
Mineral charts	Water cycle
Animal classification charts	Rock cycle
Periodic table	
Rock identification chart	

MANAGING TIME AND THE CLASSROOM

Sometimes managing the classroom during hands-on science investigations may seem to be one of your most challenging roles as a teacher of elementary science. Groups are working away, people are out of their seats, materials are everywhere, and the time is galloping by. For this to be a positive experience for all involved, a good deal of planning and monitoring is necessary. Your lesson plan will need to have a clear focus for the day, and estimated times for each part of the activity. On the other hand, science often involves unexpected "teachable moments." You will need to be flexible enough so you can take the time to explore a special event with your children, if one arises.

Points you may want to consider in planning and managing your class during science can include:

- Plan your science instruction carefully. Know what you want your children to accomplish in the time they have available, but be flexible.

- Set times for group work; rotate tasks from group to group, or from child to child.

- Know when to let children explore, and when to pull them together to summarize or explain.

- Integrate science into other areas (maximizing instructional time).

- Monitor children as they work on a task; circulate around the room, helping and listening.

- Mix hands-on with research tasks (splitting the group if materials are in short supply).

- Monitor noise level and activity level, especially if you are in an open-space setting.

USING EXISTING TECHNOLOGY

In addition to using computers and audiovisual equipment in your science centers and resource center, your children (and you) will also be using it in science investigations, in data collection and analyses, and in preparation of presentations, reports, and projects. To that end, it would be useful to have:

- Computers with:
    Word processing
    Desktop publishing
    Spreadsheets
    Internet/email/World Wide Web
    Database software
    Graphing capabilities
    Peripherals to measure temperature, light, other factors
- Televisions and videotape recorders
    Science broadcasts
    Science tapes
- Science laser discs and players
- Tools with which to build and make other tools
- Calculators and graphing calculators
- Tools for measuring
- Telephones to access outside information

Of course, all of this is expensive, and your school may not have the wherewithal to purchase all this equipment. In that case, check with your school system's media center for what is available on loan. It is important also to check with your own school's media center. Often, such unusual equipment as a laser disc player will have been purchased years ago, and not really used.

If your school has a computer specialist, talk with this person to determine what software and hardware are available for your class to use. The ideal situation would be for you to have a number of computers in your classroom, but that's not always possible. If you are unsure about how to use any of the software yourself, or how to access the Web, for example, ask for help with this after school.

Contact adult volunteers to your class, or your school's parent/teacher group, to find out if anyone can donate tools for your children to use in building projects, or even an old VCR that is unwanted. Families today are often puzzled about how to dispose of electronic equipment and you may find useable items readily available when you reach out to your support groups.

12 Planning a Science Investigation

INTRODUCTION

Planning an effective and stimulating science experience for your children requires knowledge, imagination, and organization. While in many cases you may have substantial help from the science program your school is using, you will still need to tailor the lessons for your own particular children and situation. In other instances, your school may not have a set science program, or may be using one that requires a good deal of input from the teacher. Additionally, your school or school system may have requirements for each lesson (written objectives, "warm-ups," journal entries) that you will need to include in your plan.

The ten science investigations in this book can give you some guidance on what constitutes an effective elementary science lesson or series of lessons. Collectively, they cover topics from a variety of science disciplines and incorporate pedagogical strategies that reflect current trends in science teaching. This is to help you see that science does not have to be taught in one set way: there are many methods of involving your children in investigations that move them from beginning understandings of concepts through to more complete and connected understandings.

The following section describes the process of planning a science lesson for your children, so that you can eventually plan your own lessons. The word *lesson* is used to describe the investigation of a science from preassessment, through a series of concept-building activities, to postassessment and reflection. The section is presented as a series of questions that you can ask yourself as you go through the lesson planning process. (You might find it useful to review Chapter 11, "The Nuts and Bolts of Teaching Science," and look back at several of the exemplars from Chapters 1 through 10 to refresh your memory about their structure and contents.)

PLANNING A SCIENCE LESSON

A science lesson can be divided into three main sections:

- *Preparing for the lesson.* A description of the preparation you will need to do prior to working with your children.
- *Teaching/facilitating the lesson.* A suggested sequence for interacting with your children throughout their science investigation.
- *Reviewing/reflecting upon the lesson.* Ways to assess your effectiveness as a teacher when the lesson has concluded.

Preparing the Science Lesson

As you think about what you want to teach, you will need to make a series of decisions. These questions will help you to focus on what you need to include as you prepare your lesson:

1. What do you want your children to know and be able to do as a result of this investigation? (decide on key concepts, processes, and skills)

- Consult your curriculum guidelines and existing science program for the key concepts, skills, and processes involved in investigating a particular science topic.
- Consult national and local science education standards that your school or school system supports. These can help you with teaching

strategies, prerequisite understandings for topics, research on how children learn this topic, and much more.

- Examine the concepts you want your children to learn. What do they need to know before they begin investigations dealing with these concepts? (Consult national standards documents for help with this. They are written in grade bands, so that you can read about what children of a certain grade level are expected to know as they build their science conceptual understanding.)

- Review the skills at which you want your children to be proficient when they finish the lesson. These can include computational skills, measuring skills, use of certain equipment, research methods, and so on. Your science program may provide help with this or, again, you may wish to consult national and local standards.

- Decide on which science processes are important as your children investigate the topic on which the lesson is based. These can include:

    Observing

    Recording

    Formulating testable questions

    Conducting initial research

    Making predictions and recording reasons for these

    Designing a fair test

    Collecting and recording data

    Analyzing data

    Verifying data

    Drawing valid conclusions

    Communicating results

    Designing and making artifacts

    Testing prototypes

    Revising prototypes based on test results

    Connecting results of investigations to a larger picture

The section entitled "Science as Inquiry" in the *National Science Education Standards,* and Chapter 12, "Habits of Mind," in *Benchmarks for Science Literacy,* are excellent in describing the processes scientists use to investigate questions.

2. How can you describe your specific goals and objectives for this lesson? (define goals and objectives) This entails reviewing what you decided on in step one of this process, and setting the concepts, skills, and processes forth in statements that reflect how your children can give you evidence that they know and can do these things.

3. What do you need to teach this lesson, and how will you get it? (list materials, facilities, and other support) This requires thinking over your situation, taking stock of what you have, and planning how you will procure the rest. It always helps to:

- List your materials (for the activities, and for any presentations your children will make).

- List audiovisual support you will use and what you need to deliver it (equipment).

- Jot down adult helpers' telephone numbers and availability.
- Note the names of print materials, with page numbers.
- Decide how many copies of support materials you will need.
- Note when the computer lab is free, if this is applicable to the lesson.
- Know how you will use the physical space in teaching this lesson.

4. What activities or investigations will best help your children achieve the goals and objectives of the lessons? (choose instructional approach) Some of the strategies included in the ten exemplary lessons presented earlier, include:

- Collaborative learning
- Use of manipulatives
- Learning cycle approach
- Project-based learning
- Child-centered learning
- Contextual learning (real-world connections)
- School to work approaches
- Use of journals to record data, thoughts, questions, growth

5. What cross-curricular connections or opportunities for team teaching can you make with this topic? See Chapter 16.

6. How long will this lesson or investigation take? (estimate, and plan accordingly) If you are planning an investigation based upon activities from a commercial curriculum, you will typically find time estimates included for each activity in the investigation. If not, you can make an estimate of how much time each activity will take by doing it yourself or consulting with a colleague who has already done it. Remember to allow extra time for setup, preassessment, discussing the preassessment, teaching prerequisites, cleanup, debriefing your children, exploring interesting questions that come up during the investigation, and helping children as they work through the activities. Most of the ten exemplars in this book are designed to take at least a week of science time (30–45 minute time slots every day).

Teaching/Facilitating the Lesson

1. What will your children do to demonstrate their proficiency in the topic? (preassessment) How will you obtain information, through hands-on experiences, interviews, or demonstrations, about your children's existing knowledge, skills, and processes on the lesson's topic? If you were teaching a lesson on soil, for example, you might ask your whole class to contribute to a whole soil sunburst diagram to determine what they already know about soil. You could save this diagram to compare to a postassessment. See Chapter 14 for more guidance in this area.

2. How can you expand and deepen the reassessment phase of your lesson? (discuss preassessment with children) Discussing the results of the preassessment with your children will begin to clarify their ideas and help you to understand more about their logic. You must be willing to take the time to have this discussion, as tempting as it will be to move on to the activities portion of your lesson. Discussing the preassessment will also help you to refine your postassessment for the lesson. In the soil lesson example above, for instance, the teacher found after discussion that her children had no ideas about how soil was formed, although they seemed to be fairly well informed about soil's role in supporting plant life. They also had few ideas about the components that made up soil. Based upon this discussion, the teacher decided to include an activity on weathering that she had hesitated about when planning the lesson.

3. How will you deal with prerequisites to this topic? (review skills, knowledge, vocabulary) This involves preteaching, or reviewing, concepts and skills that are integral to the current lesson, but in which your children have shown some deficiency during the preassessment. You must be prepared to set aside what you planned, for the moment, if your children really need instruction in skills or knowledge they are lacking. Some teachers, for example, don't realize their children's lack of proficiency in using the metric system for measuring until they start a science lesson. In a lesson on soil, for example, they may need children to perform a task such as measuring the height of soil layers in a plastic column, but know in advance that children have difficulty in using metric rulers. They can either teach the skill in advance of the lesson, or use the soil layer activity as an opportunity to teach the skill in that context.

4. How will you get your children quickly engaged in the investigation? (initial activity) This is the *exploring concepts* aspect of a learning cycle approach. To help your children quickly become interested in the investigation topic, you need a beginning activity (preferably hands-on) that allows children to explore concepts freely and immediately. This can be something that involves part of their everyday lives (clothing, sports, music, soil, food); something highly visual (a video, CD-ROM, or demonstration); or something that involves intriguing manipulatives (magnets, lenses). Most good commercial curricular materials will suggest such activities. It is important, however, that the engagement activity is not only a "grabber" but is also one that helps begin the conceptual building process. Following the soil lesson example, the engagement activity might involve putting soil samples immediately into (and onto) the hands of the children, so that they can explore the characteristics of soil first-hand.

5. How will you help your children to build the key concepts and skills for the investigation? (exploration activities) This is the *focusing on and explaining concepts* part of a learning cycle approach. It will be an activity, usually hands-on, that builds understanding of the lesson's topic by allowing children to refine their ideas. To build on the soil example, you could structure your lesson so that, after your children have explored the properties of soil (using their senses), they could generate questions that they would like to investigate about soil. They could also investigate one or two questions that you selected in advance. Possibilities are: What makes up soil? or, How can we separate soil? or, What role do earthworms play in soil? All three of these investigations would help to build some of the key concepts related to soil: (a) Soil is made of a variety of basic materials. (b) Soil is composed differently in different geographic areas. (c) Soil can be separated into its layers by putting it into a water-filled container, shaking, and settling. (d) Earthworms help to enrich and aerate the soil. And so on. It is important, as your children progress through an activity sequence, that you constantly set aside time for them to review what they have done, look ahead to the next investigative question, and connect the entire experience to a larger picture: How did this activity help me to understand more about soil?

6. How will you help your children to apply their new knowledge or skills? (enhancement) This is the *applying concepts* part of a learning cycle approach. It is an activity, usually hands-on, that gives children opportunities to apply their new knowledge and the skills they may have acquired through the investigation. An application or enhancement activity can involve a design-and-make aspect that lets children put their new knowledge to work. If the children investigating the soil had learned to use a soil test kit, they could apply this knowledge to testing samples of soil from around their homes or school. They could then interpret the results of this test, using the guidelines that come with the test kits. To take the example one step further, children could design and make their own soil test kits based upon what they did in preceding exploration activities.

7. How can your children incorporate their new knowledge? (post-assessment) This may be an additional *applying concepts* lesson. It is a summative activity designed to give children the opportunity to demonstrate their proficiency in the key concepts, processes, and skills of the lesson. It can be one activity that occurs at the end of a lesson, or it can be an ongoing project that builds throughout the lesson. It is important, in a postassessment, to revisit the preassessment at some point. This doesn't mean that the revisitation is the only postassessment, however. Project work, presentations, and other activities can also contribute powerfully to your assessment of how well your children mastered the concepts and skills you designed the lesson to teach. In the soil lesson example, the children analyzed the soil around their school and planned a garden with plants chosen to match the qualities of the soil. The children were asked to support their choice of plants with data from their soil analyses. See Chapter 14 for more guidance on assessment.

8. How will your children communicate what they have discovered? (sharing results) These are small-group and whole-class opportunities to discuss what children have found out through their investigations of the lesson topic. You may want to schedule these as part of a presentation sequence in your class, or after presentations and other final assessments. It is vital that your children see science investigations as a collaborative effort, not as a competition. Scheduling sessions during which your children share results helps to emphasize this aspect of science.

9. How will your children make connections between what they have just learned and a larger, more global, picture? (making thoughtful connections) This can work as an *expanding concepts* part of a learning cycle lesson. This is a whole-class discussion, either child- or teacher-led, that gives children the chance to see how their investigations connect to the whole world. This section also gives children the opportunity to ask questions that can lead to future investigations. The importance of this type of closing discussion cannot be underestimated. Many children turn off to science because they can't see how it fits into their lives. If they can see direct and useful connections to the world, they will not only continue with science investigations but will also become more and more intrigued by all there is to find out about the world.

Reviewing/Reflecting On the Lesson

1. What work did my children do that best reflects their understanding of the lesson topic? (reviewing children's work) Take time, both during and after the lesson, to assess your children's progress, as well as any problems they had with their work. You need to set aside time on your own to read what your children have produced as a result of their investigations: to analyze their skill proficiency, review their development of conceptual understanding, and synthesize what they have learned as a whole. This can involve using portfolios, journals, lab reports, presentations, articles, and stories. The work your children produced as preassessments and postassessments is also important in gauging their learning.

2. How well did I do as a teacher, judging from the work that my children produced? (assessing your teaching and their learning processes as a result of the lesson) Take a look back after the lesson and evaluate your own teaching in light of your children's learning. How well did you accomplish the goals of the lesson? What evidence have you collected that your children know and are able to do what you expected?

3. What could I do differently next time to make this a better learning experience for my children? (planning any alterations for next time) This entails making any revisions of your teaching style, classroom setup, materials, or team-teaching partners that you feel will improve the learning situation the next time you teach science. You may wish to consult with a colleague (sharing samples of your children's work) to get an independent estimate of how you could improve your science teaching. Videotaping a lesson, or asking a colleague to sit in as you teach, is another way of monitoring your progress and getting advice.

SUMMARY

There are many variations on the theme of planning an effective science lesson for your children. You will need to try different methods out to find what works best for you and your situation. As you become more experienced in teaching science, you will find that many parts of the lesson will become second nature to you. You will automatically build in reflection and sharing sessions as children finish activities. You will become more and more adept at managing time, people, and materials during hands-on investigations. You will build a collection of assessment strategies that fit well with your teaching and provide useful information about your children's progress. You will feel more and more comfortable in team teaching with colleagues and making natural cross-curricular connections. The lesson-planning format and questions presented here were meant just to get you started. They are designed to help you think through what it takes, instructionally, to build science concepts and skills with your children.

13

How Children Learn

INTRODUCTION: PIAGET

Psychologists and educational researchers have, over the last century, studied how children learn. One of the most notable and respected researchers to receive attention was the Swiss child psychologist, Jean Piaget. Over many years, Piaget observed and questioned children as they engaged in activities such as manipulating objects, making drawings, listening to and telling stories, and making judgements. He found ways to get children to describe their reasoning, noting how it was based in their behavior and their language. From his observations and analyses, Piaget identified four sequential stages of intellectual development in children, which he defined as:

- *Sensorimotor stage* (birth to 2). Starting with their innate motor reflexes, children progressively learn to deal with their world through the stimuli they receive through their senses. Their intelligence is not linked to language.

- *Preoperational stage* (ages 2 to 7). Children who are in the preoperational stage respond to and use language as part of their thinking, but they are unable to use logical thinking or operations. In this egocentric stage the world truly seems to revolve around them. Thought largely exists in the here and now. Preoperational children learn by direct experiences, such as handling and manipulating objects, and by personalizing this experience.

They can begin to classify objects and events, and gradually they begin to think of things that are beyond their direct observations.

* *Concrete operational stage* (ages 7 to 11). In this stage, children begin to use logic. They also understand *conservation* (that is, that certain elements such as area, weight, and substance do not change if their positions change). They also understand the inverse of actions they may take (*reversibility*). They are able to see something from another's point of view. However, they are largely restricted in their thinking to concrete objects and events. They cannot think in terms of overall principles, theories, or abstractions. They are limited by the "what is" and cannot yet focus on "what could be."

* *Formal operational stage* (after age 11). At the formal operational stage, children can engage in *metacognition*, that is, they can reflect on their own thinking processes. They can now reason in abstract terms and generalize about principles. Where formerly they might think "that

person's behavior is bad and should be punished," now they can think more globally: "All bad behavior is wrong, but sometimes it can be justified for other reasons."

The key point of Piaget's theories is that the four stages of development are *sequential*. Children cannot reach a new stage until they have gone through and come to terms with the experiences of the preceding stage. At the same time, it is important to note that some children reach the stages earlier or later than the age indicated. Children act upon new objects, events, experiences, and ideas using the experience they already have in a process that Piaget terms *assimilation*. In acting upon the results of these new stimuli, Piaget says they are *accommodating* them by learning and incorporating new ideas and behaviors. The relationship between assimilation and accommodation, which has its origins in biology, is at the heart of Piaget's theory of intellectual development. Years after Piaget developed his theory, it remains at the heart of what is today termed *constructivism*.

In the earlier grades (K–2), most children are still preoperational. This means that their science experiences must take into account that they see the world as "me-focused." They need a great many hands-on experiences using simple, everyday objects and materials such as magnifiers, containers, nonstandardized measuring tools, building blocks, leaves, fabrics, water, and sand. It is important that you offer science experiences for preoperational children that allow them ample time to explore items, as well as to talk about their discoveries. In this way, you can help them to understand such ideas as: liquids are conserved no matter what the size of their container; or, it is possible to group objects in many different ways.

Older children, those at the concrete operational level, are able to investigate a number of simple science questions, but should do these using as many direct experiences as possible. Such experiences should involve measuring tools, simple laboratory equipment, plants and animals in the classroom, everyday objects, field experiences, videos, and much more. Having children work in collaborative groups as they investigate gives them the opportunity to talk about what they are investigating and what they have found out. In this way, they begin to recognize patterns and relationships in data—an important step along the path to the formal operational level.

While most older elementary children are in the concrete operational stage, you may encounter some who have some formal operational abilities. Children at this level are ready to learn about hypothesis testing as a mechanism for investigating science questions. They may be able to understand that scientific theories are based upon the results of many experiments, and can be used as the starting points for further experiments.

THE LEARNING CYCLE

A number of instructional approaches have built upon the work of Piaget and other researchers. One of the most widely used of these approaches is called the *learning cycle*. There are variations to the steps of the learning cycle, but one version consists of these steps:

- *Exploring a concept.* Children do this by hands-on experiences.
- *Focusing on and explaining a concept.* The teacher focuses the children's explorations, and helps them to clarify and understand a concept.
- *Applying a concept to a new situation.* Children apply their knowledge to a new situation, thus reinforcing their understanding.
- *Expanding a concept.* Children think about other questions they could investigate. This helps them to expand their understanding of the concept.

When using a learning cycle approach, it is important to understand that its steps put into clear and simple language what are really a series of complex intellectual processes for both students and teachers.

The learning cycle is just one research-based approach used in science teaching. The ten exemplary lessons in this book use a modified learning-cycle approach to help students learn science through inquiry. The inquiry aspect of the lessons is based upon the body of research that supports the definition of *inquiry* in the *National Science Education Standards* and the *Benchmarks for Science Literacy*. Students who learn science through inquiry may begin with their own question to investigate, or someone else's question, but, eventually they need to find answers, in a systematic way, that:

- Fit with their existing understanding and developmental level
- Make sense
- Are scientifically correct (even if only at a very simple level)
- Help them to understand their world
- Lead to new questions

SUMMARY

While hands-on experiences are a vital part of the inquiry method, children also need to draw upon the information they can find in books, videos, the World Wide Web, CD-ROMs, magazines, field trips, experts (including their teacher), and each other. It is the job of the elementary teacher to craft or select experiences for children that allow them to investigate science questions in a rich and supportive atmosphere. This includes giving children time to explore science, access to information technology, interesting items to investigate, opportunities to discuss and share, and the chance to investigate questions of their own.

14 The Role of Assessment in Elementary Science Teaching

INTRODUCTION

Why Assess Students?

As a beginning teacher of elementary science, you will find that you are constantly making judgments, or *assessments*, of how well your children are learning what you teach. This happens in an ongoing and informal sense, as you listen to their responses to questions, watching their faces as they explore ideas and pose questions to you. This *formative assessment* helps you to adjust your teaching to their needs and keeps you tuned in to your children's interests, questions, and challenges. You will also be assessing your children at key points in their science educational experience with you. This may happen at the end of a unit, module, project, or topic. Such *summative assessment* helps you to make judgements about what your children have learned and are able to do as a result of your teaching and their own explorations.

In general, assessment can be defined as a measurement of progress along a pathway. In elementary science education, children can be assessed, both formatively and summatively, in terms of their levels of content understanding, proficiency in science processes and skills, attitudes toward science, collaborative efforts in solving problems, and a number of other areas. The types of assessment that you yourself may have experienced as a student of science probably included responses to test and quiz questions, laboratory practicals, science projects, class presentations, science notebooks and/or journals, and, possibly, performance tasks.

Currently, the issue of student assessment in science education is under debate. Most of the recent elementary science programs include assessment tasks that are designed to measure how well children can use their science knowledge and skills in solving a particular problem or addressing a particular issue. This type of *performance assessment* (also called *authentic assessment* in some cases) frequently involves a hands-on component, group work, and extensive written or oral responses. Performance assessment tasks, as well as standardized science tests, are important parts of assessment programs in many school systems, districts, and states. It is important for you as a beginning teacher to find out what the district or state assessment practices entail and what their implications are, so that both you and your children can be well prepared.

Implications of Assessment Practices and Scores

Once you begin your teaching, you will quickly get a sense of what assessments are important in your school and your school system. Reading and mathematics scores are typically given a pre-eminent place in the assessment scheme, but assessment in science, as supported by national and state standards, is rapidly coming to the fore. The scores that result from such assessments, whether from standardized tests or performance-based instruments, are used by a number of entities for a variety of purposes. *Students* use the information from assessments to judge their own progress in science (if the scores are sufficiently explained so that the students can make sense of them). *Parents and guardians* use scores to judge the proficiency of their children, the efficacy of the science curriculum used in the school, and the effectiveness of the science teaching methods used to prepare their children for the assessments. *School administrators* use scores to judge students, teachers, and the "success rate" of their science program.

Beyond the school level, *school system administrators* review scores as they evaluate the science programs in different schools, and the progress of the students in those programs. This score-based evaluation can influence such things as funding for science programs, institution of professional development programs in science, and review of the instruments and methods used to make the assessment. At the *state level*, assessment scores can be used by officials to support decisions about science funding for curricula, materials, and staff development. Scores can also be used to evaluate the usefulness of the assessment instrument itself.

Assessment Politics

Assessment in elementary science—or, indeed, in any of the subject areas—is a politically charged topic. Ideally, assessment scores are used to give children a measure of what they know and are able to do at a particular point in their educational careers. In the best of all possible assessment worlds, the science assessment tool:

- Is clear in its intent and language to the children being assessed (and the teachers administering it)
- Reflects good science teaching practice as defined in national standards and supported by research
- Takes into account a variety of learning styles, that is, allows different response methods to reflect those learning styles
- Is unbiased in its content and administration in terms of gender, ethnicity, and socioeconomic status
- Gives as accurate a picture as possible of what children know in a subject, and are able to do
- Is supported by funding for staff development and materials
- Includes valid and reliable scoring methods
- Allows teachers to judge their students' progress and proficiency against a standard or against the students' own record of achievement
- Results in a report of student progress that is understandable to children, their parents or guardians, teachers, and administrators.

While these points may seem to be tied closely to performance assessment, they also apply, for the most part, to standardized testing methods, curriculum-based assessment tools, and teacher-designed assessments.

Assessing Science Teaching

Science content understanding has, for many years, been one of the main areas upon which students were assessed. Many of the current performance-based assessments, however, blend assessment of content understanding with use of science processes, application of skills, and students' abilities to evaluate science issues. This comprehensive approach to assessment, while challenging to develop, administer, and score, offers a more holistic method of evaluating student performance in science. Its intention is to reflect the practice of science as it is—a connected endeavor, not a series of unrelated tasks or content pieces.

Another area that can be assessed in the elementary classroom is children's *attitudes* toward science. This is not an easy area to explore, and, typically, is not one mandated by schools or school systems. It is, however, an important area in terms of students' willingness to become scientifically literate, as well as in terms of their interest in science as a possible career.

ASSESSMENT METHODS

There are many ways to measure your students' progress in science. Some of these are easier to administer and score than others, but they may not give you, or your students, an accurate and useful measure of the students' proficiency. When selecting and using an assessment (assuming it *is* one you are selecting, and not one mandated by the state or system), you need to consider what it is measuring and how well that fits your current assessment requirements. Following are brief descriptions of some assessment methods that can be useful in an elementary science program.

Preassessment

A preassessment task or set of questions is used to determine the level and quality of your students' understandings, skills, attitudes, and science processes before you enter into an investigation, project, or new topic in science. Preassessments can be as simple as asking students to write down what they know about a topic, or they can include a hands-on experience, video, or other prompt. You might find it useful to have students record their responses to preassessment questions or tasks in a journal, portfolio, or laboratory notebook. In this way, their progress and understanding can be tracked over time. It is important, at the end of a topic, module, or unit, to revisit the preassessment task or question and see how student responses have altered during the course of the instruction.

Student Interviews

One of the most direct ways of finding out what your students know about a topic is to ask them questions about the topic in a structured interview. This entails taking time from whole-class teaching to talk to students as individuals or in small groups. Interviews can be managed when the rest of the class is engaged in independent work or when you are team teaching with a colleague. In the interview setting, ask children what they think about specific science events, issues, or phenomena, and listen carefully to what they have to say. Often, it helps in an interview to have manipulatives (magnets, lenses, batteries and bulbs, ramps and cars, vinegar and baking soda) available for children to use when working through their ideas.

Quizzes and Tests

These are the most traditional forms of assessment, in which students are given questions, diagrams, graphs, or situations and make their responses in a written or oral format. Questions can range from multiple choice (a statement followed by a list containing several incorrect and one correct response), to completion ("fill in the blank"), matching (putting pairs of related terms together), labeling diagrams, filling in charts or tables, graphing data sets and interpreting the results, short answer (few sentence response) to essay (extended verbal answer to a question). Tests typically come at the end of chapters, units, or modules, or at certain set time periods. Quizzes are shorter and can come more frequently. Students can do tests or quizzes as individuals, or in groups.

When selecting or devising tests or quizzes for your elementary science students, you need to ask yourself what you are trying to assess and how well your test or quiz reflects good science practice. Is it important, for example, for your students to memorize items or terms that they can easily look up? Or is it more important that they can perform such tasks as recognizing patterns in graphs, connecting ideas, applying knowledge, and evaluating issues or situations? Tests can be designed to do the latter, and it is best to examine examples of tests that do this well before devising your own. For example, it can be confusing to your students to have them work in cooperative groups to solve science problems, then assess their progress at the end of six weeks with a test requiring an individual effort. Doing this sends a mixed message about what you consider important in learning science.

Projects

Projects are long-term efforts in which your students investigate a science question or issue, make an artifact to solve a problem, or collect and analyze related objects or events, among other tasks. Students can work as individuals or in small groups on projects, which usually have a presentation aspect at their conclusion. It is important, before your students embark upon a project, that they are clear about the purpose of the project, the criteria upon which they will be judged, their timeline for the project, and any procedure they are to follow in completing the work. The advantage in using project work for assessment is that you can determine how well your students can apply their science knowledge and skills to solve a problem. Projects also allow students who may excel in nonscience areas to contribute to the effort (research, drawing, presentation). The criteria for judging student project work can include areas such as completeness, accuracy of concepts, clarity, support for ideas, logical methods of solving the problem, development of working prototypes, and evidence of teamwork. Students should receive a copy of such criteria from you before they begin, and they should be given a thorough introduction to what is expected. The project deliverable can include a presentation, poster, notebook, collection, mural, dramatization, artifact, or a number of other methods of communicating results.

Presentations

Presentations are communications of results to others so that the results can be clearly seen and understood. While presentations often come at the end of project work, they can also be a part of a hands-on classroom investigation, a library research endeavor, a field experience, or any other occasion when information needs to be communicated to a group of people.

Students should be encouraged to use highly visual and auditory methods of presenting whenever possible. These can include posters, murals, skits, overhead transparencies, videotapes, closed-circuit television, and computer-driven presentations. If students have prepared their presentation as a group, you may feel it important that each group member have a role in making the presentation. For students who have a problem doing this, you could suggest a panel approach, whereby the presenting groups sit behind a table to make their presentation. The criteria for using presentations as assessment tools are very much the same as for using project work. You might find it useful to have peer input when offering feedback to presenting groups. You will need to prepare your students to do this, so that the feedback is offered in a constructive, fair, and inoffensive manner.

Portfolios

Portfolios are collections of student work. These can be useful in assessing student progress in science, particularly because they show development of thought, skills, and ideas along the way. If you are using portfolios for assessment, it is important that your students understand how the portfolio will be kept and used, what can go into it, and what their role is in maintaining and building it. Items that can be included in a portfolio are project reports, labs, journal entries, lab notebooks, problems solved by collaborative groups, reflections on science issues or careers, understandings of science concepts, and more. A portfolio is an excellent tool to use in an interview with a student at key points in the learning process. Together, you can evaluate a student's growth and understanding in science, as well as any areas that need work. Portfolios are also valuable to students as they move to middle school and high school. They give the teachers in these higher grades evidence of what your students have done and are able to do.

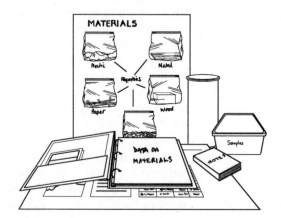

Performance Tasks

Performance tasks are science problems that your students attempt to solve by applying their knowledge, processes, and skills. These can be problems that are part of your current science curriculum, problems that you devise, or separate tasks that are part of a state or local performance assessment program. They may include a hands-on component, video piece, or other prompt. Students respond in writing, or sometimes by building something and evaluating how well it answers the problem. Student proficiency in content understanding, skills, and processes is judged by rating student responses against scoring keys or rubrics. From these ratings, levels of proficiency are determined and reported back to students.

Teacher Observations

Teacher observations can be used to collect data on a number of areas: how well your students work in collaborative groups, how well they handle science equipment, what their levels of content understanding are, and so on. As your students work on science problems or discuss science issues, circulate around the room to make notes of what they do, how they do it, and where there are gaps or misunderstandings. This type of *formative assessment* can help you plan your teaching as well as help individual students in need.

Self-Assessments

Students can assess their own progress and science understanding by making entries in notebooks or journals, or meeting with you as individuals or in small groups to discuss their progress. You may be surprised to find that students tend to be tougher on themselves than you would imagine. One of the major advantages in self-assessment with students is that they feel a part of the assessment process and can contribute their own feelings about their progress freely.

Journals

Journals are written records that students can keep throughout their science program. Journals can be used to: record initial and developing understandings of science ideas; note questions students may want to investigate; list things they have discovered; record points they want to make about science issues; contain lab reports; and include daily records of observations (especially useful in longitudinal studies.) Journals help to develop recording skills, narrative style, and organizational abilities. As with portfolios, journals can be used as tools to evaluate student progress along the way. It is important that you make clear to your students from the start what the purpose or the journal is, how it can be used, and what role it will play in science assessment.

Practicals

A laboratory practical is a method of assessing student proficiency in using science equipment. You may want to find out, for example, if your students can read a thermometer properly, or measure volume using a graduated container. Typically, practicals are set up in stations around the room, and students circulate through, making measurements and responding to questions designed to reveal their knowledge of instrument use. You may want to set up a practical as a stand-alone type of assessment, or you may want to incorporate aspects of it into performance assessment tasks. Practicals are easy to score, in that students either know how to use an instrument properly or they do not.

Surveys

Surveys are sets of questions used to determine opinions or factual information from a set of respondents. You may want to use a survey format to assess your students' attitudes about science, science careers, or science issues.

Such a survey can help you get a sense of how well informed your students are about issues, what their feelings are about science careers, and what their biases might be about science in general. Once you know this, you can use the information to help your students become more informed about areas in which they reveal a bias.

CONSTRUCTING AN ASSESSMENT TASK

When constructing your own assessment for your children, whether it is a test, quiz, performance task, project, portfolio, or whatever, the following method can act as a guide:

1. Decide what skills, processes, content understandings, or attitudes you want to measure. (Refer to national, state, or local standards for this, as well as to the science program you are using.)

2. Decide what evidence your children could produce that would let you know they are proficient. (Can they interpret graphs, build a prototype, analyze information from a variety of sources, identify next steps in a protocol?)

3. Decide what task, instrument, or questions would elicit the information. (Should they be charged with building something that will solve a practical problem, arrange a protocol in sequence, find information on the Web, then synthesize it?)

4. Decide what level of performance would be excellent (proficient), good (approaching proficiency), average (attempting proficiency), or poor (nonproficient). (Have they constructed and administered a survey that has resulted in valid information? Is their survey unclear, incomplete, off-topic? Did they fail to do the task at all, or do it so incompletely that it makes no sense?)

5. Devise sample responses (answer key, scoring key, rubric) that will be the standard against which you judge your students' performance. An answer key or scoring key is specific to one question or one task ("The plant in the closet eventually died because it received no light, though we gave it water and it had air. The plant in the window lived because it had water, air, and light.") A rubric is a written guide that can be used to assess student performance in a *class* of skills or processes (graphing, finding information, interpreting graphs, arriving at conclusions).

6. If possible, pilot the assessment with a small group of students, or with volunteers from another class. This allows you to refine the assessment instrument before you give it to your whole class.

7. Administer the assessment. (Allow enough time for students to complete the assessment without being rushed. Arrange for alternative methods of administration for students with learning variations.)

8. Score the results. (Devise the scoring method based upon your levels of proficiency. For example, proficient: 4 points; approaching proficiency: 3 points; attempting proficiency: 2 points; nonproficient: 1 point. Or, 90–100 points, A, etc. Or, Pass/ Try Again. Or, provide your students with a written narrative feedback set or a rating scale.

9. Report results to students. (Be sure that students have feedback in writing, and that they understand the scoring method. It is usually a good idea, especially with a long-term assessment, to confer with students

either individually or in small groups about their progress. Also, be sure that parents and administrators understand how you are assessing and what the feedback means for the student.)

10. Allow opportunities for students to repeat the assessment as they work toward proficiency. (Give students the opportunity to try the assessment again after they have understood what is required to become more proficient.)

11. Revise the assessment based on your students' performance and your own sense of how well the instrument measured what you intended it to measure. (You may find, after devising, administering, and scoring an assessment tool for the first time, that it poses problems for your students and for you. It may have been unclear or unfair, or it may not have resulted in the data you needed to evaluate your students' performance. In that case, revise it and retry it with other groups of students.)

SUMMARY

You may feel that assessing student progress is a burden, or an "add-on" to your science teaching. Actually, it is the core of what you do with children in science. If you cannot measure what they have learned and what they can do, what evidence do you have that they have achieved anything as a result of your teaching? As a beginning teacher and professional educator, you need to be informed about what assessment practices are current, what they tell you and your students, and what implications they have for you. Here are a few questions you might want to ask when faced with a choice of assessment practices, or when a new state or system-wide assessment is going to be implemented in your school:

- What is the instrument assessing? (Is this what we want our children to know and be able to do in science?)
- How does the method of assessment reflect accepted science teaching practice, as defined by standards and supported by research?
- In what ways does the assessment method reflect how people's performance is evaluated in the workplace?
- How does the assessment scoring method inform the learner about strengths and weaknesses, successes and failures?
- In what ways does the assessment provide a useful tool for students to take beyond elementary school?
- What is driving the assessment (politics, standards, new curriculum)?
- Who supports this form of assessment?
- How valid and reliable is this assessment? (Who has developed it, how has it been tested, does it yield results we can count on?)
- How are students informed in advance of what will be assessed, how it will be assessed, and what will happen to the results?
- How are teachers prepared to administer the assessment?
- How will the baseline of performance for students be established?
- How will the scores be used?

These questions (and others that will occur to you) will help you to take a critical and informed look at assessment practices as they affect your teaching.

Discuss new assessments with colleagues and members of science education organizations. Read research articles on assessment to find out what is current, what appears to yield useful results, and what has been found to be tortuous and difficult to implement. Remember the bottom line for assessment in elementary science: A good assessment tool informs you and your students about what they know and are able to do as a result of your science program.

15 Selecting a Science Curriculum for Elementary Children

INTRODUCTION

A wide variety of elementary science programs is available, both commercially and at the school district level. Sometimes the decision on which science program to use is made at the county, district, or school level. Other times, the decision is made by the individual classroom teacher. (Even then, however, the programs available from which to choose have usually been screened at some higher level.) As a beginning teacher, you may find yourself in the position of selecting which program to use in your classroom. It is important to have clear criteria upon which you can judge if a program will fit your needs and those of your students.

To get a sense of what is on the market, you can visit curriculum centers at colleges or universities, or check with your district science supervisor for review copies of materials. Once you have found a few "approved" programs that excite you, you can contact publishers either by telephone, fax, mail, or Web site, for more information. When you do make contact with a publisher carrying an attractive curriculum, ask for:

- Review copies (both student and teacher editions)
- Program goals and objectives
- How the program intends to accomplish its goals and objectives
- How the program recommends assessing student achievement

- How the program meets national science education standards
- Where the program is being used and with what types of students
- Pricing information
- Information about adjuncts (kits, CD-ROMS, videotapes, laserdiscs, teacher editions, test banks)
- Information about training sessions.

You will need time to review the program thoroughly before deciding whether it is right for you and your students. A simple flip through a book or module does a disservice both to your students and to the developers of the curriculum. To get the best possible feel for how a science program could work, you need to have your students try out activities from the program, read sections from it, answer questions, and review the layout. Often, a program will look very good on paper, but once your students start using it you find that the explanations are overly simplistic (or too difficult), the activities are not engaging, or there are inadequate methods of assessing student progress.

SELECTION CRITERIA

You need to look critically at a prospective curriculum with clear criteria in mind. Some of these criteria can include (depending upon what is important in your area, and what is important to you as a professional):

science education standards (national, state and local)

activities

language level

safety

illustrations

tables and graphs

resources

assessment

durability

innovation

philosophy

pedagogy

integration of related subject areas

ethnic and gender balance

concept development

global outlook

layout

The following can help you to make an informed decision about a new program. Try evaluating your current elementary science program using these criteria, to see how well it fares.

STANDARDS

You might find it useful to read Chapter 19 on Science Education Standards first. Then look at the following:

* How does the program address science education standards? (Derived from them, keyed to them?)

* On which standards is the program based?

* How are national mathematics standards (*Principles and Standards for School Mathematics, 2000,* National Council of Teachers of Mathematics, or NCTM) addressed by the program?

* How does the pedagogy of the program support the *National Science Education Standards* or the *Benchmarks for Science Literacy*?

* How does the program address district, county, or state science education standards?

ACTIVITIES

How are the activities designed to engage children in hands-on investigations of science questions?

What evidence do you have that the activities are developmentally appropriate for the students?

How do the activities build conceptual understanding?

How do the activities help children to make connections between science ideas?

How thoroughly have the activities been tested by children in elementary classrooms?

How do the activities help to move children away from informal ideas toward more scientifically accepted ideas?

LANGUAGE LEVEL

How would you assess the appropriateness of the language level for your students?

SAFETY

How is safety addressed in the program (cautions with activities, special safety section, use of safety icons)?

ILLUSTRATIONS

How would you assess the usefulness of the illustrations in the program—do they give you content information, teaching suggestions?

How would you assess the appropriateness of the illustrations in the program?

TABLES AND GRAPHS

How would you assess the usefulness of the tables and graphs in the program—do they give valuable information, show relationships clearly?

How would you assess the quality of the tables and graphs in the program; e.g., are they clearly labeled, large enough to be easily read?

RESOURCES

What types of resources (glossaries, CD-ROMs, teacher's guide, videotapes, laserdiscs, kits, training) are included in the program?

How would you rate the usefulness of each of the resources to your teaching of science?

How necessary are the resources to the success of the program?

ASSESSMENT

How is student progress and proficiency assessed with this program?

What resources does the program offer for assessment?

How current are the assessment techniques in terms of research and practice?

How well do the assessment techniques fit with those supported by your school? District or county? State?

DURABILITY

How durable are the various components of the program (hard cover, soft cover, kit cases)?

INNOVATION

How would you characterize an innovative elementary science program?

How well would you assess the developers' attempts to produce a program that is innovative and engaging to students?

What evidence can you find in the program's materials to support such innovation?

How comfortable do you feel with the depth of innovation? Why is that?

PHILOSOPHY

What is the stated philosophy of the program?

How well does your analysis of the program match the stated philosophy?

How well does the philosophy of the program fit with the national standards' definition of good science teaching? What is your evidence for that?

PEDAGOGY

What is the stated pedagogical approach used in the program?

How well does your analysis of the program match the stated pedagogical approach?

How would you describe the pedagogical approach used by this program, based on your analysis?

INTEGRATION OF RELATED SUBJECT AREAS

Are relevant subject areas explicitly integrated into the program where appropriate? What is your evidence for that?

ETHNIC AND GENDER BALANCE

Does the program, explicitly and implicitly, promote the idea of "science for all"? What evidence can you find for this in textual examples, career references, illustrations?

CONCEPT DEVELOPMENT

How are concepts developed in the program? (Choose one concept, and follow it through from introduction to final assessment of understanding.)

How does the method of concept development used in the program fit with current research into how children learn science?

GLOBAL OUTLOOK

How global is the program? (Assess examples, illustrations, graphs)

How important is a global approach to your students' learning of science?

LAYOUT

Is the program easy to follow and understand?

Is the program attractive and motivating to students?

One of the best ways that you can discover what is important to you in a science program is by evaluating one with the above criteria. You will probably find that you don't really know what you like and don't like in a program until you read it through carefully, think about it, try it out with your students, and discuss it with your colleagues. Often a program using a nontraditional pedagogical strategy, or one with an unusual philosophy, will take quite a long time to evaluate fairly. You and your students will need to adjust to the program's innovative approach before you can evaluate how well they are learning science concepts and skills.

TEACHING SCIENCE IN CONTEXT

An example of an innovative elementary science approach is teaching science "in context." This means that students learn the science they need to know to be able to solve a real-world problem or address an issue. The advantages of this approach are:

- Students are immediately engaged by the relevance of the topics.
- Students can make clear connections between the science and technology they learn.
- Students can demonstrate their proficiency by performance assessment tasks adapted from the activities in the program.

The possible disadvantages to a contextual program include:

- Establishing the program's scope and sequence so that it makes "approved" curriculum lists
- Covering the complete amount of subject matter required by district and school guidelines
- Assessing student achievement in ways that parents and guardians clearly understand

Other innovative approaches include programs that:

- Are based on a strict constructivist approach
- Are focused on key science events as beginning points
- Use a science/technology/society approach
- Include a strong communications network to exchange data
- Are CD-ROM- or Web-based, rather than print-based
- Include a satellite broadcast component
- Have a "school-to-work" aspect
- Are strongly cross-curricular
- Are modular, rather than textbook-based
- Explicitly promote cooperative grouping strategies
- Include embedded assessment

- Are based upon national science education standards at the start of their development

All of these approaches have their strengths and weaknesses. It is important, therefore, that, before you make a decision about curriculum, you be as well informed as possible. The World Wide Web is an excellent resource in learning about curriculum projects, as are science education journal articles, other teachers, conferences and conventions, science and science education associations, and the developers of the programs themselves.

SUMMARY

Unfortunately, suitability to you and your students is not the only consideration you have in selecting a science program. Your school, and school district, budget only certain amounts of money for elementary science. A program that is wonderful, but too expensive (due to adjuncts or other reasons), could result in your making a second or even a third choice. It is up to you to find out how much of the school's budget is available for your science program, and to try to work within that budget. Sometimes schools budget for different programs to purchase materials on alternate years. This means that you might not get enough money for science one year, but you will be able to make up for that in the following year. The budget cycle in your school is another important factor to find out from your administration.

As an education professional, you also need to find out what support is available, either from the developers or the publisher, for each program in which you are interested. A deciding factor in whether you go with one program or another may be whether training is available, where the training is, if it costs anything, what it entails (time and resources), and if it fits into your schedule. Another factor to consider is the nature of the adjuncts available. If a program is kit-dependent, for example, you may find that is exactly what you need, or you may find the kit makes the program cost-prohibitive. A program may have a laserdisc, CD-ROM, or DVD, but your school might not have the technology to support it. A curriculum could provide an extensive test bank of questions, but if your school system is 100 percent performance-based assessment in its approach, you have a problem. All of these items are things that you need to consider when you research, evaluate, test, and eventually select a science program that will create a rich science experience for your students.

16 Cross-Curricular Teaching and Learning

INTRODUCTION

It is important to distinguish between two approaches to teaching and learning: a *cross-disciplinary* approach, and a *cross-curricular* approach. Scientific understanding has grown steadily over many centuries. Historically, it became organized into a number of distinct bodies of knowledge, usually called disciplines. The main disciplines are usually thought of as physics, chemistry, biology, and the geosciences (the Earth sciences). Recently, space science has been recognized by some as a distinct scientific discipline.

Most of the key disciplines can be further divided into subdisciplines. For example, biology can be subdivided into zoology, botany, entomology, microbiology, and others. Some subdisciplines represent combinations of more than one discipline, like biochemistry or geophysics. Geoscience can be subdivided into many different but related subdisciplines, including geology, oceanography, geomorphology, paleontology, volcanology—up to about 25 in total. As scientific knowledge increases, new disciplines establish themselves, often as a combination of other disciplines.

A Cross-Disciplinary Approach

In the work of many scientists, disciplines often overlap. For example, a geologist's study of soil (Earth science) may involve studying chemicals within soil (chemistry) and living organisms in soil (biology), along with gravity's effect on water moving through soil (physics). Professional scientists, working mainly in one major discipline, often have to apply or refer to science ideas located within a different science discipline.

At the elementary level, where the basic building blocks for later scientific understanding are being laid down, the broad distinctions between science disciplines are of minor importance. Scientific inquiry—that is, the process of scientific investigation—is common to all science disciplines. Some curriculum initiatives, recognizing that the links between disciplines can be as important as the disciplines themselves, take an integrated approach, even at high school level. In the quest to develop scientific literacy for all in society, an integrated approach would seem to fit more comfortably with all students. In contrast, a traditional approach, where each discipline is taught and learned separately, would seem more appropriate for students who aspire to become professional scientists (chemist, physicist, biologist, geologist).

For elementary students, however, a cross-disciplinary approach, at least for the main part, is more appealing and appropriate. To a great extent this is implicit in the *National Science Education Standards* (NSES), with their heavy emphasis in scientific inquiry. An integrated approach to science teaching and learning is therefore *cross-disciplinary*.

A Cross-Curricular Approach

Science education involves far more than just science content. Language and mathematics are the two most obvious examples, in that science ideas are expressed in written and spoken language, and scientific inquiry frequently makes use of mathematics as a tool for measurement, data collection and analysis, and so on. In the broadest sense, science can be seen as relating to almost every other curricular subject. Music is composed of sound waves (physics) that are detected and interpreted as sound by ears and brains (biology).

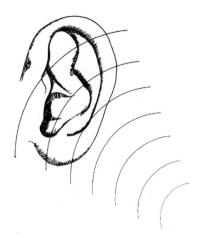

Social studies not only links to science in terms of history and the effects on humans of scientific knowledge and invention but also represents the social context within which scientific development takes place. The relationship between science and technology is especially strong, perhaps inseparable, in the application of scientific ideas in solving human problems.

A cross-curricular approach takes all this into account. It recognizes that opportunities to learn science are present in all other subjects, and that opportunities exist to learn other subjects while working with science. For example, when children are gathering data and trying to interpret them, there are opportunities for them to use, and thereby learn, mathematics (applying percentages, calculating averages, using fractions). As they record their observations, and as they present their results to others, they are developing their language skills, and possibly their graphic art skills. In everyday life, humans are constantly using knowledge and skills that cover a variety of subject areas. Here is just one simple example.

Buying food in the grocery store may involve thinking about a meal at home. This may be a special meal, perhaps where the extended family is gathering or guests are coming for dinner. There will be social interaction before, during, and after the meal (social sciences), and the buying of food and other items takes this into account. The food itself needs to be attractive to those who will eat it, but also needs to represent a balanced, healthy combination (home economics and health education). The cost must be affordable, the amounts of different foods needed figured out to avoid waste, and at the checkout the amount owed will have to be calculated and paid (mathematics).

In the crowded store, the shopper may have to read signs to find the intended purchases and read labels to distinguish one product from another, check contents and ingredients, and determine measures. Shoppers may also need to consult with a store staff member and will certainly have to communicate with the checkout assistant (language arts). Products often come from many different regions or countries, and the buyer may want a specific product that comes from a particular place, or the intended meal may have a particular ethnic food tradition (geography).

Perhaps flowers are needed for decoration (biology) and candles, disposable cooking containers, napkins, and cleaning items will be used (chemistry). The buyer may also be influenced by the way the store's merchandise is laid out and by some of the in-store advertising (creative arts). Shopping also involves physical effort, pushing a cart, avoiding others, carrying and lifting (physical education). Music may be playing in the store (creative arts). Temperature is important for many foods, and we tend to eat different foods according to weather conditions (mathematics, geoscience). Time will also be a factor, especially when the buyer estimates which checkout line promises to be quickest. In fact, the list of subjects being juggled by the shopper seems endless—a constant interaction between different forms of human understanding. The same can be said of most human activities.

A cross-curricular approach reflects this interaction of subjects. It combines two or more subjects—perhaps in part, possibly in total—in a way that the outcome is seen to add up to more than the sum of the parts. It can also involve two or more teachers working together as a team. Practical and different ways of doing this are discussed later. For now, it is important to take a few steps back and reflect for a moment on the bigger curriculum picture.

ORIGINS OF OUR PRESENT CURRICULUM

Curriculum subjects represent the separation of whole human knowledge into smaller discrete categories. This has come about historically, not always because of logic but often through social history. The nineteenth-century school curriculum generally recognized only three subjects: reading, writing and arithmetic. Arithmetic, a subcategory of mathematics, was included in the curriculum because of the Industrial Revolution, which produced an urgent need for numerate workers. Since those days, the range of curriculum subjects has grown substantially. Physical education was added because societies realized the value of healthy bodies. Social studies was added because societies believed that citizens needed to be informed in order to contribute wisely to political decision making. Recent additions, such as health education, computer literacy, and multicultural education also reflect particular societal concerns as translated into curricular obligations. Perhaps it is extraordinary that school organization has hardly changed at all as new subjects were added. Schools are still generally organized around a collection of subject-specific periods on a daily timetable.

As the subject range increased to near bursting, some became defined as core subjects (reading, language arts, and mathematics) to be taught every day, while others were relegated to alternate days (science, social studies, health, physical education, art, music, computer studies).

Change is often a difficult process. Changing the school organizational structure has become extremely difficult to contemplate. It is important to recognize how pervasive and deeply rooted the traditional school structure has become for most members of society. Perhaps this is partly because almost everyone is an "expert" in schooling. Parents' and guardians' understanding and expectation of schools are greatly influenced by their own school experience. A dramatic change would certainly produce a great deal of parental concern. Students themselves come to school for the first time with a very fixed set of expectations, and would no doubt find something different quite disturbing, at least at first. Teachers also tend to focus their work and expectations along clear structural lines. A radical change in their role would certainly trigger anxiety for many, especially if this change were imposed from the outside. Administrators rely on the current structure as the basis of their organizational arrangements, procedures, policies, and—most of all—the management of human and financial resources.

At a much broader level, think what would happen if children did not go to school. How would family management work? How could parents sustain their incomes through work? What would children do all day? Besides education, the schooling system has traditionally been seen as a safe haven for the nation's young, allowing adults to get on with their lives. Finally, schooling is rather like a permanently revolving fairground carrousel. You can't stop it to fix it. Only in extreme circumstances has a school system been put on hold for restructuring. The best example was during the Chinese Cultural Revolution, when schools were closed for two years while a total revision was made. Even then, what emerged was not structurally different, but more a revision of curriculum content.

We also need to keep in mind that school curriculum arrangements have far-reaching consequences. At the top end, a student's measured success in a curriculum subject can become crucial for entry to higher education or the job market. The road to success or failure begins much earlier, in some senses even before children start school. Nevertheless, the school experience of each person from kindergarten through grade 12 is a crucial factor in terms of life chances. The school curriculum can legitimately be seen as the key instrument by which society sorts its citizens into different socioeconomic groups. It can be seen as a social stratification process as well as an educational process.

In the popular imagination, school structure and the curriculum are viewed as deeply fixed systems, like the political system, the rules of football, money, and taxes. Small changes, especially if they can be shown to be beneficial in some way, are tolerable. Dramatic changes seem to be virtually impossible.

It is within this mix of deeply held structures, systems, and expectations that a cross-curricular approach operates. Its impact in this context is relatively small. Certainly a cross-curricular approach is not revolutionary, nor does it challenge the heart of traditional values. The benefits of working this way can be argued logically, and its benefits can be demonstrated in practice. It is, nevertheless, a change that will prompt surprise, questioning, concern, criticism, and even hostility from some quarter. As a teacher, you need to be prepared for this if you are contemplating working in a cross-curricular way. You need to be sensitive to the views of others, especially parents, children, and teacher colleagues. That said, let's look at how a cross-curricular approach can play out in an elementary school, and what your part in it might be.

BEING ALIVE TO CROSS-CURRICULUM OPPORTUNITIES

As you work through any science program, and especially as you use the exemplars given in this book, you are likely to come across moments where a cross-curricular opportunity presents itself. This will be particularly true with mathematics and language arts, because your children will inevitably be making use of these subject areas as they explore science ideas. Here are some obvious examples.

Your students are investigating the properties of container materials (see Chapter 3). You have asked them to devise tests on several materials, such as:

* Thin cardboard (from file folder)
* Strong plastic sheet (from zipper plastic bag)
* Aluminum foil
* Plastic wrap
* Brown paper (from grocery bag)
* Plastic foam (from meat tray, washed)

They are going to devise tests for these materials that will show comparative properties of:

* Strength
* Water resistance
* Stretch
* Elasticity
* Density
* Moldability
* Any other property they think interesting or important

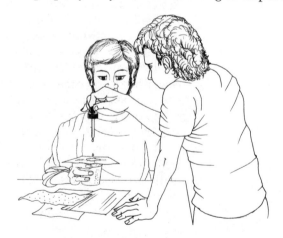

Mathematics

Mathematics will very quickly enter the picture. To make the testing fair, some children may think that all the samples should be exactly the same shape and size. Others may feel that the samples should all have the same mass/weight. Measurements needed to ensure this could include area, length, width, and mass/weight, among others.

The tests they design will need to have a fair means of comparing the materials. For example, with strength testing, what is the force needed to break or pull apart each different material? With elasticity, how great is the material's ability to return to its original shape? With moldability, what shapes can a material hold? Again, mathematical concepts and measurement can quickly become involved.

Comparing and contrasting the results of the tests for different materials may well need to go further than "more than/less than." Children may find ways to use numbers as a means of making more accurate comparisons. "The result for plastic wrap is almost twice as much as for strong plastic sheet" or "It took less than half the amount of force to break the plastic foam that was needed to break thin cardboard." Statements like these are inherently mathematical. Moreover, by applying mathematics in the form of numbers, children can quantify their results.

Communicating findings to others, in a form that can be easily understood, demands that your children use number ideas. Mathematics focuses on patterns and relationships, and exactly the same can be said of interpreting the results of scientific investigations. There is an obvious cross-curricular opportunity here. For example, findings can be expressed as whole numbers, fractions, decimals, ratios, percentages, averages, ranges, or even approximations or estimates—all key mathematical concepts. Most also present good opportunities for making calculations. It is not difficult to see the range of possibilities. Moreover, there are two distinct approaches that you could use:

* Ask your children to apply their current mathematical knowledge to their science investigations.
* Use the children's need to find a good way to interpret their scientific investigation results as a means of introducing a new mathematical concept (fractions, percentages, averages, and so on).

The key point with either of these approaches is that the children will have a clear focus as they combine science and mathematics to solve the problem. From a science point of view, they are using mathematics to clarify their science ideas. From a mathematics point of view, they have a clear reason for understanding a particular mathematical idea, concept or operation. It is a mutual enhancement of both subjects.

Children often have difficulties learning mathematical concepts when they are taught in isolation. They can "learn" a mathematical concept and operation but totally fail to recognize a situation where the concept can be applied. Scientific investigations present one of the best opportunities for overcoming this problem, because children can easily see how the mathematics relates to solving their problem.

As a teacher, you need to be alive to opportunities to bring science and mathematics together. If having children learn how to calculate percentages is on your mathematics agenda, why not consider linking this to a science investigation where calculating percentages would be most useful?

Language Arts

The subject of language arts—listening, talking, reading, and writing—offers similar cross-curricular opportunities. Science involves communicating with others at every stage. Children need to articulate and compare their initial thoughts about a science idea. They need to discuss possible questions to investigate, record and share observations, figure out ways of testing and experimenting, choose ways of recording data, and, at the end of their work, find ways of communicating their results in a form others can see and understand. Clearly the language arts are key tools for science.

Science, like all areas of human knowledge, also has its own very special language. There are many words in the science vocabulary that are unique to science. In addition, words and phrases used in general conversation can have specialized meanings within science. The role of language arts in science is therefore a two-way process, similar to mathematics.

From a biological point of view, human communication skills mark us as highly developed animals. The links between the ability to think and the ability to talk are very closely intertwined. So language is, of itself, a scientific phenomenon.

The opportunities for cross-curricular approaches between language arts and science teaching and learning are perhaps too numerous to count. The following are just some of the possibilities.

LISTENING AND TALKING

Listening to the ideas of others

Verbally expressing one's own ideas

Raising questions

Responding to questions

Discussing ways of observing, predicting, investigating, recording and reviewing

Discussing results and their implications

Discussing the best way to communicate information to others

READING

Gathering information, from a variety of written sources (books, newspapers, magazines, other people, computer information, Web sites)

Reviewing observations, ideas, explanations, data, questions that colleague students have written

Referring to notes, recordings, and ideas

Interpreting the findings of investigations completed by other students

WRITING

Making personal notes in a form that one can refer to later and understand

Making notes and recordings that peers can read and understand

Using written language in a technical way (designing charts, formulating a question for investigation, formulating unambiguous predictions, expressing findings in an accurate form, drafting a clear explanation from evidence)

Using language in a descriptive way, to help others see and understand

Using language in an entertaining way to excite the interest of others in investigation results

Developing a sense of audience for one's writing, and different ways of writing for different audiences and different purposes

Writing collaboratively with others to produce joint statements

These few examples demonstrate just some of the possibilities. You will no doubt easily find more if you keep alive to the possibilities.

As with mathematics, there are good opportunities either to make science or language arts your starting point. The former is obvious, but the latter also offers interesting possibilities. For example, in language arts you may want to have children learn how to write a formal letter. If you can, focus this toward an investigation where students need to write a letter (for example, in investigating the properties of materials they might write a letter to a paper manufacturer asking how cardboard is made). Or, you may need to develop children's abilities to phrase precise questions. Formulating questions for investigation, or questions for a survey, can be a key part of an associated science inquiry. Once again, the advantage is that children are not learning these things in isolation. Rather, they are learning the language arts within a meaningful and functional context. It becomes "real" for them, with clear outcomes and consequences.

Helping Children Understand Cross-Curricular Relationships

As teachers, we often get so involved with the detail of individual subjects that we forget to help our children see why these subjects are part of their curriculum. Equally, we can forget to help children see the connections between subjects. If you regularly draw children's attention to the ways in which science, mathematics, and language are integrated, they will grow to understand the richness of this interaction. The advantage of a cross-curricular approach is that it provides children with a meaningful context within which to enhance their understanding of these subtle relationships.

OTHER CROSS-CURRICULAR POSSIBILITIES

Although the links among science, mathematics, and language arts are the most likely subjects for a cross-curricular approach, this does not mean that there are no possibilities with other subjects. There is science to be found in all aspects of human knowledge and understanding. Perhaps a good way of showing this is to look again at the example of the properties of materials, and specifically those used in containers. The following sunburst diagram shows how containers' materials can be related to most other areas of the curriculum.

Container Sunburst (filled in)

Looking at this diagram, one might be tempted to plan an integrated curriculum around the theme of containers. Thematic approaches have been tried in the past, especially in the United Kingdom during the so-called progressive education period in the late 1960s and early 1970s. As with most innovations, there are advantages and disadvantages. Taking a central theme, and customizing all the different subjects toward that theme, certainly can help your children to see the integrated nature of human knowledge because they can see the connections and links between subjects.

For some children, this thematic approach delivers subjects in a more understandable context and offers an engaging approach toward learning. Not all children, however, respond readily to the thematic approach. From a teaching perspective, this approach can be extremely difficult for an individual teacher to manage alone. It almost certainly needs a team of two or more teachers to be adequately delivered. Moreover, there is likely to be some artificial "bending" of subject content toward the theme. A major problem is ensuring that the content of the separate curriculum subjects is adequately covered, and in a coherent way. It is unlikely that you will find yourself working in this way as a beginning teacher. If you were to join a school that had adopted this method or organization across the board, then you would likely be part of an existing teaching team, not thrown into the deep end on your first day!

COLLABORATING WITH OTHER TEACHERS

Working with Colleagues

There are many opportunities for teaming with colleague teachers beyond the totally integrated curriculum approach. In most elementary schools, individual teachers rarely teach all subjects to their classes. Often, specialist teachers teach subjects such as physical education, sports, music, art, and sometimes science. Generally, though, the elementary teacher can expect to cover most of the curriculum subjects.

Opportunities exist for working with a colleague teacher when common interests are apparent. For example, when dealing with the human body as part of your science curriculum, there may be a common interest with the physical education teacher. Another example might arise if you are working with food chains in science. If you have a colleague teacher for health education, there are some distinct overlaps where expertise could be combined. Again, if you are dealing with sound, then a music teacher might be able to work with you in a complementary or collaborative way.

It is clear that teaming can be very effective. Its basic requirement is mutual interest on the part of the participating teachers, especially from yourself. The other teacher, or teachers, need to share a common enthusiasm and commitment toward working in this way. The advantages are clear. Each teacher brings a particular set of strengths into the mix which, combined with those of others, can enhance the learning possibilities.

Working in a team approach can produce other benefits for the teachers. With two or more minds sharing the teaching experience comes much discussion and idea sharing. The focus is sharpened, and each teacher gets to consider possibilities that might not easily surface otherwise. Teaching can be a relatively lonely, even isolating, experience when you are confined just to yourself and your class. Teaming also helps to blend experience with current learnings. It can be especially helpful to a beginning teacher, provided it does not interfere with a sense of professional status. After all, it is important that you feel comfortable on your own as a teacher as well as when working as a team.

At the very least, you should feel able to talk to other teachers about curriculum matters. Even if collaborative teaching, or team teaching, does not seem a possibility, it is important to realize that there is still great expertise residing in colleague teachers. Consulting with colleagues should be normal practice, and an experienced teacher can help beginning colleagues with advice and information. It is important to see consultation with colleagues as a positive thing. Sometimes it is hard to ask for advice, especially when you feel the need to establish yourself within the closed society of a school. Other professionals such as medical doctors, lawyers, and research scientists, see this as normal professional practice.

Planning with Colleagues

Planning is, of course, essential for all teaching. For a cross-curricular approach, you can expect to spend extra time in planning, anticipating how the plan will work, and then ensuring that all the pieces are in place. You will have to consider the resources required, the classroom arrangements, and the management of learning. If there are colleagues who have used a cross-curricular approach, you need to ask them for advice. Working in this way places extra demands on the teacher, both in planning and execution, and the experience of others will be very helpful to you.

If there is a prospect of a team approach—perhaps because the school is eager to work in this way, or other teachers approach you about it—or if the initiative is coming from you, planning will take on a whole new dimension. Working with others in a team raises extra planning questions and issues. Everyone in the team needs to be very clear about how the work is to be shared and who is going to do what, when, and how.

As a beginning teacher, you may at first feel apprehensive about working with experienced teachers. It is important that you not bite off more than you can chew. Be sure to admit, up front, any concerns you have about working in this way for the first time. All teachers remember how they felt in their first teaching experiences, and chances are that colleagues will be sympathetic to your concerns. Equally, you need to feel able to contribute to the planning in a real way.

This may become a careful balancing act for you, but it is important to everyone that the approach succeed and that potential risks and problems be fully discussed ahead of time. You may want to stress the need for a careful approach, perhaps one step at a time, to ease yourself into this new way of working. Remember that the children may also have to adapt to this change if they have not experienced it previously.

In planning for team teaching, the most crucial aspect is time. You and your colleagues will need to set aside adequate time for meetings. This may involve some after-school effort, since the busy elementary curriculum often has little space for colleagues to meet. Everything needs to be discussed in detail, including:

What are the reasons for team teaching?

With what curriculum areas are you going to be dealing?

What specific content will be covered?

How will different aspects of the content be covered?

What kinds of experiences do you want children to have in this approach?

How can you best ensure that all students profit from the experience?

Who is going to take responsibility for what?

What special skills does each teacher have and how can they best be used?

Will there be a common teaching learning style or strategy across the team?

What constraints are there in terms of time and organization?

How will this team approach fit with the normal school timetable?

What resources will be needed?

What administrative support, agreement or permission is needed?

How will children be introduced to this approach?

How will on-going evaluation of the approach be managed?

How will you know that the approach is working satisfactorily?

What will you do if problems arise?

How will you build in opportunities to change, or adjust, the approach in the light of experience?

Do you need to alert parents to this approach?

What will happen if a team member is absent, through illness, for example?

Is there a contingency plan if problems arise?

Is everyone comfortable with the plan?

How will you know that the plan has been successful when it is completed?

These and other similar questions are the basis of good planning. At the first meeting with colleagues, you might suggest that you formulate a list like the one above as a means of getting the planning started. Certainly, you yourself will need to feel assured that all these questions have been carefully answered in order to proceed with confidence. Raising questions and discussing them is the best way to overcome uncertainty.

SUMMARY

Working with others in a team can be both exciting and professionally rewarding. You will learn a huge amount from your colleagues, and they in turn will learn from your contribution. Remember that all of you will be sharing both responsibility and achievements, as well as the normal ups and downs of any approach. At its best, team teaching in a cross-curriculum way can take the learning enterprise to a new and exciting level—one that you will find professionally inspiring.

17 Evaluating Your Science Teaching and Professional Growth

INTRODUCTION

Teaching is such an intensive enterprise that it may seem there is never enough time to reflect on how you are doing. You will get feedback from your students as you observe their degree of involvement in class activities, their faces when you are explaining something to them, and their comments about how much they like (or don't like) what is happening. You will also get feedback, especially in your first two years, from parents, supervisors, colleagues, principals, and visitors to your classroom. As useful as all of this will be to you, it is really only a part of the picture. As a beginning teacher, you need to plan for evaluating your own progress, both in the classroom and as an active member of the professional education community.

EVALUATING YOUR SCIENCE TEACHING

There are many ways to evaluate your progress as a teacher. One possible method uses the following steps.

1. Think carefully about your goals as a teacher of elementary science. Discuss these goals with colleagues and supervisors. These questions can help to get you started:

- Why did I want to become an elementary teacher in the first place?
- Why do I think science is an important part of every child's educational experience?
- How comfortable do I feel with teaching science, and what steps could I take to feel more comfortable?
- How do I see myself growing as a teacher of elementary science over the next five years?
- What could I do now to help me grow in this way? How can I track my progress?
- What experiences do I think that my students need to have in science, and why?
- What concerns do I have about teaching science, and how could I alleviate them?
- What excellent science teachers have I had in the past, and what did they do that made science a good experience for me?

You may find it useful to interview your fellow teachers using adaptations of the above questions. Compare to your own the ideas and feelings they have about teaching elementary science to children.

2. Write down your goals and objectives for science teaching.

If you feel comfortable about it, share the list with your colleagues. The following are some examples of possible goals and objectives that might give you ideas about your own list.

Objective: Set aside time every week to talk to my students about their science ideas.

Goal: Learn more about my students' understandings of basic science concepts so I can improve the way in which I create learning opportunities for them.

Objective: Take a college course in animal science [as an example area].

Goal: Expand my own knowledge about an area in which I have always had a great interest.

Notes: This will help me to plan lessons about animals for my students that will be informative, accurate, and exciting. I'll learn more about the possibilities of working with animals in the elementary classroom.

Objective: Join a professional science or science teaching organization.

Goal: Learn about the types of services that such organizations provide for science teachers, and become a part of the professional science teaching community.

Notes: This can help me with professional development opportunities, and provide a support group of teachers who can help me out.

Objective: Find a really good elementary science program that has a strong cross-curricular focus.

Goal: Maximize the connections between science and the other curricular areas.

Notes: A cross-curricular program not only helps show my students that science is linked to many areas but it also increases the amount of time that I can spend on science. My students will be working on science-related topics in reading, math, and social studies, as well as in formal science time.

Objective: Establish (or patch into) a network of new elementary teachers with a strong interest in teaching science.

Goal: Have colleagues with whom I can share ideas, lesson plans, problems, and successes as I teach science to my students.

Notes: I might be able to do this through Internet connections, or through my state science teacher organization.

Objective: Provide my students with "real world" science experiences.

Goal: Help children to realize that science (and technology) are important parts of their lives (understanding how things work; balancing risks and benefits; knowing about human effects on the environment; science and safety; the aesthetic nature of science; what the needs of living things are).

Objective: Become part of a staff development team in science education.

Goal: Expand my own professional skills to the point where I can share useful ideas and knowledge with colleagues.

Notes: This will help me have the impetus to gain as clear an understanding as possible of a variety of science concepts. It will also give me a forum to learn from the experiences of my fellow teachers of elementary science.

Objective: Set up a classroom resource center in science for my students.

Goal: Provide my students with as many sources of information that I can so that they are learning about science that is current, accurate, and exciting.

Notes: The resource center should include print materials, computer-based information (the Internet, including World Wide Web connections; CD-ROMs), videos, kits, and anything else that will help my students to find out things on their own.

EVALUATING YOUR PROFESSIONAL GROWTH

1. Make an action plan with a timeline for each objective or goal, and keep it in a safe place. An action plan will help to make your ideas "real" and possible. Because it is essential to your success, put your plan in a permanent notebook or journal, or back up your computer files to prevent the plan's being lost or deleted. Here's an example of how your action plan can work for two of the points above.

Objective: Join a professional science or science teaching organization.

Action plan:

- Call the district science supervisor to get membership information on your state science teachers association and order a copy of their latest newsletter.
- Review the materials, contact the membership chair, and, if the organization fits your needs, join up.
- Look into other state and national science education organizations to see what services they offer.

Objective: Find a really good elementary science program that has a strong cross-curricular focus.

Action plan:

- Visit the curriculum center housed in the board of education building, since they have samples of all of the elementary curricula that have been commercially available since the 1960s.
- Read reviews of new curricula in the science education journals and get copies of reviews done by national science education organizations.
- Discuss the pros and cons of various programs with fellow [fourth-grade] teachers and the science and elementary supervisors.
- Request examination copies of promising programs from the publishers.

2. Revisit the plan monthly (perhaps same day each month) to assess your progress. Write comments about how well you are meeting each one of your objectives, and what you could do to improve. Use the following table as a guide.

Sample Record of My Action Plans

Objective: Set aside time every week to talk to my students about their science ideas.
Goal: Learn more about their understandings of basic science concepts so that I can improve the way in which I create learning opportunities for them.
Action plan: 1. Research children's understandings of key science concepts (journal articles located through ERIC search). Note: Could double as Master's research project (summer). 2. Focus on concepts that seem to be commonly misunderstood by children and draft interview questions based on clinical interview research (summer). 3. Practice interviewing children about their ideas during the first quarter. 4. Devise a plan for regularly interviewing students and using the interviews to plan and monitor my science teaching. Discuss this plan with my mentor teacher (fall semester). 5. Implement the plan over the rest of the year.

Action date	Comments
July 5–25	Found articles by Fisher, Finley, Gabel, Resnick, Hewitt, Anderson, Smith, Osborne, and Novak. Listed some of the key ideas that I'd like to focus on for my research project and in my teaching. Need to find more articles related to upper elementary students. This took longer than I thought.
Late July	Drafted sample interview questions (using some of the questions used in clinical interviews in the research articles).

A document of this sort can be a great help in your first years as you try to keep on track as a growing professional. It can also be something that you can share with a mentor teacher, a science supervisor, or your principal. It is your evidence, both for yourself and for others, that you are a thoughtful, reflective professional.

Creating a list of your goals and objectives, and using these on a regular basis to monitor your progress, may seem like a daunting task. Actually, most of the work takes place on the front end of the process. It is accomplished in the time it takes to think things out and decide what you really want your students (and yourself!) to gain from your science teaching. Once you have established your key goals and objectives, as well as your preliminary plans for achieving them, the rest is a matter of monitoring your progress regularly. This takes discipline, time, and reflection, but the rewards will be great. You will have a strong sense, at all times, of where you are in some of the most important aspects of your teaching.

Continue to add, change, and expand your goals and objectives with time and increasing experience. The teacher who had the goal of taking the college course in animal science, for example, decided that, after the course, he would work as a volunteer at the county animal shelter on weekends. This led to a symbiotic relationship between the teacher and the shelter personnel. They visited his classroom once a month to work with his fifth graders on the proper care of pets. He, in turn, gained hands-on experience with handling and caring for animals, as well as observing how they were treated for injuries and disease. This teacher brought his new knowledge back into the classroom when teaching about the needs of living things, and about how diseases are spread and controlled. As he grew, his students benefited.

SUMMARY

Self-evaluation involves a commitment from you in terms of time, thought, preparation, and follow-up. This can help you monitor your progress, in the classroom as a teacher of elementary science, and in your overall growth as a professional. Self-evaluation entails:

- Honing in on your professional goals as a teacher of science
- Recording those goals and objectives in a systematic way (either in a journal, or in electronic format)
- Deciding on a written action plan that will help you to achieve each goal
- Revisiting your goals, objectives, and action plan regularly to assess progress
- Identifying your strengths and weaknesses as a teacher of science
- Making adjustments to your plan to build on your strengths and work on weak areas
- Sharing your self-evaluation periodically with supervisors, mentors, colleagues, and others with an interest in your growth as a professional.

18 Using Curriculum Standards as a Teaching Resource

INTRODUCTION

As a result of activities in grades K–4, all students should develop understanding of:

- The characteristics of organisms
- Life cycles of organisms
- Organisms and environments

National Science Education Standards, 1996, p 127

This is just one example of a science content standard. Curriculum standards are relatively recent in U.S. education, but their introduction and implementation marked a major turning point in the nation's educational development. Moreover, curriculum standards are here to stay, at least for the foreseeable future, and they will directly affect your teaching. This chapter attests to their significance in science education. To make the most of it, you should obtain copies of the *National Science Education Standards* from the National Research Council (1996), and *Benchmarks for Science Literacy*, which were produced by the American Association for the Advancement of Science's Project 2061, and published by Oxford University Press in 1994.

WHY DO YOU NEED TO KNOW ABOUT CURRICULUM STANDARDS?

As a beginning elementary teacher, you will quickly find that schools have undergone significant curriculum changes since you were an elementary student yourself. Few of these changes have been more dramatic than the changes in science education. When you were in elementary school, science education was not likely to have been seen as a core subject like mathematics and language arts. The chances are that your teachers had little expertise or background in science. If you did have science lessons, they were probably more oriented to life science than physical science or earth science. At a national level, all this has changed. Science is now seen as a key subject for all students K–12. States, and school districts, have been translating this into structures for curriculum change, and most elementary schools have felt the resulting impact.

In the school where you begin your teaching experience, you are likely to find that science now occupies an important place in the curriculum. This change that has taken place is systemic. It has become enshrined, largely because of the introduction of curriculum standards for science that define what students should know and understand as a result of their learning experiences. To be able to teach science well, you need to understand what these science standards are, how they have come about, and how they can be used as both a curriculum baseline and a teaching resource.

WHAT ARE STANDARDS?

In the past, textbooks often drove the curriculum. They defined what content was taught, when it was taught, and (often) how it was taught. Student achievement was largely measured by tests designed to show how well students had acquired that content knowledge.

This began to change after a series of worldwide studies in the 1980s suggested that U.S. student achievement— especially in science and mathematics —was lagging behind that of many other countries. At about the same time, U.S. industrialists voiced growing concern about the educational competence of graduates joining the job market, and universities expressed similar worries about freshmen students. The Third International Mathematics and Science Study (TIMSS) reports in 1995 and 1999 spotlighted the mathematics and science deficiencies of U.S. students (National Center for Education Statistics, U.S. Department of Education).

This mixture of concerns stimulated a political climate that encouraged new thinking about school curricula, with a stronger focus on what became known as *student outcomes*. Gradually the emphasis shifted from ideas about what *content* students should be taught and tested on, toward defining what student *performance* should be. The question became what should students understand and be able to do by the time they complete their schooling. From this, the idea of developing sets of curriculum standards was born. Today, the term *curriculum standards* usually describes a set of statements detailing what students can be reasonably expected to know and apply by certain stages in their school career. They are essentially statements of educational expectations and outcomes.

At the national level, key organizations worked on producing educational standards for various curriculum areas. One of the first was the National Council for Teachers of Mathematics (NCTM), which researched, developed, produced, and published new curriculum standards for mathematics in 1989. They have recently released a revised version of their standards, *Principles and Standards for School Mathematics, 2000.*

National Science Standards

In science education, the American Association for the Advancement of Science (AAAS) produced *Science for All Americans* in 1989, which articulated the need for all U.S. citizens to be scientifically literate. This was followed by *Benchmarks for Science Literacy* (BSL) in 1993, which states what students should be expected to know at the end of grades 2, 5, 8, and 12. Another body, the National Research Council (NRC), produced in 1996 the *National Science Education Standards* (NSES), statements of what all students should understand as a result of their activities in grades K–4, 5–8, and 9–12.

In some sense, the BSL and NSES compete with each other as being the recognized national standards. However, there is broad agreement about what scientific understanding students should have at a given stage. Beyond their statements of student outcomes, each publication also focuses on other aspects of science education. The BSL gives relevant background and also research references about students' acquisition of science concepts, and contains a variety of sections that deal with such things as the nature of science, mathematics and technology, the designed world, and habits of mind.

The NSES offers a range of other standards in addition to content standards. These include science teaching standards, standards for professional development for teachers of science, assessment in science education, science education program standards, and science education system standards. Taken together, these two publications represent a formidable resource for science education in general and a rich resource for teachers of science. Although these are now well established national curriculum standards documents, they are essentially advisory. Individual states and school districts usually develop their own science curriculum standards. However, BSL and NSES generally are a strong influence in this process.

Local Science Standards

Local standards either originate from a state department of education or a county/school district. Although individual states and school districts vary in their approach to setting and implementing science standards in schools, it is unusual to find any that are far removed from national standards. In some cases, the school standards can be more specific on a grade by grade basis, and may even have keyed standards into curriculum scheduling for particular semesters.

Local standards represent key educational curriculum policy and can be seen as a public statement of intent on the part of the area's educational entity. These standards may become a set of criteria for testing purposes, with educational achievement assessed or demonstrated on the basis of student testing against these standards. Most school districts also use their standards to determine their adoption of basal and supplementary curriculum resources. Typically, they look for science curriculum products that demonstrate a good match with their standards. Teachers are required to implement activities and learning experiences that target these standards.

As a beginning teacher of science, it is crucial that you become familiar with the science standards that apply in your school. This is a professional responsibility that may also be a legal obligation in some areas.

BECOMING FAMILIAR WITH SCIENCE STANDARDS

Given the fact that most local standards are informed by the national standards, a good starting point is for you to study these two publications:

- American Association for the Advancement of Science, *Benchmarks for Science Literacy* (BSL), Oxford University Press, 1993. Web site: www.project2061.org/tools/benchol/bolframe.html.

- National Research Council, *National Science Education Standards* (NSES), National Academy Press, 1996. Web site: www.nap.edu.

The BSL groups its elementary outcome statements K–2 and 3–5. These two sets of statements neatly cover the normal elementary range, since most school systems encompass grades K–5 (though in some districts grade 6 is also included). The NSES, however, presents a slight difficulty for the elementary grade level range because it groups its standards statements K–4, then 5–8. So, in looking at the standards, two group levels have to be considered. It is important to note that the statements represent an achievement level that students should begin to have by grade 4, and later be completing in grade 8. The first educational period, grades K–4, fits well into the elementary range. For grades 5–8 statements it is necessary to judge what elements are appropriate for grade 5, the last year of elementary education, from a set that are designed to be reached by grade 8.

SHARED THEMES IN BSL AND NSES

It is helpful to identify and track two broad themes in these publications: (1) science as inquiry, how students should engage with scientific processes, and (2) science as content, or concepts that children need to understand.

Science as Inquiry

Both BSL and NSES have important things to say about scientific inquiry. Here is a look at them in order.

BENCHMARKS FOR SCIENCE LITERACY

Benchmarks devotes a separate section to scientific inquiry (see BSL pp 9–12). Following a general introduction to the nature of scientific inquiry, BSL then details specific benchmarks for different grade levels, including this:

> By the end of the 5th grade, students should know that:
> * Scientific investigations may take many different forms, including observing what things are like or what is happening somewhere, collecting specimens for analysis, and doing experiments. Investigations can focus on physical, biological, and social questions.
> * Results of scientific investigations are seldom exactly the same, but if the differences are large, it is important to try to figure out why. One reason for following directions carefully and for keeping records of one's work is to provide information on what might have caused the differences.
> * Scientists' explanations about what happens in the world come partly from what they observe, partly from what they think. Sometimes scientists have different explanations for the same set of observations. That usually leads to their making more observations to resolve the differences.
> * Scientists do not pay much attention to claims about how something they know about works unless the claims are backed up with evidence that can be confirmed and with a logical argument.

NATIONAL SCIENCE EDUCATION STANDARDS

The NSES places science as inquiry as its first *content standard* (see NSES, pp 121–23). The NSES sees science *processes* as part of, and not separate from, science concepts. This was no accident on the part of the NSES authors. Rather, it represents a clear statement from them: that engaging in scientific investigation is of equal importance to understanding the science concepts that make up the body of scientific knowledge. Here's how NSES spells it out this standard using two key points:

> As a result of activities in grades K–4 (and 5–8), all students should develop
> * Abilities necessary to do scientific inquiry
> * Understanding about scientific inquiry

Each of these points is later explained in more detail:

> Guide to Content Standard: Fundamental abilities and concepts that underlie this standard include
> Abilities necessary to do scientific inquiry, grades K–4:
>
> - Ask a question about objects, organisms, and events in the environment.
> - Plan and conduct a simple investigation.
> - Employ simple equipment and tools to gather data and extend the senses.
> - Use data to construct a reasonable explanation.
> - Communicate investigations and explanations.

Note: See NSES, p 122, for expanded explanations of the above points.

The NSES standards on scientific inquiry for grades 5–8 are really an extension of those just noted. In thinking about student progress, it is helpful to see elementary students as successfully reaching a grade 4 understanding, and being at least on the way toward these grade 8 levels:

> Abilities necessary to do scientific inquiry, grades 5–8:
>
> - Identify questions that can be answered through scientific investigations
> - Design and conduct a scientific investigation
> - Use appropriate tools and technology to gather, analyze, and interpret data
> - Develop descriptions, explanations, predictions and models using evidence
> - Think critically and logically to make the relationships between evidence and explanations
> - Recognize and analyze alternative explanations and predictions
> - Communicate scientific procedures and explanations
> - Use mathematics in all aspects of scientific inquiry
>
> Understanding about scientific inquiry, grades K–4:
>
> - Scientific investigations involve asking and answering a question and comparing the answer with what scientists already know about the world.
> - Scientists use different kinds of investigations depending on the questions they are trying to answer. Types of investigations include describing objects, events, and organisms; classifying them; and doing a fair test (experimenting).
> - Simple instruments, such as magnifiers, thermometers, and rulers, provide more information than scientists obtain using only their senses.
> - Scientists develop explanations using observations (evidence) and what they already know about the world (scientific knowledge). Good explanations are based on evidence from investigations.
> - Scientists make the results of their investigations public; they describe the investigations in ways that enable others to repeat the investigations.
> - Scientists review and ask questions about the results of other scientists' work.

Again, the statements for grades 5–8 build upon the earlier standards, and are more sophisticated and lengthy. Only two examples follow, but it is important that you review them all (NSES, p 149).

> Understanding about scientific inquiry, grades 5–8 (partial):
>
> - Different kinds of questions suggest different kinds of scientific investigations. Some investigations involve observing and describing objects,

organisms and events; some involve collecting specimens; some involve experiments; some involve seeking more information; some involve discovery of new objects and phenomena; and some involve making models.

- Scientific explanations emphasize evidence, have logically consistent arguments, and use scientific principles, models, and theories. The scientific community accepts and uses such explanations until displaced by better scientific ones. When such displacement occurs, science advances.

Note: There is a wide difference in level between the K–4 and 5–8 standard statements. Obviously, elementary students at grade 5 can only be expected to be making the first steps toward this level of understanding.

HOW CAN WE INTERPRET BSL AND NSES VIEWS?

The overall message from both BSL and NSES is that science education in schools should operate through students engaging in their own science investigations. In effect, this means children need to behave as scientists so that they can become familiar with science concepts and, ultimately, be scientifically literate. Firsthand experience in scientific inquiry is seen as the key learning method for science understanding.

Embedded in this view is a veiled criticism of the ways in which science often has been taught in the past. That is, having children learn factual information (what gravity is, how photosynthesis works, how to define density, the elements in the periodic table). This direct teaching method is no longer considered supportable by the standards.

Key processes in science investigations include children developing and using such skills as:

- *Observing* scientific objects, organisms, and events
- *Asking questions* about those things they observe that they can then investigate
- *Finding information* from reliable sources that will help to generate answers and explanations
- *Planning and conducting investigations* that include predictions of likely outcomes and use systematic observations, simple experiments, and tests that are fair
- *Gathering data* using simple equipment and tools
- *Constructing reasonable explanations* using the data as evidence
- *Communicating the results* of their investigations, and explanations, in a form that they can be seen and understood by others

These processes closely mirror the scientific procedures used by scientists in their professional work.

WHAT ARE THE IMPLICATIONS FOR MANAGING SCIENCE CURRICULA?

It is fairly obvious that working with children in this way is time-intensive. Investigations cannot be rushed, nor do they fit easily into a conventional fifty-minute lesson. Most of all, it is unlikely that the range of science content can be fully covered. (An ever-growing list of content has produced a crowded science curriculum in the recent past.) Both BSL and NSES answer this problem by the maxim *less is more*. They both recognize that learning through inquiry methods will cause some content areas to become casualties in the process. That is, the content cover will inevitably be reduced. However, their firm view is that engaging with *less* content, through an inquiry-based approach, will produce *more* in terms of *scientific literacy*. Their shared concept is that an experiential understanding of the scientific processes will equip young citizens with the skills they need to interpret the broad mass of science content areas, at least to a reasonably informed level.

This shared view has huge implications at the classroom practice level. Traditionally, teachers have planned to present certain content in the day's science lesson. They could take that content and shape it into a form that they thought the children would understand. They could also see a clear way of assessing how much of the content their children had learned by using a traditional test or quiz. Often they could use an established textbook to achieve all this.

Today's teachers have to think in a radically different way: "Tomorrow my children are going to observe an [object, organism, event] and plan their own investigation into it" requires a very different role from the teacher, who has become much more an organizer of student-centered learning than an information provider. The amount of preplanning, classroom organization, and resource management, coupled with close attention to student interactions and learning dynamics, can seem overwhelming, at least at first.

Changes are also implied for children. Scientific inquiry puts them into a much more creative role than the traditional one of being recipients of information given by the teacher. They have to work in collaboration with other children, often in small groups. They have to share ideas, and take responsibility for their share of the work. Teamwork, communication, organization, and appropriate behavior all become key elements in this student-centered enterprise. There is a huge shift of *ownership of the learning experience*, away from the teacher and toward each individual child.

HOW CAN YOU COPE WITH THIS APPROACH TO SCIENCE EDUCATION?

As a beginning teacher, you may find all this daunting. However, working with children in this way produces rewards, for both teacher and children alike, that far outstrip traditional methods. Nor is this approach completely new to most elementary teachers, for it is broadly used in other curriculum areas—creative arts, for example. Coping with a scientific inquiry approach in the classroom will be easier for you if you have experienced, for yourself, all or some of these elements:

- A science inquiry approach in your college methods course that mirrors an elementary school science classroom.
- Attending science education workshops given by school districts, science education organizations or publishers.
- Observing and participating in classes already using this method.
- Teaming with an experienced teacher acting as a mentor.
- Becoming familiar with and using curriculum materials that have been specifically developed to help teachers use a scientific inquiry approach.

HOW CAN THIS BOOK HELP YOU WITH SCIENTIFIC INQUIRY?

This book has been specifically designed to help you develop skills in working with scientific inquiry. In particular, the ten Exemplars of Chapters 1 through 10 have been conceived as tools to ease you into this way of working during your first year of teaching. They provide an easy to follow way to infuse a scientific inquiry approach into a classroom where both teacher and children are coming to grips with it for the first time. The aim is that, by the end of your first year, you and the children you teach will have become proficient and comfortable with a scientific inquiry approach. Beyond that, it will be up to you to maintain your own teaching development by availing yourself of all opportunities to further your professional abilities as an educator, through in-service workshops, college programs, appropriate journals, science teaching organizations, new curriculum materials, and, most of all, working with colleague teachers in your school to make science education the best it can be.

CONTENT-SPECIFIC STANDARDS

There are certain science concepts that all students need to understand. Remember that NSES includes scientific inquiry as its first content standard, so what follows now concerns the remaining content standards. The BSL, in contrast, treats science inquiry in a separate section from content areas. The following table shows how the two publications have arranged these content statements.

Comparing BSL and NSES Content Standards*

Benchmarks for Science Literacy	National Science Education Standards (Ch. 6 / Science Content)
Note: In BSL, content benchmarks (standards) are included under chapter themes (Chs. 4–8).	*Note:* In NSES, content standards are included in Chapter 6, which has 7 sections.
Chapter 1. The Nature of Science (includes scientific inquiry)	Science as Inquiry
Chapter 4. The Physical Setting	Physical Science
Chapter 5. The Living Environment	Life Science
Chapter 6. The Human Organism	Earth and Space Science
Chapter 7. Human Society	Science and Technology
Chapter 8. The Designed World	Science in Personal and Social Perspectives
Chapter 9 The Mathematical World	History and Nature of Science

(continued)

Comparing BSL and NSES Content Standards* *(continued)*

Benchmarks for Science Literacy	National Science Education Standards (Ch. 6 / Science Content)
Chapter 10. Historical Perspectives	
Chapter 11. Common Themes	
Chapter 12. Habits of Mind	

*Shaded areas in BSL also contain student achievement benchmarks (standards), but these refer to the more general science ideas than to specific content concepts. You will find an orientation to BSL Chapters 9–12 later in this chapter.

The following examples will help you get a flavor for both BSL and NSES statements.

National Science Education Standards (NSES)

Physical Science: Content Standard B,
As a result of the activities in grades K–4, all students should develop an understanding of:
- Properties of objects and materials
- Position and motion of objects
- Light, heat, electricity, and magnetism

NSES, p 123

This is what NSES terms a *content standard*. As you can see, it is a short, yet very specific, statement. The NSES follows each standard with a narrative discussion of what experiences and understanding children are likely to have in this content area. Each standard is then spelled out in more detail. Here's one example:

Properties of Objects and Materials:
- Objects have many observable properties, including size, weight, shape, color, temperature, and the ability to react with other substances. Those properties can be measured using tools, such as rulers, balances, and thermometers.
- Objects are made of one or more materials, such as paper, wood, and metal. Objects can be described by the properties of the materials from which they are made, and those properties can be used to separate or sort groups of objects or materials.
- Materials can exist in different states—solid, liquid, and gas. Heating or cooling can change some common materials, such as water, from one state to another.

NSES, p 127

Here the NSES details the level of understanding, about this specific concept area, that all students should be working on during K–4 activities, and should have achieved by the completion of grade 4.

Remember, students are expected to gain this understanding through a process of scientific inquiry. Teaching these ideas as straight information is not the objective. Instead, students need to interact with materials and engage in investigations about their properties as a means of reaching this level of understanding. The chances are that this level of understanding cannot be achieved in just a few lessons; it will probably be necessary to investigate the properties of materials on many different occasions during K–4. So, you can't simply take the standard, design a few lessons to cover it, and expect students to have a clear understanding of it by grade 4. This is not the purpose of a content standard, nor is it the function of the collective content standards. To help you see this more clearly, it is worth looking at the standards for assessment.

STANDARDS FOR ASSESSMENT

The BSL has little to say about assessment practices. In contrast, the NSES discusses and sets standards for assessment in general, and teachers in particular. For example, there are sections of standards dealing with:

- Design of assessments in terms of their purpose
- Relationships between decision and data, and consistency (Assessment Standard A, pp 78–79)
- Achievement and opportunity to learn (Assessment Standard B, pp 79–83)
- Matching the technical quality of the data collected with decisions taken on the basis of their interpretation (Assessment Standard C, pp 83–85)
- Fairness of assessment practices (Assessment Standard D, pp 85–86)
- Soundness of inferences made from assessments about student achievement and opportunity to learn (Assessment Standard E, pp 86–87)

Much of this sets forth general principles about assessment for state departments of education, school districts, and schools, and relates less specifically to the teacher's role. However, it will help for you to read these sections so as to understand the broad frame of reference of assessment standards. This way you will be able to relate your professional responsibility to the "big picture."

A special section is devoted to Assessments Conducted by Classroom Teachers (pp 87–89). This is a crucial part of the NSES for you, especially in your first year of teaching, so be sure to study it carefully. It is divided into the following five elements:

- Improving classroom practice
- Planning curricula
- Developing self-directed learners
- Reporting student progress
- Researching teaching practices

Even a quick glance at these items clearly shows that the assessments you should be doing are far more than a paper-and-pencil quiz could possibly give. Here's just one element to illustrates this point:

Developing Self-Directed Learners
Teachers have communicated their assessment practices, their standards for performance, and criteria for evaluation to students when students are able to:

- Select a piece of their own work to provide evidence of understanding of a scientific concept, principle, or law—or their ability to conduct scientific inquiry. (Note how science concepts and scientific inquiry are linked here)
- Explain orally, in writing, or through illustration how a work sample provides evidence of understanding.
- Critique a sample of their own work using the teacher's standards and criteria for quality.
- Critique the work of other students in constructive ways.

NSES, p 88

The key point being emphasized here is that there should be an integrated relationship between:

- Scientific inquiry
- Understanding scientific concepts (principles and/or laws)
- Assessment practices

The NSES recognizes and promotes the crucial need for all three of these to be practiced in harmony. That is: learning *scientific concepts*, through *scientific inquiry processes*, with *assessment practices* that are appropriate for letting students *show scientific understanding*. Within the text, NSES highlights quotable statements in large type. In the assessment section they include the following:

When teachers treat students as serious learners and serve as coaches rather than judges, students come to understand and apply standards of good scientific practice.

NSES, p 88

SCIENCE TEACHING STANDARDS

All the standards discussed above relate to children learning science. The NSES also has an important section entitled Science Teaching Standards. These describe what teachers of science at all grade levels should understand and be able to do, so they are particularly relevant for you. Here is how NSES introduces them:

The standards for science teaching are grounded in five assumptions:
- The vision of science education described by the standards requires changes throughout the entire system.
- What students learn is greatly influenced by how they are taught.
- The actions of teachers are deeply influenced by their perceptions of science as an enterprise and as a subject to be taught and learned.
- Student understanding is actively constructed through individual and social processes.
- Actions of teachers are deeply influenced by their understanding of and relationships with students.

NSES, p 28

It is within the context of these five assumptions that the teaching standards are designed. They fall into six categories, as follows:

Teaching Standard A:
Teachers of science plan an inquiry-based science program for their students.

Teaching Standard B:
Teachers of science guide and facilitate learning.

Teaching Standard C:
Teachers of science engage in ongoing assessment of their teaching and of students' learning.

Teaching Standard D:
Teachers of science design and manage learning environments that provide students with the time, space, and resources needed for learning science.

Teaching Standard E:
Teachers of science develop communities of science learners that reflect the intellectual rigor of scientific inquiry and the attitudes and social values conducive to science learning.

Teaching Standard F:
Teachers of science actively participate in the ongoing planning and development of the school science program.

You can see at a glance how these teaching standards are consistent with, and dovetail into, all the student-oriented standards given earlier. Once again, these standards pick up on *inquiry, scientific concepts,* and *assessment* as key components. But they say much more than this. They define the responsibilities of a teacher of science for planning, guiding learning, developing appropriate attitudes and values, and taking an active role in the school-wide development of the science program.

Note: Self-assessment of your own teaching is also included (Teaching Standard C). In this regard, see Chapter 17 of this book.

As usual, each of these individual standards has a list of key points. It is very important that you understand and appreciate them because they detail what NSES defines as *your responsibility* as a professional teacher of science. It is toward these standards that your professional training should be oriented, and against which your professional abilities are likely to be judged. Once again, you need to take time to study these standards in the NSES publication and reflect upon their implications for you as a teacher of science. The standards are too long to include here, but the following sample will alert you to their character and depth:

Teaching Standard E
Teachers of science develop communities of science learners that reflect the intellectual rigor of scientific inquiry and the attitudes and social values conducive to science learning. In doing this, teachers:

- Display and demand respect for the diverse ideas, skills, and experiences of all students.
- Enable students to have a significant voice in decisions about the content and context of their work and require students to take responsibility for the learning of all members of the community.
- Nurture collaboration among students.
- Structure and facilitate ongoing formal and informal discussion based on a shared understanding of rules of scientific discourse.
- Model and emphasize the skills, attitudes, and values of scientific inquiry.

NSES, pp 45–46

Bear in mind that these teaching standards are for all teachers of science at all grade levels, not just elementary school. It is also important to realize that many experienced teachers will also be struggling to meet these standards, especially if they have earlier taught in a more traditional manner. Even secondary teachers who have a deep scientific understanding may not be used to teaching science in this way. In fact, this teaching style may be more familiar to elementary teachers than to their secondary counterparts (though possibly through other curriculum areas). This reflects the standards' far-reaching nature and their underlying mission of *curriculum reform*. In many ways, you, as a beginning teacher, are entering the profession during a process of radical educational change. In can be considered an advantage to start out in this fashion, unencumbered by prior experience of working with a different system.

Although this chapter began by focusing on student-oriented standards, you need to be aware that the science teaching standards are crucial for you. Moreover, it is very likely that a school you apply to for a position will expect you to have a good grasp of them and their implications. You are urged to study them carefully so as to become completely familiar with what they are saying.

ADDITIONAL STANDARDS AND SUPPORTING SECTIONS

So far in this chapter, we have covered the three standard areas that are likely to be of most importance for you as a beginning teacher. One way to think of them is the *How?* (inquiry), the *What?* (scientific concepts), and the *How well?* (assessment). These are standards that both BSL and NSES address. We have also stressed the importance of the NSES Science Teaching Standards. However, both BSL and NSES contain a number of other standards and supporting sections with which you will need to become familiar. The key remaining sections appear in the following tables. It is imperative that you acquire your own copies of the BSL and NSES and gain a proper understanding of these sections. Note that *Benchmarks* online are available at Web site www.project2061.ord/tools/behcnol/bolframe.html. You will also find it useful to have the actual publications available for reference as you plan science experiences for your children.

Benchmarks for Science Literacy (BSL)

Chapter	Title	Chapter content
	• Introduction	*Benchmarks for Science Literacy* (BSL) derives from the Project 2061 *Science for All Americans* (SFAA). Science, technology, and mathematics will be central to radical changes in the next generation, and education is required to ensure that all Americans become *scientifically literate*. Substance and character of such education? BSL was introduced to provide answers.
1	• The Nature of Science	Sets benchmarks for what science is, in terms of an intellectual and social endeavor. Deals with scientific processes in *Scientific Inquiry*.

Benchmarks for Science Literacy (BSL)

Chapter	Title	Chapter content
		Other sections: *Scientific World View, Scientific Enterprise.*
2	○ The Nature of Mathematics	Mathematics is the science of patterns and relationships. Examines relationships among mathematics, science, and technology, as well as mathematical inquiry.
3	○ The Nature of Technology	Explores technology (the way we extend our abilities to change the world) in *Technology and Science, Design and Systems, Issues in Technology.* Gives benchmarks.
Note: Chapters 4–8, covering benchmarks for specific scientific content areas, were addressed earlier in this book.		
9	○ The Mathematical World	Benchmarks deal with basic mathematical ideas, especially those with practical applications. BSL acknowledges importance of National Council of Teachers of Mathematics (NCTM) standards.
10	○ Historical Perspectives	Benchmarks that address development of student understanding of selected episodes in the history of science. Important for students 6th grade and beyond.
11	○ Common Themes	Ideas used by mathematicians, scientists, and engineers, but not the intellectual property of any one discipline: *Systems, Models, Constancy and Change, Scale.*
12	○ Habits of Mind	Broad themes that go beyond acquiring knowledge and skills and are important in the real world. Benchmarks: *Values and Attitudes, Computation and Estimation, Manipulation and Observation, Communication Skills, Critical Response Skills.*
13	○ The Origin of Benchmarks	Background events and research that led to the BSL.
14	○ Issues and Language	Development of language and form of BSL: *Benchmarks, Curriculum, Hands-On, Interdisciplinary,* discussed and clarified.

(continued)

Benchmarks for Science Literacy (B S L) *(continued)*

Chapter	Title	Chapter content
15	• The Research Base	Research that informed BSL, including school district teams, learning specialists, and published research. Lists research findings that underpin BSL.
16	Beyond the Benchmarks	Intended steps, beyond BSL, toward science education reform: *Designs for Science Literacy, Blueprints for Reform, Resources for Science Literacy, Curriculum Design.*

National Science Education Standards (N S E S)

Chapter	Title	Chapter content
	• National Science Education Standards: An Overview	Describes NSES standards and gives rationale for organization.
1.	• Introduction	Discusses need for national science standards, establishes goals for school science, traces developmental history of the standards, and gives guidance for readers.
2.	• Principles and Definitions	NSES explains principles upon which standards are based: • *Science is for all students.* • *Learning science is an active process.* • *School science reflects the intellectual and cultural traditions that characterize the practice of contemporary science.* • *Improving science education is part of systemic education reform.* Includes references for further reading.
3.	• Science Teaching Standards	What teachers need to know, and be able to do, to deliver good science education in schools. Standards for teaching listed and explained. **Note:** This is an important section. Strong implications, not only for the classroom, but also for teacher preparation, continuing professional development, and in-service teacher education.

National Science Education Standards (NSES)

Chapter	Title	Chapter content
4.	• Standards for Professional Development for Teachers of Science	Criteria for judging the quality of professional development opportunities that teachers of science will need to implement the NSES. Encompass preservice teacher education and in-service programs plus teacher's responsibility for continuing professional development.
7.	• Science Education Program Standards	Criteria for quality and conditions for school science programs. Directed toward those responsible for design, development, selection, and adaptation of science programs: teachers, department chairs, curriculum directors, administrators, publishers, and school committees.
8.	• Science Education System Standards	Criteria for judging components of the science education system that are responsible for providing schools with necessary financial and intellectual resources.

SUMMARY

This has been a rapid tour through the national standards. Please remember that this chapter is nothing more than an orientation. It is *crucial* that you obtain and study the BSL and NSES publications to fully appreciate their significance and the special demands standards place upon you as a *professional* teacher. These documents will provide you with the insight you need to grasp today's science education. Most of all, you will find them to be an invaluable daily resource for your own teaching.

Because of the national standards, and the ways in which they are strongly influencing local standards, gone are the days when a teacher's responsibility was to teach lessons based on textbooks, give quizzes, and go home. The word *professional*, applied to teachers, is finally coming of age. That you are entering the teaching *profession* now is truly a privilege in terms of timing.

19 Dealing with Diversity

INTRODUCTION

As teachers, we rarely select the members of our classes. It is our professional, and sometimes legal, responsibility to provide the highest educational experiences for every student we are assigned. As a beginning teacher, you can expect to have classes containing children with a wide range of abilities. Even if the range is fairly narrow, there will still be more diversity than similarity among individual students. A class may also reflect a wide range of other diversity factors with which you will have to deal. The most obvious is gender, but there may be many others, including socioeconomic status, ethnicity, race, cultural background, special educational needs (both challenged and gifted), physical disability, non–English speaking, possibly strongly held religious beliefs, and—not least—family mores and circumstances.

It is important to recognize that diversity among the members of an elementary school classroom represents a rich resource that can be drawn upon for the benefit of all. It is also important to be sensitive to these differences in order to ensure a positive and inclusive experience for each child in your class. The nature of science makes it a particularly useful subject for this purpose. Science is universal. It seeks to investigate and interpret all aspects of the real world on the basis of fair evidence. It welcomes and is especially interested in diversity and has no particular political position. Science is a subject to which all can contribute and from which all can benefit. This is reflected by the National Science Education Standards:

The intent of the Standards can be expressed in a single phrase: Science standards for ALL students. The phrase embodies both excellence and equity. The Standards apply to all students, regardless of age, gender, cultural or ethnic backgrounds, disabilities, aspirations, or interest and motivation in science.

In terms of diversity, you yourself are not neutral in the classroom. You represent only one gender group, come from a particular cultural background, and may include other diversification elements within your personal repertoire. This will not be lost on your children, and they may have certain expectations of you as a result. The big difference is, you are in charge!

In the diverse classroom, you may have to address many things that go beyond the straightforward teaching of science. Keep in mind that what children bring to any learning experience is crucial. Children with different life experiences can be counted on to bring different interests and ideas, interpretations of phenomena, beliefs, and expectations. Your job is to harness these differences and help your children view them and draw upon them in a positive way.

There are, of course, no hard-and-fast rules, other than having an open mind. You must deal with student diversity without prejudice and without stereotypical assumptions. That said, there are some ideas worth considering. The following is merely a preliminary guide, but it may help you to think about diversity in broad educational and science education terms.

ELEMENTS OF DIVERSITY

Gender Differences

In teaching science, it is particularly important to be alert to how the boys and girls in your classroom work together in groups as they do hands-on investigations. Observe who takes the lead in assembling the apparatuses and who does the writing. It has been noted, in studies on gender differences in science education, that boys have a tendency to take over the manipulatives in investigations, leaving the girls to do the recording or display making. You can help your girls to build their skills with manipulatives, and your boys to gain practice with recording and displays, by assigning and rotating roles in groups. You can also have your children find out about famous *women*, as well as men, who have been scientists and inventors. These could include Marie and Pierre Curie (physicists); Rosalyn Yalow (chemist); Jane Goodall (animal biologist); George Washington Carver (chemist); Charles Darwin (biologist); Rachel Carson (environmentalist); and many others. The list lengthens with each passing year.

Ethnicity

Children of different ethnicities can bring many interesting experiences to your science lessons. For example, if you are teaching lessons on food science and nutrition, or even on plants people use as foods, ask your students to bring in recipes that are typically prepared in their homes. You could support such an activity with a display of fruits and vegetables that are used in the recipes, and sort these according to their type of plant part (root, seed, fruit, stem, flower, leaf). Fruits or vegetables that would be suitable for this type of exercise would be gingerroot, chayotes, taro root, fennel, napa, plantain, bok choy, mango, kale, collards, papaya, daikon, jicama, and many others.

You might also find that children from different ethnic backgrounds can, with their own experiences or those of their parents, augment lessons on fabrics and fibers (different clothing from around the world), musical sounds, animals, beverages, art, and many more.

Cultural Background

Children from different cultures may have unexpected perspectives on science topics. Many tribes of Native Americans, for example, have a rich culture of living in harmony with the natural world. Legends explaining natural phenomena (weather, earthquakes, seasons) have long been part of the Native American life, as they have for people of many other cultures (Caribbean, African). When teaching science, it is important that you be sensitive to the fact that other cultures have such stories and legends and they may crop up during science time. You will need to be gentle in helping children to differentiate between fact and legend. Both have validity of their own kind.

Special Educational Needs

You may have children in your class who are achieving at levels much higher or much lower than the norm. It can be demanding to meet the needs of both types of children, since a gifted child typically thrives with challenges, while a less able child needs instruction that meets him where he is, and helps him to learn at his own pace.

Many schools have special programs for gifted children, so that they are challenged outside the regular classroom. If this is the case in your school, find out the details of the program so that you can support its efforts by your own teaching to the gifted children. Such programs as Odyssey of the Mind, for example, encourage gifted students to work together to solve problems and share their results in a public forum. You could mirror such a program with smaller-scale efforts in your own classroom.

The same thing goes with less able children. Those who are receiving special out-of-class help need continuity with your in-class instruction. If you have any special students who are mainstreamed in your class, you may receive the help of an instructional assistant. Inform assistants regularly about what you are planning on doing for science instruction, so they can support what you are doing with the special student(s).

Physical Disability

You may have students with temporary or permanent physical disabilities that require such assistive devices as wheelchairs, crutches, braces, or the like. You may also have students with auditory or visual impairments. It is important that your classroom is set up to allow these students to participate fully in any activities, but particularly in the hands-on activities that are so critical to creating an understanding of and enthusiasm for science. This may mean that you have certain students placed closer to visual displays (boards, flipcharts, monitors) or to instructional sources of sound (including you!). It may also mean that you need to arrange your room for wheelchair access or for students with assistive walking devices to get to a seat in the easiest manner possible, without weaving around desks, chairs, or tables.

Non-English Speakers

Depending upon where you teach, you may have children for whom English is their second language. Different states and districts have different laws regarding how students who speak English as a second language (ESL) are taught. Some locales support an English immersion approach, while others have versions of science curricular materials in both English and other languages (typically, Spanish). You might find it useful to pair non–English speaking children with those who are bilingual; this will depend upon the regulations of your school, district, and state. No matter what the regulations are, however, non–English speaking children will benefit from an extensive use of graphics to explain things, as well as from many hands-on experiences.

Religious Differences

It is important to be aware that some religions do not support the teaching of evolution, believing it is at variance with a strict interpretation of the Old Testament of the Bible. You will need to discuss this with your team leader, principal, or science supervisor, if the teaching of evolutionary concepts has been an issue in your school in the past. Take official advice on how this is dealt with in your school.

You also may have students whose religion espouses reincarnation as a tenet. Again, with such sensitive topics, it is important to talk to those in authority in your school so that your way of teaching doesn't inadvertently offend any of your children, or the adults in their lives.

Family Circumstances

Some of your children may come from family situations that are "nontraditional." These can include single parents, gay couples, grandparents or other relatives raising children, adoptive parents, guardians, foster parents, and others. You will need to be sensitive to this, especially when discussing life science topics such as genetics and reproduction, if these are part of your curriculum. Asking a question such as "How many of you have eyes the same color as your father's eyes?" could be problematic for some children.

Nontraditional families might also be an issue when requesting chaperones for field trips. It might be very difficult for a single parent to get release time from work to attend trips, so it is vital that you don't pressure children who seem reluctant to ask a parent to volunteer.

SCIENCE ORGANIZATIONS

National Science Teachers Association
1840 Wilson Boulevard
Arlington, VA 22201-3000
703-243-7100 (voice)
www.nsta.org

From this Internet source you can get information about science materials and currcula, as well as guidelines for using animals in the classroom.

American Association for the Advancement of Science
1200 New York Avenue, NW
Washington, DC 20005
202-326-6400 (voice)
www.aaas.org

American Association of Physics Teachers
One Physics Ellipse
College Park, MD 20740-3845
301-209-3300 (voice)
301-209-0845 (fax)
www.aapt.org

American Chemical Society
1155 16th Street, NW
Washington, DC 20036
800-227-5558 (voice)
www.acs.org

American Geological Institute
4220 King Street
Alexandria, VA 22302-1502
703-379-2480 (voice)
703-379-7563 (fax)
www.agiweb.org

American Institute of Physics
One Physics Ellipse
College Park, MD 20740-3845
301-209-3100 (voice)
301-209-0843 (fax)
www.aip.org

American Society for Microbiology
1752 N Street, NW
Washington, DC 20036
202-737-3600 (voice)
www.asmusa.org/eduscr/edu3.htm

Association for Educators of Teachers of Science
P.M.B. 302
740 Greenville Boulevard, Suite 400
Greenville, NC 27858
www.aets.unr.edu/

Council for Elementary Science International (C.E.S.I.)
http://unr.edu/homepage/crowther/cesi.html

International Technology Education Association
1914 Association Drive, Suite 201
Reston, VA 20191-1539
703-860-2100 (voice)
703-860-0353 (fax)
www.iteawww.org

National Association of Biology Teachers
12030 Sunrise Valley Drive, Suite 110
Reston, VA 20191
703-264-9696 (voice)
703-264-7778 (fax)
www.nabt.org

National Association of Geoscience Teachers
PO Box 5443
Bellingham, WA 98227-5443
360-650-3587 (voice)
www.nagt.org

National Council of Teachers of Mathematics
1906 Association Drive
Reston, VA 20191-9988
703-620-9840 (voice)
703-476-2970 (fax)
www.nctm.org

National Institute for Science Education
University of Wisconsin Madison
1025 West Johnson Street
Madison, WI 53706
608-263-9250 (voice)
608-262-7428 (fax)
www.wcerwisc.edu/nise/

PREPARING STUDENTS FOR SCIENCE FAIRS

If you decide to ask your children to participate in a science fair, they will need your guidance on what constitutes a science fair project. Essentially, a good science fair project is one in which your children are interested and that is within their abilities to investigate. There are differing thoughts about adult participation in science fair projects. Some educators think that science fair projects should be completely the work of the children, with only very minimal participation by adults. Other schools of thought value the involvement of adults (parents, guardians, grandparents) as investigative partners in the science project experience. It will be up to you and your school's tradition as to what is acceptable.

There are a variety of ways to organize the parts of a science fair project. The following list represents just one way of going about it:

1. *Title of the project*
2. *Investigative question* (What do I want to find out?)
3. *Research* (What do other people already know about my question?)
4. *Predictions* (Based on my own experience and my research, what do I think might be possible answers to my question?)
5. *Limitations* (What and who are available to help me answer my question?)
6. *Materials* (What supplies will I need to investigate my question?)
7. *Procedure* (What did I do, step by step, to investigate my question?)
8. *Safety* (What special safety precautions did I take as I investigated my question?)
9. *Data* (What information did I collect about my question?)
10. *Analysis* (What patterns and relationships in the data help me to answer my question?)
11. *Conclusions* (What answers to my question are supported by my data?)
12. *Recommendations* (What would I pass on to others about what I found out?)

Although each of these items have "titles" (research, data, analysis), depending upon the ages and readiness of your children, you may prefer to have them organize their projects just by the questions in the parentheses. It is always a good idea to give your children explicit examples of each of the elements so that they know what is expected of them when they do their projects. Here is one example that you could use:

1. *Title:* Investigating Garden Soil
2. *Investigative question:* What types of plants would grow well in my backyard garden?

3. *Research:* When I called the local gardening society, they said that the soil in our area is mostly clay, and acidic. They weren't sure, however, if this were true for the soil in my backyard. I looked up the soil in our area on the Web and found out that the Geological Society of America puts my area into a zone where the soil can be clay but can also be sandy. The local garden center suggested that I test my soil with a soil test kit.

4. *Predictions:* Based upon what the local and national experts have told me, I would predict that my soil has clay in it. I don't know what else the soil might have in it, though.

5. *Limitations:* I am limited by what I can test with my soil test kit. I am also limited by the information I can get from local sources such as the Cooperative Extension Service. I plan to take my soil samples there for testing.

6. *Materials:* Soil test kit, soil samples, digging tool, paper towels, plastic containers to hold the soil samples, labels, safety goggles, pen to write labels for the sample containers, coffee can with no top or bottom for the percolation test, hammer.

7. *Procedure:*

    a. Buy soil test kit.

    b. Read directions on kit for collecting samples and running the tests.

    c. Collect soil samples as directed on the kit. Label containers with samples in them.

    d. Put on safety goggles, then run the tests as described on the soil test kit. Record test results.

    e. Repeat the tests to check results.

    f. Wearing goggles, run percolation test. Record results and repeat the test.

    g. Examine the soil for its appearance. Record the results.

8. *Data:* Put test results into a data table that is clear enough so that others can understand what I did.

9. *Analysis:* Look for agreement between first and second tests. My soil is mostly clay, has a pH of 6 (acidic), and contains X ppm of potassium, X ppm of nitrates, and X ppm of phosphorus. It took 15 minutes for the water in the percolation test to get to the bottom of the coffee can.

10. *Conclusions:* In comparing the data analysis to gardening books, some of the plants that would grow in my garden (for our growing zone) would be herbs such as basil and sage, hostas (in the shade), daffodils, hyacinth, grasses, baby's breath, and a number of others.

11. *Recommendations:* I could recommend any of the plants on the list above, but some take more care than others. I would like to focus on plants that don't take much care, since I'm new at gardening.

BIBLIOGRAPHY

Abruscato, J., & Hassard, J. (1977). *The Whole Cosmos.* New York: Scott, Foresman.

Andersson, B. (1990). "Pupils' conceptions of matter and its transformations (age 12–16)." In P. Lijnse, P. Licht, W. de Vos, & A.J. Waarlo (eds.), *Relating Macroscopic Phenomena to Microscopic Particles* (pp. 12–35). Utrecht: CD-þ Press.

Baird, J., Fensham, P., Gunstone, R., & White, R. (1989). "A study of the importance of reflection for improving teaching and learning." Paper presented at the annual meeting of the National Association for Research in Science Teaching, San Francisco.

Bar, V. (1989). "Children's views about the water cycle." *Science Education, 73,* 481–500.

Bar, V. (1986). *The Development of the Conception of Evaporation.* Jerusalem: Hebrew University of Jerusalem, The Amos de-Shalit Science Teaching Centre in Israel.

Barker, M. (1985). "Teaching and learning about photosynthesis." Hamilton, New Zealand: University of Waikato, Science Education Research Unit, Working Papers 220–29.

Bell, B. (1981). "When is an animal not an animal?" *Journal of Biological Education, 15,* 213–18.

Bell, B., & Brook, A. (1984). *Aspects of Secondary Students' Understanding of Plant Nutrition.* Leeds, UK: University of Leeds, Centre for Studies in Science and Mathematics Education.

Bentley, M., Ebert, C., & Ebert, E.S. (2000). *The Natural Investigator.* Belmont, CA: Wadsworth.

Ben-Zvi, R., Eylon, B., & Silberstein, J. (1986). "Is an atom of copper malleable?" *Journal of Chemical Education, 63* (1): 64–66.

Bernstein, A.C., & Cowan, P.A. (1975). "Children's concepts of how people get babies." *Child Development, 46,* 77–91.

Bishop, B., & Anderson, C. (1990). "Student conceptions of natural selection and its role in evolution." *Journal of Research in Science Teaching, 27,* 415–27.

Black, P., & Solomon, J. (1983). "Life world and science world: Pupils' ideas about energy." In G. Marx (ed.), *Entropy in the School: Proceedings of the Sixth Danube Seminar on Physics Education* (pp. 43–55). Budapest: Roland Eotvos Physical Society.

Blum, L.H. (1977). "Health information via mass media: Study of the individual's concepts of the body and its parts." *Psychological Reports, 40,* 991–99.

Bouma, H., Brandt, L., & Sutton, C. (1990). "Words as tools in science lessons." Amsterdam: University of Amsterdam, *Chemiedidactiek.*

Bransford, J.D., Brown, A.L., & Cocking, R.R. (eds.) (1999). *How People Learn.* Washington, DC: National Academy Press.

Briggs, H., & Holding, B. (1986). *Aspects of Secondary Students' Understanding of Elementary Ideas in Chemistry.* Leeds, UK: University of Leeds, Centre for Studies in Science and Mathematics Education.

Brody, M.J. (1992). "Student science knowledge related to ecological crises." Paper presented to AERA, San Francisco.

Brook, A., Briggs, H., & Bell, B. (1983). *Secondary Students' Ideas about Particles.* Leeds, UK: The University of Leeds, Centre for Studies in Science and Mathematics Education.

Brook, A., & Driver, R. (1984). *Aspects of Secondary Students' Understanding of Energy: Summary Report.* Leeds, UK: University of Leeds, Centre for Studies in Science and Mathematics Education.

Brook, A., & Wells, P. (1988). "Conserving the circus: An alternative approach to teaching and learning about energy." *Physics Education, 23,* 80–85.

Brumby, M. (1982). "Students' perceptions of the concept of life." *Science Education, 66,* 613–22.

Clough, E.E., & Wood-Robinson, C. (1985). "Children's understanding of inheritance." *Journal of Biological Education, 19,* 304–310.

Curtis, H. (1983). *Biology,* 4th ed. New York: Worth.

Darwin, C. (1998). *The Origin of Species.* Suriano, G. (ed.) New York: Grammercy Press.

Driver, R. (1984). "Cognitive psychology and pupils' frameworks in mechanics." In Ljinse, P. (ed.), *The Many Faces of Teaching and Learning Mechanics in Secondary and Early Tertiary Education.* Proceedings of a conference on physics education, August 20–25, Utrecht. GIREP/SVO/UNESCO, WCC, Utrecht, 1985: 227–33.

Driver, R. (1989). "Students' conceptions and the learning of science: Introduction." *International Journal of Science Education, 11* (5): 481–90.

Driver, R., & Millar, R. (1985). *Energy Matters.* Leeds, UK: University of Leeds, Centre for Studies in Science and Mathematics Education.

Driver, R., Squires, A., Rushworth, P., & Wood-Robinson, V. (1994). *Making Sense of Secondary Science: Research into Children's Ideas.* London: Routledge.

Duit, R. (1984). "Work, force, and power: Words in everyday language and terms in mechanics." In Ljinse, P. (ed.), *The Many Faces of Teaching and Learning Mechanics in Secondary and Early Tertiary Education.* Proceedings of a conference on physics education, August 20–25, Utrecht. GIREP/SVO/UNESCO, WCC, Utrecht, 1985: 221–33.

Erickson, G., & Hobbs, E. (1978). "The developmental study of student beliefs about force concepts." Paper presented to the annual convention of the Canadian Society for the Study of Education, June 2, London, Ontario.

Gellert, E. (1962). "Children's conceptions of the content and functions of the human body." *Genetic Psychology Monographs, 65,* 293–305.

Gunstone, R., & Watts, M. (1985). "Force and motion." In R. Driver, E. Guesne, & A. Tiberghien (eds.), *Children's Ideas in Science* (pp. 85–104). Milton Keynes, UK: Open University Press.

Gunstone, R., & White, R. (1981). "Understanding of gravity." *Science Education, 65,* 291–99.

Harlen, W. (1988). *The Teaching of Science.* London: Fulton.

Hewson, P.W., & Thorley, N.R. (1989). "The conditions of conceptual change in the classroom." *International Journal of Science Education, 11* (5): 541–53.

Holman, J. (1995). *Chemistry.* Walton-on-Thames, UK: Thomas Nelson.

Holman, J. (1996). *The Material World,* 2nd ed. Walton-on-Thames, UK: Thomas Nelson.

Hone, E., Joseph, A., & Victor, E. (1971). *A Sourcebook for Elementary Science.* New York: Harcourt Brace Jovanovich.

Lederman, N. (1992). "Students' and teachers' conceptions of the nature of science: A review of the research." *Journal of Research in Science Teaching, 29,* 331–59.

Lucas, A. (1971). "The teaching of adaptation." *Journal of Biological Education, 5,* 86–90.

McCormick, R., Hennessy, S., & Murphy, P. (1993). "Problem-solving processes in technology education." Paper presented at the 55th annual conference of the ITEA, April, Charlotte, NC.

Minstrell, J. (1989). "Teaching science for understanding." In L. Resnick & L. Klopfer (eds.), *Toward the Thinking Curriculum: Current Cognitive Research* (pp. 129–49). Alexandria, VA: Association for Supervision and Curriculum Development.

National Council of Teachers of Mathematics. (1989). *Curriculum and Evaluation Standards for School Mathematics.* Reston, VA: author.

National Research Council. (1996). *National Science Education Standards.* Washington, DC: National Academy Press.

National Science Resources Center. (1988). *Science for Children.* Washington, DC: National Academy of Sciences.

National Science Teachers Association (1991). *Guidelines for Responsible Use of Animals in the Classroom.* Reston, VA: author.

Novak, J.D., & Gowin, D.B. (1984). *Learning How to Learn.* Cambridge, UK: Cambridge University Press.

Osborne, R.J., & Freyberg, P. (1985). *Learning in Science: The Implications of "Children's Science."* New Zealand: Heinemann.

Penick, J.E., & Yager, R. E. (1993). "Learning from excellence: Some elementary exemplars." *Journal of Elementary Science Education, 5* (1), 1–9.

Pfundt, H. (1981). "Pre-instructional conceptions about substances and transformations of substances." In W. Jung, H. Pfundt, & C. von Rhoneck (eds.), *Proceedings of the International Workshop on Problems Concerning Students' Representation of Physics and Chemistry Knowledge* (pp. 320–41), Pedagogische Hochschule, September 14–16, Ludwigsburg.

Piaget, J. (1952). *The Origins of Intelligence in Children.* New York: International Universities Press.

Project 2061, American Association for the Advancement of Science. (1993). *Benchmarks for Science Literacy.* New York: Oxford University Press.

Raizen, S.A., Baron, J.B., Champagne, A.B., Haertel, E., Millis, I.V., & Oakes, J. (1990). *Assessment in Science Education: The Middle Years.* Washington, DC: National Center for Improving Science Education.

Roberts, M. (1996). *The Living World,* 2nd ed. Walton-on-Thames, UK: Thomas Nelson.

Roth, K., & Anderson, C. (1987). *The Power Plant: Teacher's Guide to Photosynthesis.* Occasional paper no. 112. Institute for Research on Teaching. East Lansing: Michigan State University.

Roth, K.J. (1989). "Science education: It's not enough to 'do' or 'relate'." *The American Educator, 13* (4): 16-22; 46-48.

Sere, M. (1982). "A study of some frameworks of the field of mechanics used by children (aged 11–13) when they interpret experiments about air pressure." *European Journal of Science Education, 7*(1):83–93.

Shavelson, R.J. (1991). "Performance assessment in science." *Applied Measurement in Education, 4* (4): 347–62.

Smith, E., & Anderson, C. (1986). "Alternative conceptions of matter cycling in ecosystems." Paper presented at the annual meeting of the National Association for Research in Science Teaching, April, San Francisco.

Solomon, J. (1983). "Learning about energy: How pupils think in two domains." *European Journal of Science Education, 5,* 49–59.

Solomon, J. (1983). Messy, contradictory, and obstinately persistent: A study of children's out-of -school ideas about energy." *School Science Review, 65* (231): 225–33.

Stavridou, H., & Solomonidou, C. (1989). "Physical phenomena – chemical phenomena: Do pupils make the distinction?" *International Journal of Science Education,* 11(1): 83–92.

Stavy, R. (1990). "Children's conceptions of changes in the state of matter: From liquid (or solid) to gas." *Journal of Research in Science Teaching, 27,* 247–66.

Trowbridge, J., & Mintzes, J. (1985). "Students' alternative conceptions of animals and animal classification." *School Science and Mathematics, 85,* 304–316.

Tyson, H. (1994). *Who Will Teach the Children? Progress and Resistance in Teacher Education.* San Francisco: Jossey-Bass.

Watt, F., & Wilson, F. (1992). *Weather and Climate.* London: Usborne Publishing.

Watts, M. (1983). "A study of school children's alternative frameworks of the concept of force." *European Journal of Science Education, 5,* 217–30.

Watts, D.M., & Gilbert, J.D. (1983). "Enigmas in school science: Students' conceptions for scientifically associated words." *Research in Science and Technological Education, 1* (2): 161–71.

Welch, W., & Walberg, H. (1968). "A design for curriculum evaluation." *Science Education, 52,* 10–16.

Williams, J. (1997). *The Weather Book.* New York: Vintage.

INDEX